TESI GREGORIANA

Serie Teologia

—————————— 42 ——————————

SCOTT M. LEWIS S.J.

«So That God May Be All in All»

The Apocalyptic Message of
1 Corinthians 15,12-34

EDITRICE PONTIFICIA UNIVERSITÀ GREGORIANA
Roma 1998

Vidimus et approbamus ad normam Statutorum Universitatis

Romae, ex Pontificia Universitate Gregoriana
die 9 mensis novembris anni 1995

R.P. Prof. JEAN-NOËL ALETTI, S.J.
R.P. Prof. ERNEST R. MARTINEZ, S.J.

ISBN 88-7652-794-X

GREGORIAN UNIVERSITY PRESS
Piazza della Pilotta, 35 - 00187 Rome, Italy

Finito di stampare il 26 giugno 1998
«a.p.» editrice tipografica
Via Ugo Niutta, 2 – 00177 Roma

ACKNOWLEDGMENTS

I would like to take this opportunity to thank those who have helped me during my years of study and the preparation of this dissertation. Many have supported me with encouragement, suggestions, prayers and friendship during this time, and in this regard I would like to thank Dennis Glasgow S.J., Robert Hurd S.J., Steven Hawkes-Teeples S.J., and Clarence Gallagher S.J., Henry Berthels S.J., John Baggarly S.J., Richard Mackowski S.J., Scott Brodeur S.J., John Welch S.J., Sr. Juliana Mishka S.C.C., and the sisters of the Missionaries of Charity.

Thanks to Ernest Martinez S.J. for his careful reading of the text and his suggestions, and to the California Province of the Society of Jesus for missioning and supporting me.

I am very grateful to my dissertation director, Jean-Noël Aletti S.J., for his encouragement, helpful comments and suggestions, and detailed criticisms of the text. Any errors or misinterpretations are mine alone.

Mr. Carlo Valentino of the Pontifical Biblical Institute has been most patient and helpful in the preparation of this text for publication.

Special thanks to my family for their constant love and support.

PREFACE

The stirring imagery of Paul's description in 1 Cor 15 of the defeat of God's enemies, especially death, was an inspiration for the Church Fathers and spiritual writers of the patristic age. The passage gives the believer hope that he or she will participate in God's final victory at the end of time and share in the resurrection of the dead. It is strange, therefore, that one rarely if ever hears a homily on this passage when it is read from the pulpit or reads of it in modern theological works. It seems to be a treasure whose life-giving power remains dormant.

Part of the problem is the language and symbolism. The passage speaks about the defeat of heavenly powers and authorities, indicative of a cosmology that the modern world does not share. Death is the last enemy to be defeated, but it is still very much with us. At the very end, God will be "all in all". Isn't God already omnipotent and in command of the universe? Even the resurrection has been interpreted and reinterpreted in ways that treat it as an allegory, symbol or myth. As far as the modern world is concerned, the parousia seems to have receded in Christian consciousness, with the exception of the more fundamentalist religious groups.

I believe that the meaning of this passage can be understood and its message appreciated if it is accepted as being apocalyptic in nature. Schweitzer was the first to draw attention to the apocalyptic nature of much of the New Testament, including the Pauline letters. Others have followed his basic insight, although this view has not won universal acceptance. It is only in the past thirty years that apocalyptic literature itself has begun to be understood and appreciated in its own right. At this point in our history – close to the new millenium – it is important that we understand and honor the apocalyptic message that this and similar passages have to give us, thereby avoiding the danger of what J.C. Beker calls neo-apocalypticism.

Chapter I will describe the problem and propose the method and limits of the study of 1 Cor 15:12-34. Attention will be given to some modern proponents of the apocalyptic interpretation, such as E. Käsemann, J. Moltmann, and J.C. Beker.

Chapter II analyzes the rhetorical structure of the passage under scrutiny. The rhetorical structure is determined by the rhetorical situation, which is the ambience of attitudes, problems, and personalities calling for a response on the part of the writer, who seeks to change attitudes and behavior. Analyzing the structure will help us to understand why Paul wrote this passage, what the symbolism means in a particular context, and what he was attempting to accomplish.

Chapter III first of all defines the terms «apocalypse», «apocalyptic», and «apocalyptic theology or movement», since these terms have been used in a very imprecise and confusing manner in the past. The second part of the chapter will examine the various Jewish views of death, resurrection and the afterlife in the period roughly 200 BC – 100 AD. For this study, it is assumed that Judaism was represented by a broad range of theologies, so apocalyptic and pseudepigraphal works outside the Judeo-Christian canon of scripture will be used. Finally, we will determine what might have been the function or role of a messianic figure at the turn of the era.

Chapter IV will utilize this definition of apocalyptic and the dominant model of death and the afterlife in asking the question, Is 1 Cor 15:12-24 an apocalypse or apocalyptic in theology and content? An analysis of the various terms used in the passage will aid in this search. The second portion of the chapter will confront the issue of salvation. Who is saved? What is the fate of unbelievers? Since this passage has played a part in theologies of universal salvation an examination of the soteriological intent is in order. Finally, the content of this passage's apocalyptic message and its practical application will be discussed.

Chapter V surveys the exegesis of this passage from the apostolic age to the late 5th century. How was this passage understood in the first few centuries of the church? Was it viewed as apocalyptic in nature? Did this view change? What were the consequences of the loss of the apocalyptic understanding of the passage? Is this passage speaking primarily of Jesus or God the Father?

Chapter VI summarizes the results of this study and touches on the fundamental question of how we can understand this passage today and what an apocalyptic understanding of it has to offer the church. I hope to show that this apocalyptic passage – along with similar ones – has a vital role to play in the Church's preaching, catechesis, and ethical life.

Since the defense of this dissertation in November 1995, several books on apocalyptic in the Pauline letters or on 1 Corinthians have been published. Foremost of these are:

Joseph Plevnik S.J., *Paul and the Parousia*, Peabody 1997.

Alexandra R. Brown, *The Cross and Human Transformation: Paul's Apocalyptic Word in 1 Corinthians*, Minneapolis 1995.

The first is a thorough study of the parousia or Second Coming in Paul's theology as well as an analysis of the apocalyptic imagery and theology in his letters. Brown's work is a study of the cross as a liberating and empowering apocalyptic symbol, and concentrates on the first four chapters of 1 Corinthians. Although these works would have been helpful in the research and preparation of this dissertation, I have not included them in the text or the bibliography, since none of them alters the fundamental thesis of this work.

CHAPTER I

Introduction and Overview

1. Introduction

The Pauline epistles of the NT were not written in a timeless, ahistorical vacuum. They were occasional letters, written in a specific historical and cultural context to deal with specific issues. In wresting the secrets or entire meaning from a text, it is important to know what circumstances generated it. This is especially true for 1 Corinthians, and at first the answer seems rather clear: disunity within the community, unacceptable ethical behavior, denial of doctrine, etc., and these are examined and analyzed by every commentary[1].

But a closer examination of the text raises a number of perplexing questions. Who were the different factions? What was the attitude and relationship of the Corinthian church to Paul? The search for answers to these questions has produced an abundance of secondary literature: Paul's opponents in Corinth were gnostics[2]; Paul himself was at least interpreted by the gnostics in a gnostic fashion if not one himself[3]; the Corinthians were enthusiasts or followed some form of pagan philosophy; or the ambiguity is caused by the fact that the letter we have is actually a conflation of more than one[4].

---

[1] E.B. ALLO, *Saint Paul Première Épitre aux Corinthiens*; H. CONZELMANN, *1 Corinthians*, 14-16; C.K. BARRETT, *The First Epistle to the Corinthians*, 1-27; G.D. FEE, *The First Epistle to the Corinthians*, 46-65; I. HÉRING, *The First Epistle of Saint Paul to the Corinthians*; H. LIETZMANN, *An die Korinther I/II*, 4-8.

[2] W. SCHMITHALS, *Gnosticism in Corinth*; ID., *Paul and the Gnostics*.

[3] Pagels shows how second-century gnostics interpreted Paul, who was often viewed as the mortal enemy of gnosticism in any form, in a gnostic fashion. In fact, they claimed him as a gnostic initiate. Cf. E. PAGELS, *The Gnostic Paul*, 53-94.

[4] For a detailed history of the various attempts to reconstruct the Corinthian correspondence, see J.C. HURD, *The Origin of I Corinthians*; H. CONZELMANN, *1 Corinthians*, 2-5; G.D. FEE, *First Epistle to the Corinthians*, 15-16.

In our own day, this letter has come under closer scrutiny, as it deals with questions of order, authority, ministry, etc., and contains the notorious *mulier taceat in ecclesia* passage in 1 Cor 14[5].

By far one of the richest chapters of the letter is chapter 15, which was apparently provoked by a denial of the resurrection by a faction within the Corinthian community. Paul's response resulted in what has been called a self-contained treatise on the resurrection of the dead[6].

Indeed, it has often been treated in that fashion, especially during the apostolic and patristic periods. The chapter was a treasure chest of proof texts for the reality of the resurrection, especially its corporeal nature. Verses which were linked in any way to the great christological controversies of the age were given great attention[7].

During the middle ages, attention was given to the passage by such theologians as Peter Lombard, Walafrid Strabo, Haymo of Halberstadt, and Thomas Aquinas[8].

During the time of the Reformation, John Calvin dealt with the same issues in this passage that concerned Marcellus of Ancyra and many of the patristic fathers: the humanity and the kingship of Christ[9].

Schweitzer «allowed Jesus to return to his own time» by interpreting the entire Jesus tradition from an apocalyptic point of view. His analysis dehistoricized Jesus, and according to Schweitzer, made the message of Jesus applicable to any time and place. Schweitzer held that Paul dealt with the problem of the delayed parousia in a two-fold manner: first, he altered the received Jewish apocalyptic tradition by proposing two resurrections, one at the parousia for the faithful, both living and dead, and the other at the end of the Messianic reign for the wicked and the rest of humanity. Additionally, through a christocentric mysticism of «being-in-

---

[5] See E. SCHÜSSLER FIORENZA, «Rhetorical Situation», 386-403; W. WUELLNER, «Paul as Pastor», 49-77.

[6] H. CONZELMANN, *1 Corinthians*, 249.

[7] «We know the temptation which 1 Cor 15.24-28 has been to theologians: the Arians found in it their thesis of the inferiority of the Son to the Father, and Marcellus of Ancyra, Evagrius and the Origenists wanted to derive from it the abolition of the incarnation and the separation of the Logos from the flesh, so that in the return of the Logos to the Father the latter became all in all» (A. GRILLMEIER, *Christ in Christian Tradition*, 399); See also J.F. JANSEN, «I Cor 15.24-28», 543-570.

[8] B. SPÖRLEIN, *Die Leugnung der Auferstehung*, 3.

[9] Calvin's ambiguity in his exegesis has led to differing views as to whether he held that Christ's humanity would cease at the end of history. His exegesis can be found in the *Inst.* 2.14.7, 1.13.26, and his eighth sermon on Ephesians, 1.19-23. Cf. J.F. JANSEN, «I Cor. 15.24-28», 543-570.

Christ» the faithful dead experienced the presence of the eternal and supernatural, enabling them to rise at the first resurrection[10].

Barth paid special attention to 1 Cor 15, holding that not only was it the key to understanding the whole letter to the Corinthians, but was crucial in unlocking the meaning of Romans, Philippians, Colossians, and even the whole NT[11].

Bultmann, in reviewing Barth's commentary, agreed with him on several points: that the main concern with the chapter was the resurrection, and that it was not apocalyptic in nature, even though some of its language was. The apocalyptic interpretation has not been favored, and writers such as Bultmann have felt that this is the husk which must be stripped away in order to reveal the «true» message of the author[12].

It is Käsemann who is credited with defending and refocusing attention on the apocalyptic nature of Paul. According to Käsemann, apocalyptic is the «mother of all Christian theology», arising out of the Easter experience. Reacting to Bultmann, Käsemann insisted on the cosmological and apocalyptic import of Paul's writings[13].

Bultmann interpreted Paul's use of the word «body» (σῶμα) as representing the «ontological nature of human existence», and its definition to be: «the ability to control oneself and be the object of one's own actions, with the possibility of having a relationship for or against God». In other words, complete autonomy and independence. The emphasis of Käsemann, on the other hand, is on the interdependence of the individual with the entire cosmos. He insisted that anthropology is by necessity cosmology, since man is never autonomous, but always stands under lordship of one type or another[14].

---

10 A. SCHWEITZER, *The Mysticism of Paul the Apostle*; ID., *Paul and His Interpreters*; For a good critique of Schweitzer see H.W. BOERS, «Apocalyptic Eschatology», 59-65.

11 K. BARTH, *The Resurrection of the Dead*, 7-8.

12 «Thus Barth's interpretation of I Corinthians 15 and Bultmann's review of this interpretation helped open the way for the non-apocalyptic eschatological interpretation that was to become so influential in the period that followed» (H.W. BOERS, «Apocalyptic», 52-53).

13 E. KÄSEMANN, «The Beginnings of Christian Theology», 82-107; ID., «Primitive Christian Apocalyptic», 108-37; M.C. DE BOER, *Defeat of Death*, 27.

14 «Man for Paul is never just on his own. He is always a specific piece of world and therefore becomes what in the last resort he is by determination from outside, i.e., by the power which takes possession of him and the lordship to which he surrenders himself. His life is from the beginning a stake in the confrontation between God and the principalities of this world. In other words, it mirrors the cosmic contention for the lordship of the world and is its concretion. As such man's life can only be understood apocalyptically» (E. KÄSEMANN, «Primitive Apocalyptic», 136).

For Käsemann, Paul's apocalyptic eschatology asks the fundamental apocalyptic question: To whom does the sovereignty of the world belong? To God or the evil powers? God has invaded the realm of these powers, and believers are in the midst of a war between these two spheres of power for sovereignty of the world. On this battleground, the believer must decide in which camp he stands. This battle began with the death and resurrection of Christ[15].

Käsemann believes that 1 Cor 15,20-28 is a description of Paul's theology of the resurrection but it is christological rather than anthropological in content, focusing on the work of the Second Adam his lordship and reign. This eventually gives way to the total reign of God, Christ acting as God's agent in a world not totally subject to God[16].

Moltmann holds that apocalyptic can be described in one sense as an eschatological and historical interpretation of the cosmos, allowing the whole world and the cosmos to be involved in God's eschatological plan of history[17].

In response to what Moltmann calls a presentative eschatology, Paul countered with his own form of apocalyptic eschatology. The resurrection appearances could not be seen merely as the presence of the eternal, but as something requiring a new eschatology:

> The resurrection has set in motion an eschatologically determined process of history, whose goal is the annihilation of death in the victory of the life of the resurrection, and which ends in that righteousness in which God receives in all things his due and the creature thereby finds its salvation. It is only from the standpoint of a presentative eschatology or a theology of the eternal present that the eschatological and anticipatory thinking displayed by Paul in I Cor. 15 can be regarded as a relapse into outmoded apocalyptic mythology[18].

---

[15] M.C. DE BOER, *Defeat of Death*, 28; E. KÄSEMANN, «Primitive Apocalyptic», 135-136.

[16] It is questionable whether its content is *primarily* christological in its intent. As Beker points out, christological interpretations are often at the expense of the apocalyptic nature of a passage. The passage is about *God's* complete victory; the resurrection and the work of Christ are defined by God being «all in all» (E. KÄSEMANN, «Apocalyptic», 133).

[17] One of the ways in which apocalyptic differs from prophetic eschatology, according to Moltmann, is that instead of overcoming evil with good, as does the latter, apocalyptic eschatology strives to separate evil from good. He uses phrases such as «determinism» and «fatalistic dualism» in describing apocalyptic. The prophet takes his place in the historical present, while the apocalypticist veils his (J. MOLTMANN, *The Theology of Hope*, 133.137).

[18] Presentative eschatology is the presence of the eternal in the present in what can be described as an *eschatologia gloriae*. This usually expresses itself in an «eschatological ecstasy of fulfillment» i.e., mystery religions and ecstatic forms of worship. Cf. J. MOLTMANN, *Hope*, 163.

Moltmann states that Paul takes the known tradition in 1 Cor 15,3-5 and makes an original contribution to it: he extends it into the distant future. Christ *has* been raised from the dead, and the believer *will* be raised. This is accomplished by the Spirit, and this spirit is an «eschatological earnest» rather than the eternal spirit itself. With a deterministic notion, Paul makes it clear that there is a preordained element in the defeat of the inimical powers in the future, for Christ *must* reign until all of this takes place. Finally, even Christ's lordship is not enough: this is «eschatologically provisional,» awaiting the complete sovereignty of God. In this sense, Moltmann is correct: apocalyptic usually describes something imminent, whereas Paul is vague and unconcerned about the timetable, and does not even include «signs» of the impending final events. Paul, on the other hand, has extended the resurrection and the eschaton into the distant and rather nebulous future[19].

The modern champion of the apocalyptic nature of this passage is J. Beker. In his reinterpretation of the Pauline corpus from the standpoint of apocalyptic theology, he takes the apocalyptic message itself seriously and presents it as a viable theological outlook for today[20].

Beker holds Paul's gospel to be apocalyptic because it looks forward to the final triumph of God in Christ over all the inimical powers in the world that resist his plan for redemption. According to Beker, the very center of Paul's gospel is his proclamation that a new future for the world has been opened by the death and resurrection of Christ. The climax of this future is in the reign of God, which brings the entire cosmos to its glorious destiny, in accordance with the promises of God[21].

The four basic components of Jewish apocalyptic form the basic structure of Paul's apocalyptic gospel: vindication, universalism, dualism, and imminence[22].

---

[19] Cf. J. MOLTMANN, *Hope*, 162-163.

[20] J.C. BEKER, *Paul the Apostle*; ID., *Apocalyptic Gospel*.

[21] J.C. BEKER, *Apocalyptic Gospel*, 19.29.

[22] By *vindication*, Beker means that «in the death and resurrection of Jesus Christ, the Covenant God of Israel has confirmed and renewed his promises of salvation to Israel and to the nations, as first recorded in the Hebrew Bible» [p.30]. *Universalism* describes the «cosmic extension of God's majesty and glory» [p.34]. This means a radical reversal of the status quo and the inauguration of new values. It is a time of leveling, and of ethical decision. *Dualism* means not a spirit-matter dichotomy, but a great contrast between the present world and the coming new one. «The forces of evil that dominate the present world are both macrocosmic and microcosmic powers: the angelic forces under Satan rule not only the world of history and nature but also the inner being of persons» [p.39]. Nature and humans will be transformed in the world to come. Finally, *imminence* is the «impending actualization of God's reign». It intensifies and heightens hope for the actualization of God's vindication and universal

An apocalyptic theology has implications for ministry: ministry must prepare the world for the coming of God's glory and the transformation of the world's structures. The method of such a ministry involves the reciprocal relationship between thought and practice which is called coherence and contingency: One shifts between the abiding center or coherence of the gospel, or that which «does not accommodate itself to the various tastes of the times», and contingency, or the «historical situations to which the gospel addresses itself so that its word becomes a word on target»[23].

Despite modern distaste for apocalyptic, Beker denies that it is obsolete; on the contrary, he insists that it is such an integral part of Paul's gospel that its excision or rejection would seriously damage the truth and the driving force of his message[24].

The church should be viewed, according to Beker, as the «avant-garde of the new creation in a hostile world, creating beachheads in this world of God's dawning new world and yearning for the day of God's visible lordship over his creation, the general resurrection of the dead». This is sacrificed when the apocalyptic nature is lost. One of the ways in which it is lost is when apocalypticism «collapses into Christology». Beker warns us that the consequences of this «collapse of apocalypticism into Christology» are manifold: individualism and spiritualization, as well as a misunderstanding of Paul's anthropology and ecclesiology resulting from the spiritualization of the «somatic worldly component of his thought»[25].

---

reign, as well as for the elimination of dualistic structures. The biggest problem is how to reconcile imminence with the continuation of chronological time (J.C. BEKER, *Apocalyptic Gospel*, 30-53). As will become clearer in chapter 4, this definition is not sufficient, for it can be applied to other types of literature as well.

[23] This theory of coherence and contingency is one way of explaining the «inconsistencies» of Paul's letters: to call them contingencies is merely another way of saying that his letters were written *ad hoc* to meet various pastoral situations. It is not entirely clear exactly how one is to determine the coherent center. It is always problematic to superimpose a theology or a plan over a mass of data; often the data is then interpreted in light of the model rather than the facts. Cf. J.C. BEKER, *Apocalyptic Gospel*, 56.

[24] «Paul's apocalyptic is not an obsolete and/or peripheral ornamental husk that can be eliminated or reinterpreted in such a way that the *core* of his gospel remains unaffected [...] Paul's apocalyptic is the necessary consequence of the truth of the gospel; he does not celebrate apocalyptic *notwithstanding* Christ but *because* of Christ. For the death and resurrection of Christ are future-oriented events, not "closure" events. Thus the gospel of Christ today becomes severely distorted when we ignore this central issue» (J.C. BEKER, *Apocalyptic Gospel*, 84).

[25] The church then becomes an «aggregate of justified sinners» or a «sacramental institute». In the past, the consequences have been negative: divorce of ethics from spirituality; a dualistic anthropology and attitude towards the created order; individualism; and a backward looking rather than forward looking theology. See J.C. BEKER, *Apocalyptic Gospel*, 108-109; ID., *Paul the Apostle*, 154-155.

In answer to those who hold that apocalyptic theology is otherworldly or not suited to the needs of the modern world, Beker insists that «apocalyptic hope compels ethical seriousness, because it is existentially impossible to believe in God's coming triumph and to claim his Holy Spirit without a life style that conforms to that faith [...] God's triumph will not take place without the participation of our "neighbors" in it, and our "neighbors" compel us to struggle together with them for the liberation of all of God's world»[26].

Not all are in agreement about the apocalyptic nature of Paul's gospel. Beker's thesis, although welcomed and praised, has also come under much criticism, some of it salutary. Beker viewed every attempt by modern biblical scholars to translate, transmute, or temper the apocalyptic nature of Paul as a betrayal of that fundamental message[27].

There is still prejudice against apocalyptic literature, and one can still see phrases such as «world-negating», «alienation», etc., as well as extensive attempts to deny that Paul was apocalyptic in his theology or world view[28].

Boers states that following the influential analyses of Barth and Bultmann, a non-apocalyptic interpretation of this chapter predominated. He holds that chapter 15 is a sort of «test case» for apocalypticism in the NT. Disproving the apocalyptic nature of this chapter results in a non-apocalyptic eschatology. It is precisely this test case that will be the concern of this study[29].

2. Proposed Study of the Passage

It is proposed for this study that 1) this passage, 1 Cor 15,12-34, is apocalyptic in its nature; 2) this passage, especially vv. 20-28, must be interpreted as a whole, rather than taking individual terms or symbols out of context; 3) these same verses are not *primarily* christological in character, but focus on the resurrection and the defeat of death, especially the resurrection of Christ as a proleptic event that initiates the end time which will culminate in the resurrection of those in Christ and finally the reas-

---

[26] J.C. BEKER, *Apocalyptic Gospel*, 110.

[27] V. BRANICK cites A. SCHWEITZER and R. JEWETT as two prime examples of this reinterpretation, which Beker feels leads to the loss of the apocalyptic perspective. See V. BRANICK, «Apocalyptic Paul?», 666-667.

[28] Witherington goes to great pains to make the distinction between «apocalyptic» and «eschatological» and opts for the latter (B. WITHERINGTON, *Jesus, Paul, and the End of the World*, 18). Many feel that to admit the presence of apocalyptic theology in Paul is to somehow detract from him. Fee, for example, denies that 1 Cor 15 has anything to do with apocalypticism. See G.D. FEE, *First Corinthians*, 752.

[29] Cf. H.W. BOERS, «Apocalyptic», 53.

sertion of the total sovereignty of God the Father. God's diminution of sovereignty is not real but apparent, since it is only through the forbearance of God that creation has been permitted to defy its creator.

In analyzing the apocalyptic structure and message of 1 Cor 15,12-34, a fourfold study is proposed: an analysis of the rhetorical structure and argumentation, a background study of death and the last things in the Jewish milieu of the period, a study of the passage from the point of view of apocalyptic literature, and finally a diachronic survey of the patristic exegesis. Prompted by the study by Beker, we shall see if the apocalyptic approach to this passage is fruitful in drawing out further meaning and determining its role in the letter as a whole. In this study, we will assume the Pauline authorship of Romans, 1 and 2 Corinthians, Galatians, Philippians, Philemon, and 1 Thessalonians. The authenticity of 2 Thessalonians is controverted, and strong arguments can also be made in its favor, but since the majority opinion is in favor of non-Pauline authorship, this will be assumed during the study. Colossians, Ephesians, 1 and 2 Timothy and Titus are considered deutero-Pauline, but they will be used in this study of Pauline apocalyptic theology for comparative purposes, since they reflect an early Pauline theological tradition.

Additionally, there are a number of questions that arise in a study of this passage: In what sense did some Corinthians deny the resurrection? What is the connection between the resurrection of Christ and that of the believer? When does the reign of Christ begin and end? When does the resurrection take place? Does it involve only believers, or unbelievers and sinners too? What is the role of death in the universe? What is meant by God being «all in all»?

2.1 *Rhetorical Critical Approach*

A rhetorical criticism of this passage can be especially helpful in retrieving the original context and meaning, since it is more inclusive and goes beyond the study of only the theological or ethical meanings of the text[30].

This type of criticism is distinguished from literary criticism in that in rhetorical criticism, the «text must reveal its context», or what is called the rhetorical situation[31].

---

[30] Its emphasis is on the social and the practical, rather than the theoretical. Other forms of criticism tend to fragment or atomize the text, but rhetorical criticism «... takes the text as we have it, whether the work of a single author or the product of editing, and looks at it from the point of view of the author's or editor's intent, the unified results, and how it would be perceived by an audience of near contemporaries» (G.A. KENNEDY, *New Testament Interpretation*, 4.

[31] Written works other than poetry are a «direct response to a specific historical-political situation and problem», and this situation «controls the rhetorical response in

The user of rhetoric attempts to influence human behavior; knowing what that behavior is will tell us a lot about the original context[32].

A knowledge of the structure of the passage as a whole and the purpose of individual rhetorical units and terminology gives a clearer picture as to the purpose of the entire passage.

2.2 *Death and Salvation in Jewish Apocalyptic*

Before moving into the cryptic world of Jewish apocalyptic literature, it is necessary to define terms: what is apocalyptic, apocalypse, and apocalyptic eschatology? There is much confusion over terms and definitions. The word «apocalypse» and «apocalyptic» are often used interchangeably and imprecisely and there is some question as to how the latter relates to or is different from eschatology. How is the genre defined by scholars? What is its purpose? What makes a term or symbol «apocalyptic»? A rapid survey of the prominent views concerning this genre will be conducted, along with the establishment of a controlling definition for the study of the apocalyptic genre and how it applies to this passage.

Many of the NT statements concerning death are difficult if not impossible to understand if viewed only against a background of canonical OT texts. With the exception of Dan 12 and Isa 24-27, along with some controverted texts such as psalms 16, 49, 73, 78 and Job 14,13-15 and 19,25-27, there is precious little concerning an afterlife or resurrection of the dead. It is necessary to turn to the Jewish milieu in its *entirety* to il-

---

the same sense that the question controls the answer». Context, according to Wuellner, means more than just the *Sitz-im-Leben*, literary tradition or genre of a text. It means «the attitudinizing conventions, precepts that condition (both the writers *and* the reader's) stance toward experience, knowledge, tradition, language, and other people». It is similar to what might be called the «ideology» of a literary work. Wuellner follows T.O. SLOAN , «Rhetoric: Rhetoric in Literature», 802-803 for his definition, in W. WUELLNER, «Where is Rhetorical Criticism Taking Us?», 449-450. Both Kennedy and Schüssler Fiorenza base their definition on that of Bitzer: «a particular discourse comes into existence because of some specific condition or situation which invites utterance. The situation controls the rhetorical response in the same sense that the question controls the answer and the problem controls the solution.» [pp. 4-6] Rhetorical situation is defined as «a complex of persons, events, objects, and relations presenting an actual or potential exigence which can be completely or partially removed if discourse, introduced into the situation, can so constrain human decision or action as to bring about the significant modification of the exigence» (L. BITZER, «The Rhetorical Situation», 1-14).

[32] By changing motivations and attitudes, the person engaged in rhetoric tries to affect the situation by persuading and motivating people to act differently. To achieve this end, persuasion and teaching engages the reactions, emotions and convictions of the reader or hearer, and the criterion by which this rhetoric is measured is praxis rather than esthetics. Cf. E. SCHÜSSLER FIORENZA, «Rhetorical Situation», 386-403.

luminate the NT texts to their fullest. Pseudepigraphal and apocalyptic texts are a rich source of comparisons with the NT. Apocalyptic eschatology itself was a way in which one could transcend death and join the angelic hosts[33].

Even a cursory reading of the apocalyptic and pseudepigraphal literature of the first century B.C. and first century A.D. discloses that for the Jews, as well as for the early Christians, death was the very symbol of all that was wrong in the world, the irrefutable evidence of the alienation of creation and humanity from God. But recent studies have shown that something which is even more clear is that there was no *one* Jewish belief on the afterlife or the resurrection. Documents of that period are a wonderful but often frustrating pastiche of images of death, intermediate existence, resurrection, judgment and punishment. These images are sometimes contradictory, even within the same document[34].

Rather than looking for specific source texts for 1 Cor 15, we will examine the pseudepigraphal and apocalyptic texts for images and symbols which would have comprised Paul's intellectual and spiritual world in the matter of death, the afterlife, and the resurrection.

2.3 *The Apocalyptic Nature of 1 Cor 15,12-34*

With the information gleaned from the survey conducted in the previous chapter, a comparison will be made with the Pauline corpus in general and 1 Cor 15 in particular to determine how Paul utilized the Jewish apocalyptic heritage and what changes, if any, he made.

Utilizing the model and definition from the previous chapter, an analysis of 1 Cor 15 will be made to determine 1) if it is an apocalypse; 2) if it is an example of apocalyptic literature or expresses an apocalyptic eschatology; 3) whether it expresses the parenetic aspect of apocalyptic literature.

This passage is often cited as evidence that Paul taught universalism or salvation for all of humanity. This is based on the «all» in v. 22 and the «all in all» of v. 28, along with different interpretations of τὸ τέλος in

---

[33] Collins contrasts biblical prophecy, which always looked upon transcendence of death in the communal context, i.e., the life of the nation, with apocalyptic, which includes the nation but focuses more on the individual. It provides the possibility for the individual to transcend death and pass to heavenly spheres, and with it the hope in the transcendence of death which is the distinctive characteristic of apocalyptic vis-a-vis prophecy. See J.J. COLLINS, «Transcendence of Death», 21-43.

[34] Cf. H.C.C. CAVALIN, *Life After Death*, 199-201; G.W.E. NICKELSBURG, *Resurrection, Immortality, and Eternal Life*, 170-176; D.S. RUSSELL, *Between the Testaments*, 143-162.

v. 24. An analysis of these terms and the role within the passage, along with a comparison with other Pauline soteriological passages, can shed some light on the question of universal salvation in this passage. The passage as a whole, however, will have to be examined in light of the theological implications of its apocalyptic message.

2.4 *Diachronic Analysis: First Five Centuries of Christian Exegesis*

During the first five Christian centuries, this passage was subjected to every sort of scrutiny. This period of theological development and turmoil functioned as a prism through which the light of this passage was refracted, producing a veritable spectrum of theological insights. Approaches to this passage varied: it was mined for proof texts pertaining to the resurrection; it was used as a weapon against the gnostics (although later it was used in turnabout fashion by the gnostics themselves); it was used as evidence for the temporal nature of Christ's reign and for his status as a creature; it was used by some for cosmic speculation. We will choose the first five centuries – somewhat arbitrarily – since most of the theological controversies seem to have been expressed during this period. To carry it through the Middle Ages and the Renaissance and Reformation would be repetitious. We will begin with the apostolic age, represented by Ignatius of Antioch, and end with Theodoret of Cyrus (d.466). This is after the last of the major christological councils – Chalcedon – in 451. The question that will be addressed is whether there was a consistent exegesis of this passage, or did it undergo change? How was the message of this passage understood, and was that understanding apocalyptic in nature? Was there a shift towards a christological interpretation that drained it of its apocalyptic force, and if so, what were the consequences?

3. Summary and Conclusion

In the concluding chapter, a summary of the results of the preceding chapters will be made for the purpose of answering the following questions: Is 1 Cor 15,12-34, especially vv. 20-28, an example of apocalyptic writing, and if so, which mode? Was there a radical shift in the first five Christian centuries in the exegesis of this passage that stressed a christological interpretation at the expense of its apocalyptic meaning? If so, what were the results of this shift? What is the message concerning death and resurrection that Paul is trying to convey? Does he intend all to be saved? What are the ethical implications of this passage?

CHAPTER II

Structure and Argumentation

1. **Purpose of the Chapter**

Why did Paul write chapter 15? In part, this will be answered by the type of argumentation or the rhetorical genre which he uses. The question cannot really be considered apart from the reason he wrote the entire letter. This chapter does not stand in isolation from the rest of the letter; indeed, Barth believed that it was very carefully integrated with the total argumentation. Barth suggests that despite the apparent looseness of the portions of the letter, that they are held together by an eschatological theme and purpose with chapter 15 as its goal. In order to determine if this is true, the focus and theme and purpose of the chapter must be ascertained. Determining the structure and rhetorical type of this chapter will help to shed light on its immediate purpose and on any relationship it might have with the rest of the letter[1].

1.1 *Type of Discourse and Purpose of Chapter*

In determining the purpose of the letter and more specifically, the chapter, it is important to ascertain to which of the three species of rhetoric, i.e., deliberative, epideictic or judicial, this chapter most likely belongs. A variety of interpretations is possible[2].

---

[1] Cf. K. BARTH, *The Resurrection of the Dead*, 7-8; J.C. BEKER, *Paul the Apostle*, 173.176.

[2] *Rhetorica ad Herennium*, I.ii.2. Kennedy states that «The species is judicial when the author is seeking to persuade the audience to make a judgment about events occurring in the past; it is deliberative when he seeks to persuade them to take some action in the future; it is epideictic when he seeks to persuade them to hold or reaffirm some point of view in the present, as when he celebrates or denounces some person or some quality» (G.A. KENNEDY, *New Testament Interpretation*, 19). At

Kennedy holds that 1 Corinthians is mostly deliberative, with some judicial passages, such as 1,13-17[3].

Mitchell declares that 1 Cor is a «unified deliberative letter urging concord», and has little if anything to do with any defense of Paul's apostolate. She differs from many in her analysis by her insistence on the total uniformity and singleness of the letter with regard to type of discourse and purpose[4].

Wuellner argued that 1 Corinthians is an example of epideictic or demonstrative discourse, but with some modifications[5].

According to Bünker, 1 Cor 1,10-4,21 and 1 Cor 15 are indicative of judicial discourse, and although the letter is formally addressed to the entire Corinthian community, Paul is in fact arguing with a handful of well-educated Corinthians of high social status[6].

---

times it is difficult to determine which type of discourse is being used, especially since many times there is a mixture of more than one, although one type usually predominates. The three types are addressed to three different audiences: the first two to those who have the power to make decisions, i.e., members of the assembly and judges; the third, to spectators. See also B.M. GARAVELLI, *Manuale di Retorica*, 26-27.

[3] Cf. G.A. KENNEDY, *New Testament Interpretation*, 87.

[4] M. Mitchell insists that «the designation of the rhetorical genre or species of a New Testament text as epideictic, deliberative or forensic cannot be begged in the analysis. It must be demonstrated and supported before the compositional or structural analysis proceeds» [p.11]. Although this may seem attractive at first, there are some problems. Many texts are unclear in their style and similar to one another in style; one could find evidence to support almost any decision. There are times when the designation of a style or species must be the result of at least some analysis, always of course being subject to refinement and/or reevaluation. The other questionable aspect of her methodology is her insistence that the style or genre of any text is «determined by the compositional whole, and cannot be correctly determined apart from it» (M.M. MITCHELL, *Paul and the Rhetoric of Reconciliation*, 10.15). This seems to ignore the complex and multifaceted aspects of many texts which deal with various issues in many different ways. Mitchell's approach seems to impose a uniformity and rigidity on the text which may not have been the intention of the author. The rhetorical unit to be examined should always be a compositional unit.

[5] Wuellner identifies Paul's digressions, 1,19-3,21; 9,1-10,13; and 13,1-13 as being carefully crafted for the purpose of dealing with the issue at hand, serving an affective function of intensifying adherence. He follows Perelman's redefinition of this type: instead of being only a display of the art of rhetorical skill and eloquence for the marketplace, the demonstrative genre is concerned with the audience's values. Epideictic discourse seeks to intensify the audience's adherence to certain values. See W. WUELLNER, «Greek Rhetoric», 177-88. Quoted in E. SCHÜSSLER FIORENZA, «Rhetorical Situation», 391.

[6] Schüssler Fiorenza objects that Bünker does not base his analysis on the entire letter, but only certain chapters. This should not present a great difficulty, however, since a document may contain several rhetorical species, changing from section to

Epideictic discourse is usually given on the occasion of something important, such as a funeral or public event, and is basically the «praise and shame» type of oratory. By extolling certain types of virtues or practices, the orator hopes to convince his listeners to continue to adhere to them. There are many elements indicating that this is the type of discourse predominant in chapter 15. It exhorts the Corinthians to stick to what they had been given and had accepted in the beginning through the apostolic preaching. Verses 29-34 appeal to everyday life and modes of behavior, and v. 34 relies heavily on shame as a tool in changing attitudes and behavior. However, as Kennedy points out, nearly every species has some epideictic color or flavor to it[7].

The purpose of the judicial style is to accuse and defend, and it is concerned with judgment about something that has taken place in the past. Kennedy has drawn attention to some examples of judicial strategy, in which Paul answers possible objections and defends his *ethos*. There are several examples in the letter; for instance, in chapter 9 Paul defends his style of ministry[8].

The goal of the deliberative type is to convince people to make a decision concerning the future, to decide on a course of action that is honorable and useful, and there are many examples of this in 1 Cor as a whole.

We have seen that Mitchell believes the entire letter to be deliberative in nature. This view is supported by 1,10 and the *peroratio* in 16,15-18: the community should be in agreement, being united in the same mind and opinion without dissensions, and submit itself to Stephanas and his co-workers. The overriding concern is that of fostering concord and healing the divisions and dissensions. Towards this end, Paul deals with a number of ethical issues: marriage and sexuality in chs. 5-7; sacrificial meat in 8,1-11,1; worship 11,2-14,40; alms 16,1-4; and resurrection in 15,12-57. In all of these instances, he seeks to redefine «advantage» by redefining a Corinthian slogan «πάντα μοι ἔξεστιν». Instead of referring to the individual, advantage is now defined in terms of the whole, the community, the body of Christ (6,12-20; 10,23-11,1). Paul takes the goals and standards by which people make daily living decisions and re-

---

section. See M. BÜNKER, *Briefformular*, 48-76, quoted in E. SCHÜSSLER FIORENZA, «Rhetorical Situation», 392.

[7] For example, when the preacher exhorts his congregation to refrain from certain types of behavior by obeying accepted norms of Christian behavior, he is engaged in an epideictic type of discourse, regardless of whether the entire sermon is of this type. Cf. G.A. KENNEDY, *New Testament Interpretation*, 74.

[8] The *ethos* is the credibility of the speaker, and is one of Aristotle's three modes of artistic proof. Cf. B.M. GARAVELLI, *Manuale di Retorica*, 27.

orients them relative to a new goal: the resurrection in chapter 15. One must consider, however, that these same passages concerning behavior and ethics can just as well be indicative of epideictic rhetoric[9].

It is fairly well established that Paul, despite his protestations to the contrary, was skilled in the use of rhetoric. He appears uneasy with rhetoric in several places in his letters, and Betz believes that in 1 Corinthians he attempts to reconcile rhetoric and theology[10].

Paul writes to the Corinthians in 1,5 that «in everything you have been made rich in him (Christ), in every form of speech (λόγῳ) and in every form of knowledge (γνώσει)». The key word in Paul's criticism of the attitudes of the Corinthians is «deed (ἔργον)», and it is found in 3,13-15 and in the *peroratio* of the letter in 15,58. The Corinthians are lacking in practical application of their theology and spirituality in the daily life of the community[11].

---

[9] In her analysis, factionalism also results from differing views concerning the resurrection. By insisting on correct belief concerning the doctrine of the resurrection, Paul relativizes many of the squabbles and power struggles of the community. The resurrection becomes the final goal of the whole letter, the τέλος. The extensive use of πάντες in vv. 22-28 signifies that the resurrection is for *all* members of the community, rather than for just a select few, and serves merely a conciliatory purpose. It is this last conclusion that is most questionable. Mitchell does not seem to appreciate the varied nature of different rhetorical units, and does not analyze this passage from the point of view of apocalyptic eschatology. As much as we like to believe that religious texts are merely political or serve communitarian goals, we must also accept the fact that for Paul and his contemporaries the cosmos and the human race were interdependent and that there was a unique transcendental aspect to their theological thinking. Paul was answering soteriological and existential questions, and was striving to explain the eschatological and apocalyptic event of Christ's resurrection in terms of the future of the cosmos and humanity. This world view is attested in other parts of the NT and in intertestamental literature; it was not something conjured up by Paul to soothe dissensions in the Corinthian community. Cf. M. MITCHELL, *Reconciliation*, 175.283.

[10] Using the rhetorical device of *synkrisis*, or opposing types, Paul contrasts his own rhetoric, that of a friend, with that of a deceiver or flatterer (1 Cor 1,5; 1 Thess 2,1-12; Gal 1,10). Cf. pp. 16-21 for a history of the research on Paul's relationship to rhetoric. Given the number and type of problems in the Corinthian community, it is unlikely that philosophy or rhetoric was Paul's primary concern. Rather, he uses rhetorical method to deal with one problem: the gap between theory and praxis. Cf. H.D. BETZ, «The Problem of Rhetoric», 16-48.

[11] «There should be a synthesis of eloquence, knowledge, and practice, however, if any claim to perfection such as the Corinthians evidently make (cf. 2,6; 3,1.18; 4,8) is to be sustained. Paul's letter with its advice on the practical matters in the church is designed to bring the Corinthians' praxis (ἔργον) up to the same standards as their "eloquence and knowledge"» (H.D. BETZ, «The Probelm of Rhetoric», 33). Before attacking those problems directly, however, he must undermine the source and foundation of their opposing claims: the superior spiritual status they claimed, which was based upon wisdom and a manifestation of spiritual gifts. Beginning in

This is in partial agreement with the views of Beker, for whom the coherent core of the gospel is the correlation of spirit and body. The Corinthians hold that the spiritual and the material in the form of the spirit and body are not fully compatible. Paul must continually integrate these two principles throughout the letter (3,16-17; 6,13-20; 9,24-27). He concludes that this chapter is the climax of the apocalyptic interpretation of the gospel. To reject this correlation of the spirit and body, expressed in the form of the apocalyptic resurrection body, is to reject the gospel[12].

We have seen that several interpretations are possible. This indicates that 1 Cor does not fit neatly into any one category. It could well be that the entire letter is deliberative in nature, but is comprised of rhetorical units of differing types (*pace* Mitchell). In a long letter such as this, the types will change many times, in order to fit the argument and the rhetorical situation, although they may ultimately serve one overall purpose of the letter. However, 1,10 and the *peroratio* in 16,15-18, together with the detailed attention to ethical issues in chapters 5-7, indicate that the letter is primarily epideictic in nature. It would appear that the bulk of this passage (vv. 1-34) is also epideictic, and intends to enhance adherence of the community to certain values and doctrines, and to influence its ethical behavior. Paul's main argument will show the connection between Christ's resurrection and that of believers, and he insists that this has concrete consequences for everyday ethical behavior.

2. **Structure of Chapter 15**

The chapter itself is divided into two parts which seem to form the two leaves of a diptych. The first half, verses 1-34, speaks of the fact of the resurrection; the other half, verses 35-58, of the mode or «how» of the resurrection[13].

A traditional approach would be to view chapter 15 as a composition of many layers and strands. Rhetorical theory, however, views the text as a unity instead of the result of a «cut and paste» method. During compo-

---

1:18 to 4:13, he contrasts his preaching of the foolishness of the cross with what the Corinthians claim is wisdom, and he will seek to show that their so-called wisdom is actually foolishness in the eyes of God. Their strength becomes weakness, their virtues, vices. He continually contrasts the wisdom of the powerful of this world, which is made foolish or doomed to perish, with God's hidden wisdom, manifested in weakness and nothingness.

[12] Cf. J.C. BEKER, *Paul the Apostle*, 176.

[13] Cf. B. STANDAERT, «La Rhétorique Ancienne», 81.

sition the author draws from many different strands of his own experience, which includes tradition, reflection, and so forth[14].

Verses 12 through 34 can be described as a literary unity, based upon similarities in syntax, style, vocabulary, and semantics[15].

The verses under consideration; that is, 12-34, must be placed in the context of chapter 15 in its entirety, since they form a sub-unit[16]:

verses 1-2	*exordium*
verse 3a	*transitus*
verses 3b-11	*narratio*
verse 12	*propositio*
verses 12-28	*probatio*
verses 29-34	*peroratio*

2.1 *Exordium*

Verses 1 and 2 comprise the *exordium*. In this section, Paul addresses the Corinthians and reminds them of their reception of the gospel[17].

Paul wins the attention of his audience by demonstrating that what he has proclaimed is of special interest to them being saved. In striving to make the audience receptive to the message about to be given, one would expect a stress on the degree of difference in information and knowledge between the writer and recipient. The opening word, γνωρίζω, is used often as a technical term with a revelatory sense, although at other times

---

[14] In the approach represented by Mußner, tradition is the basic layer, and is augmented by personal experience and theological reflection or speculation, with the layers of tradition not always being clearly delineated. Mußner's analysis is as follows: vv. 1-2 introduction (with «reminder»); vv. 3-7 tradition; vv. 8-10 personal experience; vv. 11-12 transition; vv. 13-32 reflection or speculation with the additions of tradition in vv. 20-22, scripture in vv. 25, 27, and 32, and experience in vv. 30-32; and parenesis in vv. 33-34. Cf. F. MUßNER, «"Schichten" in der paulinischen Theologie», 59-70.

[15] The unity is demonstrated as follows:
a = vv. 12-19 v. 13a if there is no
resurrection of dead;
v. 16a if the dead are not raised
b = vv. 20-28 affirmation of resurrection of
Christ and the dead
a¹ = vv. 29-32 if the dead are not raised:
vv. 29b and 32c
Cf. J.-N. ALETTI, «L'Argumentation de Paul», 64.

[16] Cf. M. BÜNKER, *Briefformular*, 72.

[17] The purpose of the *exordium* is to render the audience attentive, receptive, and benevolent (*benevolum, attentum, docilem*). Cf. *Rhetorica ad Herennium*, I.iv.6-7; B.M. GARAVELLI, *Manuale di Retorica*, 63-65; G.A. KENNEDY, 23; B.L. MACK, *Rhetoric*, 56.

a more mundane meaning is intended. Despite the fact that the kerygma that is to be discussed is already known, the revelatory sense is still valid: this is a doctrinal instruction, so something new will be given or disclosed[18].

He appeals subtly to the emotions of his audience by provoking doubt and anxiety concerning their existential status, especially in the phrase ἐκτὸς εἰ μὴ εἰκῇ ἐπιστεύσατε[19].

Being saved is made contingent on holding firmly to what has been preached and received (v.2b); not to do so is synonymous with believing in vain. This stipulation addresses directly the concerns of vv. 3-28: a) it introduces vv. 3-7; namely, the tradition of the death and resurrection upon which Paul will base the argument of vv. 12-28; b) demonstrates the logic of vv. 12-19; namely, if those who say that there is no resurrection are correct, then faith in this proclamation is futile[20].

This verse also anticipates vv. 3-5, the same gospel which he will reiterate for them[21].

The Corinthians owe their very existence to the gospel which Paul himself preached to them. This serves not only to emphasize the message which he preached, but also to show their particular relationship with him and his authority. Paul also stresses the fact that they stand in this tradition (1a) and that they are being saved (or will be saved if it is taken as a futuristic present), thereby establishing common ground with them and affirming their Christian status[22].

---

[18] The basic meaning is «to make known» although a literal English translation is rather awkward, «I remind you» being chosen by the NRSV, RSV and REB. Other possible translations: «I draw your attention to,» «I inform you,» etc. The word is used extensively in the Pauline and deutero-Pauline literature: 1 Cor 12,3; 15,1; 2 Cor 8,1; Gal 1,11; Phil 1,22; 4,6; Rom 9,22.23; 16,26; Eph 1,9; 3,10; 6,19.21; Col 1,27; 4,7.9; as well as the gospels in John 15,15; 17,26; Luke 2,15.17; Acts 2,28; 7,13. See M. BÜNKER, *Briefformular*, 62.

[19] Cf. M. BÜNKER, *Briefformular*, 62.

[20] Fee argues for an «A-B-A-B» structure. A^1 repeats the basic message of A; B describes their response to the gospel, with B^1 being their present negative attitude towards it.

A I make known to you the gospel, which I preached to you,
B which also you received,
   in which you also stand,
   through which also you are being saved, (that is)
A^1 with what word I preached to you,
B^1 provided you hold fast, unless you received it in vain.
See G. FEE, *Corinthians*, 720-721.

[21] Cf. G. FEE, *Corinthians*, 720.

[22] Cf. C.K. BARRETT, *Corinthians*, 336; H. CONZELMANN, *1 Corinthians*, 250; G. FEE, *Corinthians*, 718-719.

The phrase ἐν ᾧ καὶ ἐστήκατε helps Paul to establish a sense of commonality with the community[23].

2.2 *Transitus*

Bünker describes verse 3a as the *transitus*, or transition between the *exordium* and the *narratio*. It serves to harmonize the two portions of the text as well as delineate clearly the ending of one portion and the beginning of another. A firm connection is made between the terms παραλαμβάνω and παραδίδωμι as being descriptive of the apostolic preaching mission, and when coupled with ἐν πρώτοις, the point is clear: What Paul is about to preach is the original kerygma received in the beginning and passed on by preaching, reaching the Corinthians through Paul[24].

This helps to establish the reliability of the message which Paul has preached and leads into the *narratio*[25].

2.3 *Narratio*

One of the functions of the *narratio* is to teach as well as persuade, and this is indicated in the opening γνωρίζω[26].

In addition to supporting the case at hand, it lays the groundwork for the further argumentation. It presents the irrefutable facts and events upon which the argumentation will be built. In this case, Paul stresses the common ground upon which he and the Corinthians stand, while at the same time placing a different accent on it for the purpose of furthering his own cause. To aid in performing this function, the rule of *brevitas* is observed: only that which is most important in forming the opinion of the hearer is inserted, in order to keep the argument tight and maintain the interest of the listener[27].

---

[23] Cf. M. BÜNKER, *Briefformular*, 62.

[24] Since tradition is the prime layer of Paul's theology, he utilizes rabbinic terminology. The terms παραλαμβάνειν (קבל) and παραδιδόνται (ממר) have parallels in the Mishnaic tractate *Abot* I, 1ff, in which Moses receives (קבל) the Torah on Sinai and passes it on (ומסרה) to Joshua, who in turn passes it onto the elders, prophets, etc. See G. FEE, *Corinthians*, 720; F. MUßNER, «Schichten», 62.

[25] Cf. M. BÜNKER, *Briefformular*, 64.

[26] The purpose of the *narratio* is to narrate in a persuasive fashion the facts and events as they happened or are supposed to have happened so that the listener is informed of the theme or subject of the controversy. These are supposed to be the facts and events that cannot be denied, and they form the foundation upon which the *probatio* will be built. Cf. B.M. GARAVELLI, *Manuale di Retorica*, 68-75.

[27] The technique of *brevitas* is the forced suppression or excision of all unnecessary words, leaving nothing to add or subtract, so that as few words as possible are

The function of verses 3b - 11 is controverted: is the emphasis on the resurrection of Christ or Paul's apostolic authority? Most commentators see verses 9-11 as attempts by Paul to justify and sustain his apostolic status and authority. At first glance, this appears to be the case, for Paul seems to be taking great pains to counter criticism. If, however, these verses comprise the *narratio*, it is difficult to see how this could be a justification of his apostolic status. In the *narratio*, hard facts and events are presented not only to bolster the case, but to provide a foundation for the *probatio*. Along with the resurrection of Christ, Paul's status as an apostle is known and accepted by the Corinthian community. In chapter 9, Paul is merely defending his style of ministry, not his status as an apostle, for it is to that status that he appeals. As we shall see, verses 9-11 are for the purpose of establishing the reliability of his witness and the word which he preaches[28].

If the emphasis is on the resurrection of Christ, it is possible that he was attempting to establish the death and resurrection of Christ as the common ground with the Corinthians. Given the primitive nature of the formula given in v. 3b-5, and his insistence that it represented what had already been preached and accepted, it is more likely that the emphasis is on Christ's resurrection, especially as a theological given in his argument[29].

---

used in argumentation. This is set forth in the *Rhetorica ad Herennium* I.ix.4. A good example of this is the string of independent subordinate clauses in the «creed»: καὶ ὅτι; followed by the terse, rapid-fire listing of the witnesses to the Risen Christ. Cf. M. Dülmen, *Driefformular*, 65; R. M. Garavelli, *Manuale di Retorica*, 69.254.

[28] Is the subject Paul's apostleship or the resurrection of Christ? Most probably the former, Lüdemann asserts, and for several reasons. Paul speaks at length of his apostolic office; he asserts in 10b that he has worked harder than all the others; and in contradiction to 7b where it is stated that Jesus appeared to *all* the apostles, Paul states that last of all Jesus appeared to him, the least of all apostles. This last argument implies that the apostolic circle was already closed before Paul's conversion. He also seeks to affirm the quality of his own vision of Christ as been equal to that of the others, thereby establishing him as one of the apostles on the list of witnesses. It may be said, however, that one cannot judge the subject or theme of a passage merely by the number of words given to a particular point; judgment must be made on the basis of the rhetorical function of a particular passage. There may also be other reasons for Paul's apologetic tone and apparent self denigration. In this case, it could well be for the purpose of showing the effects of his encounter with the Risen Lord and the quality of his witness to the resurrection. See G. LÜDEMANN, *Opposition to Paul*, 72-73.

[29] In dealing with the question of the reason for Paul's listing of the eyewitnesses and the views of Paul's Corinthian opponents, Sider focuses on pages 152-8 of Barth's *The Resurrection of the Dead*. According to Barth, Paul's opponents accepted the resurrection of Christ as an isolated fact without an appreciation of its importance

2.3.1 The Primitive Kerygma: Common Ground

It is fairly certain that Paul cites part of the proclaimed tradition but enlarges on it for the sake of his argumentation. The extent and form of the original, however, is most difficult to determine. Verses 3b-5 probably comprise the primitive kerygma which Paul uses for two reasons: first of all, in following a fundamentally deliberative style of argumentation, he appeals to an authority prior in time and superior to his own, of which he was a faithful transmitter (3a), and which the Corinthian church had already accepted and adhered to (1b); secondly, the death, burial and resurrection of Jesus will form the *sine qua non* of Paul's teaching on the resurrection of the dead.

The language of vv. 3b-5 has been described as un-Pauline in style, reflecting the primitive nature of this formula[30].

The phrase «according to the Scriptures» probably refers to the Scriptures taken as a whole, since no particular passage is specified, although the statement that he «died for our sins» is most likely a reference to Isa 53. This supports the view that the events listed in the creed are in accordance with God's salvific plan; additionally, they add authoritative weight to Paul's main argument. The reference to the Scriptures is repeated when referring to the resurrection, and it raises many questions, since there is no clear reference in the OT to either the resurrection of the Messiah or other individual taking place on the third day[31].

---

and ramifications. Without understanding the integral connection between the resurrection of Christ and the general resurrection, they were able to deny the resurrection of the dead while still holding the resurrection of Christ. So far, Barth is correct. He then uses this to deny emphatically that Paul listed the witnesses to prove the historicity of Christ's resurrection, but to show that all the apostles agreed that the church was founded on Christ's resurrection. Although undoubtedly Paul does want to show as much support from others as possible, Sider rightly rejects the second part of Barth's analysis, pointing out that even if the apostles do agree on the centrality of Christ's resurrection, it is not out of place to reaffirm its historicity and to use this as the basis of further argument [pp. 126-8]. Cf. R.J. SIDER, «St. Paul's Understanding», 124-141.

[30] Non-Pauline words and phrases are those which do not serve the needs of the immediate occasion, and those which are self-sufficient. It may include vv. 6-7, but these appear to have been added by Paul to serve his own purposes. According to Kloppenborg, vv. 6b and 8 as well as the connectives are from the hand of Paul. Verses 3b-5 remain the core of the pre-Pauline tradition. Based upon the parallelism of the members and the «Semitic coloring» of the language, Jeremias and others argue for a Semitic source, although no one argument is conclusive. Cf. J. KLOPPENBORG, «Analysis of the Pre-Pauline Formula», 351-367. See also H. CONZELMANN, *1 Corinthians*, 251-253; G. FEE, *Corinthians*, 722-723;

[31] The only possible OT passage evocative of the Christian resurrection event is Hos 6,2. Passages such as Dan 12,1-2 describe the general resurrection. Cf. G. FEE,

The reference to the appearance (ὤφθη) is a traditional formula. The separate appearance to Cephas is noteworthy; in the gospels, it appears only in the proclamation in Luke 24,34[32].

The fundamental structure of the formula is two-fold: a) ἀπέθανεν, ἐτάφη (he died, he was buried); and b) ἐγήγερται, ὤφθη (he was raised, he appeared). The references to being buried and appearing can be looked upon as elaborative proofs of the statements that he died and was raised[33].

Several commentators judge that the ἐτάφη is emphasizing the ἀπέθανεν, rather than the ἐγήγερται, thereby giving additional support to the fact that Jesus suffered a corporeal and definitive death[34]. From the standpoint of the eschatological event of the resurrection, however, all the verbs are of equal importance.

2.3.2 Witnesses to the Risen Lord: The Reliability of Paul's Witness

From the original circle of chosen apostles who were the prime witnesses (note that the prior appearance to the women is not mentioned), Paul constructs his string of witnesses, linked together by a series of particles (εἶτα, ἔπειτα): the 500 brothers at once, James, and to «all the apostles». Paul is not trying to prove the different aspects of Christ's

---

Corinthians, 726-727; H. CONZELMANN, *1 Corinthians*, 254-255; J. KLOPPENBORG, «Analysis of the Pre-Pauline Formula», 354.

[32] The tradition of an appearance to Peter is very early, and as some would see, the basis for his status within the Christian community. Conzelmann holds that the term the «Twelve» proves that the group arose after the death of Jesus, since there were clearly less than twelve present. It is more likely, however, a collective term for the whole group, regardless of how many were present at the time: Judas had already departed, and Cephas is here referred to as if he were distinct from the Twelve. Cf. H. CONZELMANN, *1 Corinthians*, 256-257; see also G. FEE, 729.

[33] This is strongly refuted by Sider, who notes that there are four clauses, and the latter three - buried, raised, and appeared - are all connected by καί. Any attempt, Sider insists, to subordinate any of the verbs to the other is «sheer speculation». Cf. H. CONZELMANN, *1 Corinthians*, 252; R. SIDER, «Nature and Significance», 134-135.

[34] Conzelmann feels that this is not connected with the empty tomb stories, and is not for apologetic reasons in the face of a docetic Christology as many others hold, but is intended to portray the death of Jesus as a positive, salvific event. Conzelmann follows a study by Hans Grass, who claims that «died and was buried» was an idiomatic phrase that must be taken as a whole. He cites Luke 16,22 and Acts 2,29 in support of this. Sider's analysis of these two passages, however, shows that the two words are not necessarily linked. See Sider, «Nature and Significance», 134-5. Citing several studies, Fee holds that this very early insistence that a corpse was laid in the tomb and was raised is definitely indicative of the empty tomb accounts (G. FEE, *Corinthians*, 725). See also H. CONZELMANN, *1 Corinthians*, 255.

death and resurrection recounted in vv. 3b-5; they are already accepted tradition and are being used as part of the narratio.

Although the resurrection is certainly the main topic of his argument, it will become obvious that in order to make any claims to be proclaiming the truth concerning the resurrection, Paul will have to establish his reliability as a witness, and therefore, the reliability of his message.

Verse 6 relates that the Risen Lord appeared to the 500, «most of whom are alive, though some have fallen asleep» (ἐξ ὧν οἱ πλείονες ἕως ἄρτι, τινὲς δὲ ἐκοιμήθησαν). But it can be asked: which part of this statement is emphasized, the first, i.e., the fact that many remain alive, or the second, which states that some have died? The first is most likely: First of all, Paul mentions the death of some of the witnesses very casually, almost as an aside. If the emphasis were on the fact that some of the witnesses had died, he failed to develop this line of argumentation. The 500 witnesses are mentioned here as added corroboration of the message that Paul is proclaiming. The readers/listeners are invited to check Paul's facts with these numerous witnesses, if they entertain any doubts[35].

Verse 7 describes the appearance to James, brother of the Lord and leader of the Jerusalem church and then to «all the apostles». This emphasizes that the kerygma is something shared by the Christian community, a common tradition to which one can appeal and with which one can verify Paul's message concerning the resurrection[36].

The reference to «all the apostles» presents a puzzle: does it mean another appearance to the assembled Twelve, or another group also referred to as apostles? Perhaps Paul lists this second appearance to the assembled apostles to emphasize that they were a closed circle, commissioned by Christ. The emphasis is not on Paul's status as an apostle, but on his experience of the Risen Lord, his witness to the resurrection; it is an experience shared not only with the apostles but with all of the other witnesses. The second appearance to all the apostles need not be understood in a sense implying special authority, for the term could be used here in a couple of different senses[37].

---

[35] He holds that the emphasis is on the fact that some have already died. Fee, however, argues for the emphasis on those living, as an invitation to the Corinthians to inquire for themselves if they have any doubts as to the reality of the resurrection. In view of Paul's almost casual aside concerning those who have fallen asleep, similar to his aside in 1 Cor 1:16, and his failure to develop this line of argumentation fully, the emphasis is more likely to have been on those who are still alive. They are further authoritative witnesses to corroborate what Paul is proclaiming. See M. BÜNKER, *Briefformular*, 54-55; H. CONZELMANN, *1 Corinthians*, 258; G. FEE, *Corinthians*, 730.

[36] Cf. Acts 1:21-26 and 1 Cor 9:1.

[37] This appearance to James is otherwise unknown in the canonical writings, there being only a possibility that he was among those commissioned in Acts 1,6-11. There

2.3.3 Paul's Conversion Experience: Commission From the Risen Lord

At the end of this impressive list of witnesses, Paul places himself (v. 8). He is a valid witness to the Risen Lord, and he refuses to compromise on this point. He appeals both to tradition and personal experience by referring to his experience on the road to Damascus, which he counts not as a vision, but as a resurrection appearance every bit as valid as the appearances to the others (note that the verb ὤφθη is repeated). His own personal experience is now closely connected with tradition and with the primitive apostolic experience[38].

He admits that it is unusual, abnormal or out of time (ἐκτρώματι), but that it is nonetheless valid[39].

Paul focuses upon himself in verses 9 and 10, and it at first appears that he is denigrating himself[40].

His narration is very tightly worded and refrains from appealing to the hearer's emotions or affect (*pathos*), but now verses 9 and 10 clearly play upon the emotions of the hearers[41].

---

is one reference in the Apocryphal Gospel of the Hebrews. «All of the apostles» can be taken several ways: as appearance to each one separately; as an appearance to the Twelve collectively; or as another, wider group in addition to the Twelve. Fee opts for the latter, claiming that «apostles» is here used as a much broader term, in a ministerial sense rather than a juridical one, and that this is different from what is referred to as the Twelve. In the gospels, there are lists of the Twelve, but the same names do not always appear. Since there are no other references to a wider group called apostles, it must be assumed that Paul is referring to another, final appearance to the assembled apostles, such as the one described in John 21. Cf. G. FEE, *Corinthians*, 732; H. CONZELMANN, *I Corinthians*, 258.

38 This is the experience narrated in Acts 9, 22, and 26, and alluded to in 1 Cor 9. Cf. MUßNER, «Schichten», 63.

39 The meaning of ἐκτρώμα is debated. It can mean «abortion», «miscarriage», or «stillbirth». It is usually translated as «abortion» or «untimely birth». It is here used with the definite article, which can also cause it to mean monstrosity or freak. It has been suggested by some scholars that this was the pejorative nickname for Paul among the Corinthians, but this is conjecture. It is also possible that it was a play on Paul's name, «Paulus» meaning «little one», or «dwarf», or that the Corinthians used this as a reference to Paul because of his personal weaknesses. It is clear that he uses the term in a self-deprecating sense, debasing himself in the eyes of the community and perhaps winning their sympathy. This will be the springboard for his account of what God's grace has done for him. Cf. H. CONZELMANN, *1 Corinthians*, 259; G. FEE, *Corinthians*, 733.

40 Bünker believes that vv. 9-10 form a *digressio*, which rather than contradicting the requirements of *brevitas*, serve to support the argument. The digression is often used to examine pertinent motivations, circumstances, and themes related to the question being examined. As will be demonstrated, however, these verses form an integral part of the *narratio*. Cf. M. BÜNKER, *Briefformular*, 66-67; G.A. KENNEDY, *New Testament Interpretation*, 24; B.M. GARAVELLI, *Manuale di Retorica*, 72.

First of all, he asserts that he is the least of all the apostles, unfit to even be called one, because of his past persecution of the church of God[42].

But rather than an apologia for his status as apostle, this must be looked upon as further factual data for his narratio. He contrasts his previous state with what he is now: he has worked harder than all of the others, and God's grace has not been wasted on him. He mentions the grace of God twice: it has made him what he is, and it is this grace in him that has made him work harder than the others. The quality of his ministry is for Paul further proof of the reliability of his witness to the resurrection. Those having doubts are invited to look at the transformation that has been effected by the grace of God in this persecutor and one unfit to be called an apostle, and to see the fruits of this transformation in his apostolic labors. When Paul then sets forth his doctrinal teaching on the resurrection, it will be as one who has been transformed and empowered by having witnessed the resurrected Christ.

In verse 11, he emphasizes that what he proclaims is what the others proclaim; he is at one with them, and that is the kerygma which the Corinthians community received and believed. This also gives further emphasis to the fact that this has been a *narratio*, for what has been given Paul holds in common with the other apostles and witnesses, and it is what the Corinthians adhered to. So far there should be no disagreement, and this sets the stage for the coming propositio.

2.3.4 Conclusion

Paul has established in the narratio that the resurrection of Christ is at the core of the primitive kerygma, and that this has already been accepted by the Corinthians. The fact that Christ is risen is a verifiable fact; there were many witnesses, including Paul, to the Risen Christ. Paul's status as an apostle is not in question; this is included with the facts of the *narratio*. Paul merely defends his reliability as a witness to the resurrected Christ. Even the negative facts of Paul's life bear witness to this reliability: the fruits of this experience and of God's grace are evident to all.

---

[41] *Pathos*, the second of Aristotle's artistic proofs, is defined as the emotional reaction experienced by the audience at the hands of the orator. This immediate expedient provokes the emotional participation of the listener. Cf. B.M. GARAVELLI, *Manuale di Retorica*, 269; G.A. KENNEDY, *New Testament Interpretation*, 15.

[42] Throughout this part of the *narratio*, he fulfills one of the fundamental rules of rhetoric: avoid even the hint of arrogance and maintain the good will of your audience. Cf. M. BÜNKER, *Briefformular*, 67.

With the resurrection of Christ firmly anchored, Paul can now deal with the issue at hand: the resurrection of the dead.

2.4 *Propositio*

In verse 12a, the *narratio* is ended with a forceful statement of its essence; namely, that Christ is proclaimed as risen from the dead. There is almost universal agreement that the Corinthians accepted – or at least until recently had accepted – the resurrection of Christ[43].

The *argumentatio* proper (verses 12-32) begins with a sudden shift in 12b to the *propositio* or issue under consideration: Some say that there is no resurrection of the dead[44].

To be noted is the fact that 12a sums up what appears to have been agreed to by using a conditional sentence. The «if» is positive, implying that Christ is indeed preached as having been raised from the dead, and this is the common starting point with the Corinthian community. He then asks, If this is true, if *Christ* is preached as having been raised, then how can some of you say there is no resurrection of *the dead*? Linking these two events, the resurrection of Christ and of the dead, will form the core of Paul's argument in vv. 12-34.

2.4.1 In What Sense Is There No Resurrection of the Dead?

The statement itself seems clear enough, but deceptively so. It raises several questions: Did some of the Corinthians actually say this, or is Paul misrepresenting or distorting their opinions? In what sense is there no resurrection of the dead; i.e., were they denying the bodily nature of the resurrection, or the afterlife itself? Most modern interpretations are very speculative or are not coherent with the rest of the letter. The letter

---

[43] In his discussion of Schmithals' *Gnosticism in Corinth*, Wilson deals with Schmithals' disagreement, for he held that Paul's opponents were gnostics who denied the resurrection of the body. Wilson refutes Schmithals' arguments chiefly by rejecting his exegetical and religio-historical methodology (J.H. WILSON, «The Corinthians Who Say», 93-94). Sider also disagrees; he holds that Paul cites the list of witnesses in order to establish the historicity of Christ's bodily resurrection, which he suspected the Corinthians of abandoning. Taking issue with Conzelmann, he believes that the mention of the appearance to the 500 is so that the Corinthians can go and verify for themselves (R. SIDER, «Nature and Significance», 131-132). See also H. CONZELMANN, *1 Corinthians*, 264-265; A.J.M. WEDDERBURN, «Problem of the Denial», 41; G. FEE, *Corinthians*, 737-738.

[44] Bünker notes the skill and careful crafting of Paul in maintaining the flow from the *narratio* to the *propositio*. Cf. M. BÜNKER, *Briefformular*, 68.

itself seems to be contradictory; in some places it appears to favor an afterlife, in other places it appears to deny it[45].

A complete and certain retrieval of the original intent and meaning of the statements of the Corinthians is not possible; however, some interpretations are more or less likely than others. Verses 12-34 should not be looked upon as a detailed counter-argument of all of the beliefs of the Corinthians; Paul merely takes one statement – there is no resurrection – and presents the radical consequences flowing from it[46].

There is the possibility that Paul, although he correctly reported what the Corinthians were saying, did not really understand what they meant by it. In fact, most discussions of these passages which put forward other possibilities are predicated on the idea that Paul either misrepresented or misunderstood the Corinthians' position. In order to prove this, however, one would have to be able to show what the misunderstood position was, and attempts so far have not been convincing[47].

In his article, Wilson groups the various viewpoints concerning the meaning of v. 12 into four general categories. The first of these is the rationalist category, prompted by the account of Paul at the Areopagus in Acts 17,19. According to this view, the Corinthians, influenced by Stoic, Epicurean, and Platonic ideas, believed in the immortality of the individual soul, but not the resurrection of the body[48].

But as is pointed out by Wilson and others, the NT does not really teach the immortality of the soul in any Greek or gnostic manner. He sees the background of the Corinthians as that of sacramentally oriented religious cults[49].

---

[45] Cf. A.J.M. WEDDERBURN, «Problem of the Denial», 233.

[46] Paul shows a striking lack of concern for the reasons for their denial, much to our frustration. He wanted only to show what that denial meant for humanity and for creation. Cf. J.-N. ALETTI, «L'Argumentation», 78.

[47] Bultmann held that Paul misunderstood when he wrote 1 Cor 15,12, since the Corinthians actually held that the soul casts off the body at death so that it can freely ascend to heaven. Discovering his error, Paul corrected it in II Cor 5,1-10. Hurd, Georgi and others have shown, however, that this hypothesis does not fit the situation in the Corinthian church. Beker states that on the contrary, Paul understood all too well what they meant: by separating the spirit from apocalyptic categories, undue spiritualizing and ethical aberrations resulted. Cf. J.C. BEKER, *Paul the Apostle*, 170-172; J.W. WILSON, «Corinthians Who Say», 92-93; A.J.M. WEDDERBURN, «Problem of the Denial», 230.

[48] Using Philo for a background model, Horsley thinks that the Corinthians believed in a form of dualism which is an expression of the spiritual elitism rampant in that community. «Death» is equated with «body», and body and soul are separated from each other at death in R.A. HORSLEY, «Spiritual Elitism», 223-225.

[49] Sacramentalism and a belief in the resurrection are not incompatible, however, and there is no reason to think that there is some sort of inherent logic that demands

As far as not believing in the afterlife at all, Wedderburn finds it implausible that there would have been Corinthian Christians with Epicurean or Sadduccean views[50] and Conzelmann points out that Greek skepticism is not really coherent with the rest of the letter[51].

A recurring idea is that the Corinthians believed that the resurrection had already taken place, basing this on 2 Tim 2,18 (ἀνάστασιν ἤδη γεγονέναι)[52].

This would be a spiritualizing of the resurrection, a «realized eschatology»[53].

As Schmithals points out, however, instead of ἀνάστασιν οὐκ ἔστιν, Paul would probably have said, ἀνάστασιν ἤδη γεγονέναι in order to make his argument coherent[54].

Despite the fact that many have rejected this view, Wilson finds it the most plausible. He sides with Bartsch, Barth and others who hold that the traditional material utilized in vv. 3-11 is for the purpose of emphasizing the death of Jesus and the death of some of the 500 witnesses to a community that overemphasized the resurrection. In some cases Paul is believed by some to be combating «Gnostic fanatics who believe they have already been resurrected and who thus despise the earthly Jesus, this earthly life, and bodily death»[55].

---

that a «sacramentally oriented religious cult» should deny the resurrection. See J.W. WILSON, «Corinthians Who Say», 91-92.

[50] Cf. A.J.M. WEDDERBURN, «Problem of the Denial», 230.

[51] Cf. H. CONZELMANN, *1 Corinthians*, 265.

[52] Chrysostom was the first to suggest this (*Hom. in Cor*, 88). Enjoying favor in the 19th century, it was revived by von Soden in the modern era. «He decisively rejects the idea that the Corinthian opponents were either libertines or rationalists and calls them fanatical believers in the Spirit who relied primarily on the Christian sacraments to give them power and guarantee their salvation. They did not deny the resurrection but believed that it had already taken place in the γνῶσις or πνεῦμα which was given to them in Christian baptism» (J.W. WILSON, «Corinthians Who Say», 95-96).

[53] Realized eschatology as the answer to the situation at Corinth is especially favored by C.K. BARRETT, F.F. BRUCE, and E. KÄSEMANN. Thiselton finds that there probably was a problem with an overly realized eschatology at Corinth, but that the claims are often overstated by scholars. Paul had to correct ethical aberrations fostered by misunderstandings of the gifts of the spirit. There is no evidence that the Corinthians believed that the resurrection had already taken place. Rather, an over emphasis on the transformation of the believer in the past and present had shifted the center of gravity in their minds so that it was no longer situated in the future. Paul's argumentation will orient both the resurrection and the life of the community towards the future. See A.C. THISELTON, «Realized Eschatology at Corinth», 510-526.

[54] Wedderburn cites page 158 of the English translation of Schmithals' *Gnosticism in Corinth* in A.J.M. WEDDERBURN, «Problem of the Denial», 231.

[55] Wilson then proposes his own extensive guidelines for a further study of the problem. Of special note is his realization that often the text with which this chapter

Wilson shows that in vv. 1-3a, 11, Paul reminds them of what has been already said. He is not preaching something new, but is presupposing that they believe in the resurrection of Christ. What must be emphasized, however, is the fact that Jesus died and was buried, and that even some of the witnesses to the Risen Lord have died[56].

He goes on to point out something curious: in v. 12a, Paul and the Corinthians are in apparent agreement that Christ has been raised (ἐγήγερται); but in 12b, they are at odds over the resurrection of *the dead* (ἀνάστασις νεκρῶν). In order to be logical, another explanation is required. He proposes that the original kerygma included the resurrection of Jesus but not of the dead; at first, an expectation of the imminent parousia would have rendered such an idea useless, for it was generally assumed that everyone would be alive at the return of Christ. It was the crisis of the 50's, the delay of the parousia and the death of believers, that Paul had to deal with in 1 Thess 4,13-17; in this passage, we have the doctrine of the resurrection of Christians[57].

In this case, the Corinthians probably understood the resurrection of Jesus as exaltation to heaven, and they believed that they experienced the same thing through the sacraments. Physical death, then, was not a problem. They probably denied the Hebraic notion of the resurrection of the entire body. It is this argument that Paul deals with in the rest of the chapter: vv.13-21, he links the death and resurrection of Christ with that of all believers, vv. 22-58, he shows that new categories are necessary to understand how flesh can enter the kingdom of God. All of this is in due order, with the last stages taking place in the future. He assumes that the Corinthians were offended by both the bodily and future nature of the resurrection[58].

There are, in fact, several parallels between 1 Thess 4,13-18 and chapter 15. Both letters were written in the early 50's. These two pas-

---

is compared has dominated the text under consideration, e.g., Acts 17; 2 Cor 5,1-10; 2 Tim 2,18. He assumes that the only reliable indicator of the situation in Corinth reflected in v. 12 is 1 Cor 15,1-16 itself; that 1 Cor is a unity; and that the situation in Corinth had changed between the writing of 1 Cor and 2 Cor. He also points out that «gnosticism» is a nebulous and slippery term, meaning different things in different times and situations. Even the term «resurrection» was still in flux, according to J.W. WILSON, «Corinthians Who Say», 97-99.

[56] Cf. J.W. WILSON, «Corinthians Who Say», 101.

[57] Cf. J.W. WILSON, «Corinthians Who Say», 101-102.

[58] As will be evident in the following chapter, there were many differing Jewish views of the afterlife and the resurrection in the first century B.C. The Corinthians could well have been holding one of these diverse views rather than rejecting anything. Cf. J.W. WILSON, «Corinthians Who Say», 103-105.

sages deal with the same basic issue: the resurrection or fate of deceased Christians and the crisis caused by the apparent delay of the parousia[59].

The difference in emphasis between this passage and 1 Cor 15, 2 Cor 5,1-10 and Phil 1,21-26; 3,20-21 has led many to posit a progression or development of Paul's teaching on the resurrection[60].

However, the rhetorical situation is slightly different in the two communities, making complete harmonization of the two passages very difficult: in Corinth, some doubted the resurrection of the dead, and Paul must convince them of a resurrection based on God's creative power; in Thessalonica, it is not the resurrection as such that is in doubt, but the «actual condition» of the dead in comparison with that of the survivor». Paul seeks to dispel the notion that the living enjoy any advantage over the dead at the resurrection[61].

Paul uses an apocalyptic framework to describe a general resurrection; the living enjoy no special advantage. Both passages are parenetic in nature: the readers are exhorted to persevere and remain steadfast[62].

Plevnik believes that part of the problem – and the apparent disparity between this passage and 1 Cor 15 – lies in the use of translation imagery

---

[59] There are many problems in interpreting the Thessalonian passage, and many exegeses, some of them contradictory: did the community not know of the resurrection, or did they hold for a chronologically or qualitatively relative priority? What exactly was happening in Thessalonica? There are also a number of difficulties presented by difficult grammatical constructions. There are several similarities between the two passages; both are seen by Delobel and Klijn as reflecting an apocalyptic background and imagery. J. DELOBEL, «The Fate of the Dead», 340-347; A.F.J. KLIJN, «1 Thessalonians 4.13-18 and its Background in Apocalyptic Literature», 67-73.

[60] See pages 263-66 for a survey of these developmental theories. Most of these theories hold that 1 Thess 4,13-18 describes a life in continuity with the earthly life and that 1 Cor 15 posits a transformation and discontinuity with this life. Gillman shows that the two are not mutually exclusive: transformation does not exclude continuity and the continuity in 1 Thess does not exclude transformation. The problem in Thessalonica was due to difficulties in integrating the parousia and the resurrection, not a failure on Paul's part to preach about the resurrection. Whatever development there is in the above mentioned passages is from a spatial image of transformation in 1 Thess to more technical descriptions of corporeal change in Phil 3,10; 2 Cor 3,18; Gal 4,19 and Rom 12,2. Cf. J. GILLMAN, «Signals of Transformation», 263-281.

[61] Cf. J. DELOBEL, «Fate of Dead», 345.

[62] Klijn compares two ideas that were never really reconciled: a) prophetic eschatology, in which those living are seen to enjoy happiness at the end; and b) apocalyptic eschatology, which envisions a resurrection of all, followed by judgment. Examples of the former: 4 Ez 6,25; 13,16; 7,27; 9,8; Ps. Sol. 17,50; the latter: ApBar 30,2b; 51,13; Ps-Philo LAB 19,20. See A.F.J. KLIJN, «1 Thessalonians 4,18», 69.

in 1 Thess. Paul seeks to show that God can restore the dead to life so that they can also share in the parousia of Christ[63].

It is fairly clear that the community accepted the resurrection of Christ. It is to this primitive kerygma that Paul appeals in his argumentation, and there is no reason to seriously question it. As regards the denial of the resurrection, there are several possible solutions, and not enough is known of conditions in Corinth to make a definitive statement. There are, however, some points that can be ascertained: 1) The deniers were not denying the afterlife itself. This would render superfluous the Christian faith as preached and lived in the NT, and there is no evidence that this was the case in Corinth. 2) Although an overly realized eschatology was probably operative in Corinth, there is little evidence that they believed the resurrection had already taken place. If they had, it would have been easy to say so. 3) The main problem seems to have been two-fold: they failed to grasp the connection between the resurrection of Christ and that of the believers, and they failed to understand (as in Thessalonica) how a dead person could be with Christ at his parousia and go to be with God. Sometimes the most obvious answer is correct: some were denying the resurrection. There is no need to resort to gnosticism or Hellenistic mystery religions to explain the situation in Corinth.

2.4.2 The Negative Consequences If the Dead Are Not Raised

Paul will strive to prove that those who deny the resurrection of the dead also deny the resurrection of Christ, and that the τίνες who are the deniers have left the common tradition. He has already established the fact that Christ has been raised from the dead, now he spins out the implications of not believing in the resurrection of the dead. The resurrection cannot be viewed in isolation, and Paul's entire argument will be an attempt to show that to deny the resurrection is to deny one's own existence. He will assume, for the sake of argument, that there is no resurrection of the dead: in that case, no one, including Christ, ever has been or ever will be raised from the dead, and the consequences which follow are annihilating[64].

---

[63] Drawing on a study of translation accounts by G. LOHFINK, Plevnik shows that much of the agitation of the Thessalonians regarding the resurrection was due to the OT understanding of a translation to heaven; namely, one had to be alive to be assumed. Paul explains that God will raise the dead to the earthly life first, so they can then be taken up with the believers to meet the Lord in the air. The emphasis in 1 Cor 15 is on the transformation by God of our mortal bodies which affects both the living and dead faithful, and does not at all contradict what is written in 1 Thess 4,13-18. See J. PLEVNIK, «The Taking Up of the Faithful», 274-283.

[64] Cf. H. CONZELMANN, 1 Corinthians, 265; G. FEE, Corinthians, 741-742.

According to Conzelmann, it is dead Christians who are under discussion in these verses, for Paul is driving home arguments based upon the creed. The fate of non-Christians is not part of the discussion, and cannot be derived from the kerygma. Conzelmann also believes that the resurrection is not a fact that can be isolated, and for this reason Paul begins from the proclamation and from faith[65].

Verses 12 and 16 utilize the type of reasoning called *enthymeme* or inferred proposition[66].

Taking the apodosis of v. 12 as the premise of his hypothesis, namely, that the dead are not raised, he begins to unwind the consequences. Verses 13-19 are a *sorites* or interlocking chain of implications, consisting of conditional sentences based upon verse 12, which function also as a *refutatio* of the opposing opinion[67].

First, Christ is not raised (v. 13), showing that there is a firm connection between the two, a point which Paul will argue repeatedly. Then, both the preaching and the faith are in vain (κενὸν). It also involves Paul as a false witness for proclaiming what did not actually occur, as well as detracting from God, who was said to have raised Jesus but who did not (v. 15).

Verses 16-19 appeal to the emotions of the audience by emphasizing the existential implications of denial of the resurrection: a futile faith and an annihilating death. This prepares the way for the *probatio* to follow. Verse 16 states again the fact that if the dead are not raised, then neither is Christ, and this becomes the premise for more consequences which follow. Their faith is worthless or futile (ματαία), since they are still in their sins (v. 17). This refers back to the creed in vv. 3-5, in which it is

---

[65] «The creed does not supply speculative theses of a general kind, but defines the existence of believers and discloses hope» (H. CONZELMANN, *1 Corinthians*, 264). In response to the emphasis on faith, it must be pointed out that Paul goes to a lot of trouble to establish a chain of witnesses to the resurrection, including those with whom the message can be verified. Paul wants to establish the reliable grounds for this faith.

[66] The *enthymeme* is a form of deductive reasoning taking the form of a syllogism, whose premises, according to Aristotle, must possess verisimilitude and not necessarily truth. For example, verse 16 would be restated as «the dead are not raised; therefore, Christ has not been raised». Cf. B. MACK, *Rhetoric*, 39; M. BÜNKER, *Briefformular*, 68; G.A. KENNEDY, *New Testament Interpretation*, 16; B.M. GARAVELLI, *Manuale di Retorica*, 79-80.

[67] In this type of chain, the last term of a proposition is the first term of the following proposition. This falls in one of the three forms of quasi-logical argumentation known as the transitive quality. Cf. B.M. GARAVELLI, *Manuale di Retorica*, 95.198.

stated that Christ died for our sins. If this is the case, then indeed there is no future and all who have fallen asleep in Christ have perished (ἀπώλοντο) (v. 18), for they are still in the power of death[68].

Verse 19 ends on almost a note of despair: «If it is in this life only that we have hoped in Christ, we are of all men most to be pitied». In the preceding verses, Paul has spun out some of the disastrous consequences of there being no resurrection. Verse 18 insists that if this is so, then all those who have fallen asleep in Christ have perished. This reflects the belief, common in Jewish apocalyptic literature, that only those alive at the time of the visitation would enjoy the eschatological life. This is the problem dealt with in 1 Thess 4, namely, the fate of those who have died before the parousia. Are they thereby excluded from the blessed life? Verse 19, then, states the obvious: unless there is a resurrection of believers, then only those alive at the time of the parousia will receive eternal life with Christ; the others will be lost. This indeed would be a cause of pity and despair[69].

2.5 God's Reconquest Of The Cosmos: VV. 20-28

The heart of the argument of verses 12-34 is contained in verses 20-28[70].

---

[68] This connection between denial of the future and past with regard to still being in our sins is also found in Rom 4,26 and 5,10, where it states that Christ died *for us*. Cf. G. FEE, *Corinthians*, 742-744.

[69] Commentators deal with what is considered a slight problem with the correct grammatical interpretation. The Greek reads, εἰ ἐν τῇ ζωῇ ταύτῃ ἐν Χριστῷ ἠλπικότες ἐσμὲν μόνον; should it be taken to mean «hoped only in this life», or «only hoped in this life»? The latter interpretation is unlikely, since for Paul, hope is a positive word (as in 13,13), and to make hope appear to be futile in itself would not be in keeping with the orientation of his thought. The former interpretation is more likely, not only for the above reason, but because it is consistent with the argument in vv. 12-19. The RSV's «If for this life only we have hoped in Christ» gives a clear sense of the message. Barrett applies μόνον to the whole clause, thereby insisting that if we have only hoped in this life in Christ, then we have lost both the enjoyment of this life and the possibility of a future life. And if this life alone is all we have, then we are no different than unbelievers, and should follow the hedonistic advice given in vv. 32 and 34. Cf. G. FEE, *Corinthians*, 744; H. CONZELMANN, *1 Corinthians*, 267; C.K. BARRETT, *Corinthians*, 349-350.

[70] Verses 20-28 are considered the point of unity because they express the conviction shared by Paul and the Corinthians, i.e., knowing the reality of the resurrection, while verses 12-19 and 29-32 only speak of unreal hypotheses. The negative consequences of a and a¹ stand in sharp contrast to the positive propositions in b (66).
  a = 12-19, denial of resurrection of dead and
  its negative consequences
  b = 20-28, affirmation of the resurrection of

This section is an affirmation of the resurrection of Christ and the dead and an emphatic denial of all of the hypothetical situations in vv. 13-19[71].

Paul will show the importance of Christ's resurrection first in relation to Christ himself, then to all of humanity, then to all of creation, and finally in relation to God himself[72].

Based upon linguistic patterns, Hill finds a chiastic structure in vv. 24-28 whose center is v.26: the last enemy to be destroyed is death:

20 Νυνὶ δὲ Χριστὸς ἐγήγερται ἐκ νεκρῶν ἀπαρχὴ τῶν
 κεκοιμημένων.
21 (Α) ἐπειδὴ γὰρ δι᾽ ἀνθρώπου θάνατος,
  (Β) καὶ δι᾽ ἀνθρώπου ἀνάστασις νεκρῶν.
22 (Α) ὥσπερ γὰρ ἐν τῷ ᾽Αδὰμ πάντες ἀποθνήσκουσιν,
  (Β) οὕτως καὶ ἐν τῷ Χριστῷ πάντες ζῳοποιηθήσονται.
23 ἕκαστος δὲ ἐν τῷ ἰδίῳ τάγματι · ἀπαρχὴ Χριστός,
 ἔπειτα οἱ τοῦ Χριστοῦ ἐν τῇ παρουσίᾳ αὐτοῦ,
24 εἶτα τὸ τέλος,
  (Α) ὅταν παραδιδῷ τὴν βασιλείαν τῷ θεῷ καὶ πατρί,
  (Β) ὅταν καταργήσῃ πᾶσαν ἀρχὴν καὶ πᾶσαν ἐξουσίαν καὶ
    δύναμιν.
25   (C) δεῖ γὰρ αὐτὸν βασιλεύειν ἄχρι οὗ θῇ πάντας τοὺς
     ἐχθροὺς ὑπὸ τοὺς πόδας αὐτοῦ.
26   (D) ἔσχατος ἐχθρὸς καταργεῖται ὁ θάνατος.
27   (C¹) **πάντα γὰρ ὑπέταξεν ὑπὸ τοὺς πόδας αὐτοῦ.**
  (Β¹) ὅταν δὲ εἴπῃ ὅτι πάντα ὑποτέτακται, δῆλον ὅτι
    ἐκτὸς τοῦ ὑποτάξαντος αὐτῷ τὰ πάντα.
28 (Α¹) ὅταν δὲ ὑποταγῇ αὐτῷ τὰ πάντα, τότε [καὶ] αὐτὸς ὁ υἱὸς
   ὑποταγήσεται τῷ ὑποτάξαντι αὐτῷ τὰ πάντα,
   ἵνα ᾖ ὁ θεὸς [τὰ] πάντα ἐν πᾶσιν[73].

Christ and its positive consequences for
all men and all creation
a¹ = 29-32, denial of resurrection of dead and
its consequences taken up again.
See J. LAMBRECHT, «Paul's Christological Use», 502; J.-N. ALETTI,
«L'Argumentation», 65-66.
[71] J. LAMBRECHT, «Paul's Christological Use», 502-527.
[72] J.-N. ALETTI, «L'Argumentation», 74.
[73] The linguistic indicators which Hill uses are:
ὅταν...
  ὅταν...
   ...γὰρ...
     ἔσχατος...
   ...γὰρ...
  ὅταν δὲ...
ὅταν δὲ...

Wallis arrives at almost the same chiastic structure, with some modifications[74].

Lambrecht also criticizes Hill's model, and denies that it is written in a «cyclic, concentric way». He sees vv. 25-28 as an explanation of the thesis stated in vv. 23-24. While these verses are certainly explanatory, there is no compelling reason to reject the basic outlines of Hill's model[75].

Despite the minor differences between these first two attempts to discover a chiastic structure, there is one very important point of convergence: both place the center of the structure where it belongs, v. 26. The whole point of vv. 20-28 is the defeat and destruction of death as a consequence of Christ's resurrection.

See C.E. HILL, «Paul's Understanding», 297-320.

[74] As with Hill, v. 26 is the center of the chiasm. However, from this point onwards he departs from the linguistic indicators. He makes 27a (all things subjected) the exact parallel of v. 26, instead of a counterpoint to v. 25. He also breaks v. 28 into three portions: all things subjected; Son made subject; and «that God may be all in all».

The end - 24
　Kingdom delivered over to Father - 24b
　　All enemies destroyed -24c
　　　All enemies put underfoot - 25 (Ps 110,1 MT; 109,1 LXX)
　　　　Last enemy destroyed - 26
　　　All things subjected - 27a (Ps 8,7 MT; 8,6 LXX)
　　　All things completely and finally subjected - 27b
　　All things subjected -28a
　Son made subject -28b
That God may be all in all - 28c

Hill points out that vv. 25 and 27 both contain scriptural proofs of Christ's universal dominion introduced by γάρ; Conzelmann sees v. 26 as an isolated thesis framed by two scriptural passages, the preceding one with πάντας and the subsequent one with πάντα. Wallis' chiasm does seem overly subtle. Linguistic indicators are more likely to indicate the presence of a pattern, and in this case they are very clear. Additionally, ὑποτάσσω is not used until v. 27a, after the destruction of death, and thereafter it is used six times. See W.B. WALLIS, «Intermediate Kingdom», 229-242.

[75] The linguistic indicators mentioned by Hill are fairly clear and obvious; Lambrecht finds difficulty by subjecting them to an overly subtle analysis (for example, the difference in function of γάρ in vv. 25 and 27a). Many of the verses he does not find to be «pure parallels». It might be pointed out that in a chiastic structure there is seldom a pure parallel. He concentrates on the subtle grammatical differences in the four ὅταν clauses, claiming that these differences affect the meaning of the clauses. Even so, the meanings are not affected enough to alter the *basic* meaning. He does not see a correspondence between v. 24 and v. 28c. This is true with regard to exact parallel wording, but the τέλος of v. 24 is certainly the parallel of πάντα ἐν πᾶσιν of 28c, the latter being a fuller expression of the former. Even though vv. 25-28 can be an explanation of a thesis presented in vv. 23-24, there is no reason why that cannot be done in the context of a chiastic structure as established by Hill. Cf. J. LAMBRECHT, «Structure and Line of Thought», 143-151.

In describing God's reconquest of the universe, primarily of those parts which had been alienated due to sin and death, Paul uses several symbols and devices. «All» (πάντες), which illustrates the totality of God's rule, is used 12 times in vv. 20-28. It begins in verse 22 with the death of all men, followed by life for all, the destruction and subjection of every power, ending in v. 28 with God being «all in all». The verbs ὑποτάσσω and καταργέω are used 6 times and twice respectively to signify the nullification and subjection of every power opposed to God. Finally, reaching into his own traditions, Paul uses Adam as a corporate symbol for humanity, both in its fallen state and the state of future glory. Midrashic exegesis is used with psalms 8 and 110,1 to describe Christ's (and ultimately God's) victory over the hostile powers of the cosmos, especially death.

2.5.1 Thesis: Christ Is Risen, The Firstfruits of the Dead

Verse 20a restates the fact of Christ's resurrection, while 20b adds what is to become the thesis of this section of the *probatio*: the firstfruits (ἀπαρχή) of those who have died. The operative term in this verse is ἀπαρχή which for Paul carried an eschatological meaning, establishing the future reality of the resurrection. An analogous principle is expressed in Rom 8,29 and in Col 1,18: Christ is the firstborn of many brothers and the firstborn from the dead. This will provide the linkage between the resurrection of Christ and of the dead, and is one pole in the long process of the defeat of death and the restoration of the cosmos to God which is explicated in vv. 21-28[76].

2.5.2 Paradigm: Adam and Christ

Paul now wishes to explain and elaborate on the image in v. 20 of Christ's resurrection as the firstfruits of what is to come. His entire purpose in vv. 21-22 is to make the connection between the old and the new, the past and the future, the dead and the living. Alternating parallels of

---

[76] The OT background of the term begins in Lev 23,9-14, which concerns the consecration of the firstfruits of the harvest to God. But its prime usage here is as a metaphor for a guarantee of the full and complete harvest. The term is used in the NT in Rom 8,23; 11,16; Jas 1,18; Rev 14,4, and a similar use of the metaphor is found in 2 Cor 1,22 and 5,5, in which the Spirit serves as a «present pledge on the part of God for the final eschatological harvest or payment». Christ's resurrection, then, makes the resurrection of the dead inevitable. In 2 Thess 2,13 and 1 Cor 16,15, the first converts in an area are looked upon as firstfruits, i.e., the first of many. Cf. H. CONZELMANN, *1 Corinthians*, 267-268; G. FEE, *Corinthians*, 749; C.E. HILL, «Christ's Kingdom», 303.

analogous symbols make the point: by a man, death; by a man, resurrection of the dead; in Adam, all die; in Christ, all will be made alive. The paradigm used in verses 21 and 22 is that of Adam, the primal man, a symbol with a venerable background in Jewish literature[77].

Adam also played a part in Jewish eschatology, for he was seen as having a role in the renewal of humanity and the reversal of human limitations[78].

Paul uses this collective symbol here and in Romans 5,12-19 to signify the common plight of humanity. This reflects the universality of sin; for both the rabbis and for Paul, death is universal because sin is universal[79].

It is the relationships of Adam and Christ to humanity that are being compared, as well as the universality of their relevancy for human existence. Adam's sin and death determined the personal destinies of all who die, i.e., all humanity; in a similar (ὥσπερ) fashion, Christ's victory and resurrection stand in relation to those who will be made alive, i.e., humanity[80].

---

[77] Adam's sin had been tied somehow with death, especially in 4 Ez: 3,7; 7,18; 54,15.19. A sort of change in man's nature is described in 4 Ez 3,26; 4,30; 7,92.116-126. See also Sir 17,17; 25,24; ApMos 28; 2 Bar 17,3; 19,8; 23,4; 54,15; 56,6. A distortion of a perfect world intended by God is found in Sir 40,1-11; Ap-Mos 8,2. Universal sin is postulated in Sir, 2 Bar and 4 Ez, but Sir (15,11-15 and Wis 1,13-16 and 2,23-3,3) stress individual responsibility. At various times Adam was called the first Israelite, an honored patriarch, a king, a *hasid*, and a bearer of the Divine Image. See R. SCROGGS, *The Last Adam*, 18-22.

[78] See TLev 18,9-12. Some equated Adam with the Messiah, others looked upon him as the symbol of righteous ones or saints. ApMos 13,2-4; 28,3; 39,2 portrays the last day as being when all flesh from Adam to the last day will be transformed to its former glory. The nature of this new humanity depends on Adam's glorious pre-lapsarian existence. Rabbinic writings do not contain abundant traces of a relationship between Adam and the Messiah; however, they discuss the possibility of a new human nature in this world in the days of the Messiah, for the end time will be like the beginning. Cf. R. SCROGGS, *Last Adam*, 29-31.

[79] In 4 Ezra, Adam is said to have been burdened with an evil heart which became permanent in his descendants (3,22.25.26; 7,63-72). An evil influence was present in man (יצר ערה) but it could be resisted and overcome. Ezra avoids overtly blaming God for this evil inclination, since he favors strongly the role of human free will in overcoming it. It is implied, although unclearly, that there will be an eschatological rectification of this condition by God. This is not the Christian doctrine of original sin as we know it. There was disagreement among the rabbis: some felt that if one were to avoid sin completely, one would not die, while others felt that death was a decree by God because of Adam's transgression, i.e., Moses died not for his own sin but because of the decree. In any case, each is still responsible for his own sin. See J.D.G. DUNN, *Christology in the Making*, 107-113; R. SCROGGS, *Last Adam*, 78; M.E. STONE, *Fourth Ezra*, 63-66.

[80] «And it is because Christ stands in such a relation to Christians as Adam does to those who die that the historical reality of Christ's bodily resurrection can furnish

This symbol is amplified in vv. 45-9, and much of the second half of the chapter will be a further reflection on this model, the purpose of which is to explain the link between humanity and Christ in the resurrection and how the body, rather than flesh and blood, can indeed inherit the kingdom of God. The body will rise, and there will be continuity with the flesh body, but it will be a body on a new level of creation. The old Adam or humanity will have to be vivified by Christ, the new Adam. The term used, ζῳοποιηθήσονται, is a soteriological term. In the NT, it almost always refers to the action of God or of the Holy Spirit in giving life to bodies. The term here is used in v. 22 and again in v. 45, to describe the action of the new Adam[81].

Salvation consists in the restoration of man to the image in which he had been created and to the glory which he now lacks as a result of Adam's sin[82].

Adam represents all humans, every man, as distinct from the animals. Paul makes a contrast between two levels of creation, the old and the new, and two races of humanity, the man of dust and the man of heaven. Christ, who is the Last Adam, becomes the source of the life-giving Holy Spirit at his resurrection and exaltation. Christ stands for man risen from the dead, for when Paul uses Adamic language in speaking of Christ, he is referring to Christ risen and exalted. To his exegesis of Gen 2,7, Paul adds «The first man Adam became a living soul»[83].

---

grounds for the Christians' hope of their own» (C.E. HILL, «Christ's Kingdom», 304-306). The phrase ἐν τῷ Χριστῷ is contrasted with ἐν τῷ Ἀδάμ. It is by incorporation into Christ that one will receive this life-giving spirit. There may be a resurrection for unbelievers, but it is not the same as this class of redemption. In response to Hill, it might be pointed out that the logical consequences of Paul's argumentation perhaps requires it. This does not mean that all will be saved, only that all will be resurrected.

[81] This term is used 11 times in the NT: John 5,21; 6,63; Rom 4,17; 8,11; 1 Cor 15,22.36.45; 2 Cor 3,6; Gal 3,21; 1 Pet 3,18. John 5,21 is striking: God raises from the dead and gives life; the Son will do likewise to whomever he wishes.

[82] Philo of Alexandria also uses this symbol in *Leg. All.* I 31,53; *Opif* 134; *Qu. Gen.* I 4. According to rabbinic thought, Adam possessed brilliance or glory (כבוד) before the fall. Death was not part of the original destiny; after the fall, Adam became the cause of the physical corruption of man and the break in his relationship with God. There were cosmic consequences of the fall too; the earth's fertility and the light of the heavens were affected. Rom 8,20 speaks of all creation being subjected to futility (ματαιότης), which stands in contrast to the τέλος, or goal which creation failed to achieve. Cf. J.D.G. DUNN, *Christology*, 105-106; R. SCROGGS, *Last Adam*, 32-37.

[83] «Christ's role as second man, or last Adam, does not begin either in some pre-existent state, or at incarnation, but at his resurrection» (J.D.G. DUNN, *Christology*,

Exalted after his death, Jesus fulfills God's intention for man, for he receives the power intended for man in the beginning but which he failed to reach because of his sin. Whereas Adam was a man of dust before, Jesus became a man of heaven; having been a living soul he became a life-giving spirit; having died, he is now the firstfruits. He had to share the lot of the first Adam, for it was by following through the negative situation of Adam to the end that he was able to form the new humanity[84].

Through the use of the word all (πάντες) and a series of three parallelisms, Paul connects both the old and new Adam and makes Adam a collective for humanity. All died in Adam, for his sin had disastrous consequences for all of humanity. In like fashion, however, all will be made alive in Christ. Christ's exaltation makes possible the giving of life to all humanity, counteracting the effects of Adam's sin. The defeat of death is the goal of the resurrection, and in the verses following, Paul will outline how and when this is to be accomplished.

Against this general Jewish background, Paul agrees: in the consummation and perfection accompanying the coming of the Messiah, man will regain Adam's glory, life and stature. He would, however, opt for a spiritual body rather than mere resuscitation of the physical body[85].

2.5.3 The Symbol of Totality: ALL

The use of «all» is crucial in this entire passage; indeed, Wallis sees the «all» in Ps 8,7 as the key to the whole section[86]. It is adopted by Paul as a symbol of comprehensiveness and completeness[87].

107-108). «The Christology of the Last Adam was primarily directed towards illuminating and assuring the Christian's hope of eschatological humanity» (R. SCROGGS, *Last Adam*, 59).

[84] «It was by playing out the role of Adam that Christ became the last Adam» (J.D.G. DUNN, *Christology*, 111-113. The continuity between the old and new Adam, according to Dunn, is maintained by use of psalm 8 in conjunction with psalm 110, which also refers to the earthly Jesus. This use became a «ready vehicle for Adam Christology», describing God's purpose and intention for man/Adam: «You crowned him with glory and honor; You put all things under his feet,» indicates that the risen and exalted Jesus completes God's intention for man by receiving what had been intended for him in the beginning (R. SCROGGS, *Last Adam*, 64-65).

[85] In regaining this δόξα, the new man will radiate the glory which shines from Christ. 1 Cor 15,43; 2 Cor 3,18; 4,17; Col 3,4. Cf. R. SCROGGS, *Last Adam*, 64-65.

[86] Wallis notes that Paul sees fit to add «all» to the corresponding psalm 110:1 in v. 25a. Cf. W. WALLIS, «Intermediate Kingdom», 233.

[87] «All» is used 12 times in vv. 20-28; as will be shown, this is important as a symbol of comprehensiveness in Paul's argument. It would seem to imply that the life-giving effects of the resurrection are for all, just as death was the common lot of

But the question arises: is the «all» in 22b as inclusive as that in 22a? It certainly is indicative of the universal role of Christ. There are some, however, who believe that «all» means that all humanity will be given life. This will be discussed in detail in chapter 4.

It seems that the «all» in Ps 8:7 (MT) quoted in 27a should interpret both uses of «all» in verse 22[88].

The logic of the two parallels in vv. 21-22 would also seem to indicate that something much greater is intended. Paul takes great pains to fill this entire passage with «all»; the conclusion in v. 28 is that nothing is outside of or alienated from God. Those who die do so involuntarily as a result of Adam's sin and their common humanity; in a similar fashion, all those in Christ, regardless of how «in Christ» is interpreted, will be resurrected by their commonality with Christ[89].

2.5.4 Thesis: Each In His Own Order

The resurrection of the dead is linked with God's salvific plan, and we see the use of an apocalyptic model in verses 23-4. There is another reference to the firstfruits image from verse 20, together with the proviso that although Christ is the promise of the remainder to be resurrected, order (τάγματι) is the key: God is at work; events are unfolding in a process that is according to God's plan, not ours. In this way, Paul explains why believers continue to die, while at the same time insisting that they must be raised, since Christ has been raised. The resurrection of those who belong to Christ (οἱ τοῦ Χριστοῦ) is placed at the time of the parousia.

2.5.5 The End: Christ Will Hand Over the Kingdom to God the Father

The parousia is the event which sets in motion the End, the time when (ὅταν) Christ gives over the kingdom to God the Father. This is the verse which was so troublesome to some of the patristic writers. The first ὅταν clause subordinates the handing over to the End; while the second refers to events anterior to the first. In fact, the RSV translates the second ὅταν as «after».

---

all. See chapter 4 for a complete discussion of the meaning and importance of πάντες.

[88] «The comprehensiveness of the «all» of Psalm 8:7 (sic) must decide the interpretation of «all» in verse 22b: In Christ all will be made alive» (W. WALLIS, «Intermediate Kingdom», 234).

[89] For Paul, to be resurrected is to be glorified with Christ, sharing in his glory. This passage speaks then of the universality of Christ's saving action, not about who will be saved and who will not.

2.5.6 The End or the Rest

The fact that τάγματα is plural, when linked with the ambiguity of τὸ τέλος in v. 24, has given rise to speculation that there are several orders of those who will be resurrected. The question of a double resurrection or salvation for non-believers depends a great deal on the interpretation of τὸ τέλος in verse 24, which is usually translated «the End»[90].

Lietzmann held that it should be translated «the Rest,» meaning the third and final class of people, i.e., non-believers, thereby making ζῳποιηθήσονται the verb. This interpretation would entail an intermediate period in which Christians reign with Christ[91]. This interpretation is also followed by J. Weiss. Others, however, have not accepted it: Kümmel, Allo, Héring et al[92].

Hill holds that there are only two τάγματα, of which Christ is the first while simultaneously being the ἀπαρχή[93].

There is a third possibility advanced: treating τὸ τέλος as an adverb meaning «finally»[94].

In this case, the adverb would begin a sentence containing both ὅταν clauses and ending only with the καταργεῖται of verse 26. Héring elimi-

---

[90] The term τέλος is used 37 times in the NT in a variety of ways. In a couple of instances, the term is used with the meaning of tribute or reverence: Matt 17,25 τέλη meaning toll or tribute, and Rom 13,7 τέλος in the sense of reverence due to someone. Several instances refer to the goal or destiny of one's moral choices: Mark 3,26 (Satan's self-division leading to end); Rom 6,21 (end of sin is death); 6,22 (eternal life end of sanctification); 2 Cor 11,15 (end of certain deeds); Phil 3,19 (their end is destruction); 1 Tim 1,5 (aim of our charge is love); Jas 5,11 (purpose of the Lord); 1 Pet 1,9 (outcome of your faith); 4,7 (end of those who do not obey the gospel; Heb 6,8 (field that grows brambles will end by being burnt). Fulfillment is the meaning in two cases: Luke 22,37 (what is written has its fulfillment in Christ); Rom 10,4 (Christ is the completion of the law). There are also various adverbial uses: 1 Pet 3,8 (finally); 1 Thess 2,16 (God's wrath has come upon them at last, εἰς τέλος); 2 Cor 1,13 (understand fully, ἕως τέλους); Heb 7,3 (neither beginning nor end of life); Matt 26,58 (Peter goes into courtyard to see how it will end).

[91] He bases this reading on ἕκαστος δὲ ἐν τῷ ἰδίῳ τάγματι in verse 23. Christ is the first, then at his coming those who belong to him, and finally the Rest, the third and final group. He quotes two sources, both of which are very ambiguous: Isa 19:15, κεφαλὴν καὶ οὐράν, ἀρχὴν καὶ τέλος and Aristotle's de gen. anim.: τὸ ἐκ τῆς τροφῆς γινόμενον τέλος. Cf. H. LIETZMANN, An die Korinther I/II, 81-82.

[92] Héring denies that this sense of the word is found anywhere in classical literature (J. HÉRING, First Epistle, 166-167); Cf. C.K. BARRETT, Corinthians, 356; E.B. ALLO, Première Épitre, 407-408.

[93] If τὸ τέλος is eliminated as another group, then there is no further mention of anyone who could fit the description. See C.E. HILL, «Christ's Kingdom», 307-308.

[94] An example of this adverbial use is found in 1 Pet 3 (Finally, be all of one mind). This translation was advanced by V. Hoffman and used by Karl Barth. Cf. J. HÉRING, First Epistle, 166.

nates «the Rest» as a possibility, and states that whatever choice is made from the other two, the resurrection of the non-elect is out of the question, given the explications of the resurrection in verses 51-55[95].

Hill denies that it can mean «the rest of the dead» both on linguistic grounds, as does Héring, and on the basis of its function. He points out, first of all, that it is a temporal word, determined by the double ὅταν clause in vv. 24b and c. Additionally, what is being discussed is not a mere resurrection, but life «which the pneumatic, risen Christ imparts to those who have the Spirit, by means of the Spirit» (1 Cor 15,45; Rom 8,11). As a clinching argument, he points out that «all the stupendous cosmic and soteriological events and processes Paul encompasses in the chiasm of vv. 24b-28 have as their point of departure τὸ τέλος. It would be strange if all of the language reflective of ultimate consummation and eternal glory were used merely to describe the resurrection of the wicked»[96].

2.5.7 An Intermediate Kingdom?

Ambiguity of the text in verse 24 gives rise to questions regarding the nature and duration of Christ's kingdom, and to the possibility of two resurrections. The point in question concerns the phrase εἶτα τὸ τέλος: is this meant in a temporal or logical sequential sense? If the former, it would seem to imply a period of time between the parousia and the end; if the latter, merely sequential aspects of the same event.

If an intermediate period is implied, many modern exegetes find a ready parallel in Rev 20: reference to Satan being bound for a thousand years; a first resurrection in which the just come to life and reign with Christ for 1,000 years, while the rest do not come to life until the end of the 1,000 years; after this, a time when Satan will torment humanity again before being destroyed. The dead are then judged according to their works, after which Death and Hades are thrown into the lake of fire along with those whose names are not found written in the book of life[97].

---

[95] Cf. J. HÉRING, *First Epistle*, 166-167.

[96] C.E. HILL, «Christ's Kingdom», 308-309.

[97] Lietzmann is probably one of the most insistent proponents of the *Zwischenreich*, which according to him, begins with the parousia and ends with the defeat of death (Cf. H. LIETZMANN, *An die Korinther*, 81). According to Barrett, the parousia of Christ, accompanied by the resurrection of Christians, ushers in the end. The handing over of the kingdom initiates the reign of God (Cf. C.K. BARRETT, *Corinthians*, 356-361). Fee denies the apocalyptic nature of this entire passage, as well as any second resurrection or *Zwischenreich*. The end is sequential in a mere logical sense (Cf. G. FEE, *Corinthians*, 752). Héring states that the messianic kingdom, which commenced at the resurrection and exaltation of Christ, ends at the parousia or soon after, when death is destroyed. The parousia of Christ causes the resurrection of

As we can see, there are some similarities to vv. 20-28: a time when the enemies of God are overcome, rendered ineffective, and finally destroyed, followed by the defeat and destruction of the last enemy, Death and Hades. It is also possible to find several parallels in Jewish pseudepigraphal literature; for example, 4 Ez 7,26-30; 13,39-50 and 2 Bar 29; 73; and 74[98].

Wallis rejects the notion that the τέλος and the parousia are simultaneous, and he holds that in between these two events the conquest of enemies, the last being death, must take place[99].

---

dead Christians and the transformation of those who are alive. The rejected simply cease to exist (Cf. J. HÉRING, *Corinthians*, 167-168). According to Conzelmann, Paul modifies some Jewish apocalyptic models: death is not annihilated until the end of the messianic kingdom. The kingdom is in the present because Christ is risen; his kingdom exists in that period of time between the resurrection and the consummation of the work of salvation after the parousia. He also insists that since this passage is christological, that the resurrection is only of believers (Cf. H. CONZELMANN, *1 Corinthians*, 270). L.J. KREITZER, in *Jesus and God* (234, note 18) points out that among commentators on the Book of Revelation, several are opposed to there being any parallel: G.B. CAIRD, *A Commentary on the Revelation of St. John the Divine*, 249-251; R. MOUNCE, *The Book of Revelation*, 357; E. LOHSE, *Die Offenbarung des Johannes*, 104. Those in favor include: M. RISSI, *Time and History: A Study on the Revelation of John*, 119; M. RIST, *The Revelation of St. John the Divine*, 519; G. LADD, *A Commentary on the Revelation of John*, 161.267; G.R. BEASLEY-MURRAY, *The Book of Revelation*, 290; and several older commentaries.

[98] He points out that these pseudepigraphal works were written several decades after 1 Corinthians, and that these texts are the first examples of a final judgment preceded by a temporary messianic kingdom on earth. That however does not rule out that this passage is one of the first, and regardless of the date of the pseudepigraphal texts themselves, they come from a literary and religious milieu that predate their writing. Cf. W. WALLIS, «Intermediate Kingdom», 312.

[99] He takes as his point of departure the exegetical results of Hans-Alwin Wilcke's work *Das Problem eines messianischen Zwischenreichs beim Paulus*, which are summarized on pages 148-9 as follows: «1. Paul in I Corinthians 15:22 speaks only of the resurrection of Christians. The basic argument for two resurrections, that Paul had all men in mind, is incorrect. 2. Verse 23 does not speak of a resurrection of several groups: up to and including verse 23, Paul has said only that at the Parousia believers will rise to the same life with which Christ arose. 3. *Telos* in verse 24 can only mean end. There is no thought of a last contingent of resurrected persons. There is no thought of the conversion of non-Christians after the Parousia, or of the second resurrection for judgment. 4. The kingdom of Christ is a present reality. It does not begin with the Parousia. The destruction of the powers does not take place in a hypothetical intermediate kingdom which begins with the Parousia. It happens in the time before the Parousia and at the beginning of the *telos* which is simultaneous with the Parousia. 5. There is in the end-historical events portrayed in I Corinthians 15:20-28 no room for an intermediate Messianic kingdom» (W. WALLIS, «Intermediate Kingdom», 229-242). Wallis concentrates his argument on the first point.

He believes that Paul and the author of Rev were working from the same eschatological scheme[100].

According to Wallis, the Parousia and the τέλος cannot be simultaneous, since the latter must be preceded by the destruction of God's enemies, and this cannot take place before the Parousia[101].

Additionally, a time is required for the reign of Christ in verse 25[102].

The question of the intermediate kingdom cannot be solved by the study of the text alone. Cogent arguments can be made for either conclusion. There is no conclusive argument preventing one from holding that Paul believed in an intermediate kingdom between the parousia and the final resurrection, but if he did, he failed to develop it in any of his works. One has to keep in mind the goal of the argumentation and the area of Paul's interest. Since he is dealing primarily with the victory over death, he mentions only that which is pertinent to that victory and its aim, the final and full sovereignty of God.

As for the meaning of τὸ τέλος: it probably does mean «the End». However, «End» is itself an eschatological term. We have seen from some of the NT uses and possible parallels in the OT, that the End itself was a process or coming to fruition of a long cosmic and divine plan. There is nothing incompatible with a belief that «the End» could include the resurrection of the rest, but it was certainly not developed.

2.5.8 All Hostile Powers Must First Be Destroyed

Christ will hand over the kingdom to God the Father, but this will not take place until *all* hostile powers (ἀρχὴν καὶ πᾶσαν ἐξουσίαν καὶ δύναμιν) are destroyed (καταργήση)[103].

---

[100] «Essential to that scheme is a transitional kingdom, having a complex and meaningful relation both to the concluding era of this Age, on the one hand, and to the Age-to-come, on the other, which begins with the Parousia and overlaps this Age» (W. WALLIS, «Intermediate Kingdom», 242).

[101] Following the structure of verse 24, he notes that the aorist subjunctive of the second ὅταν clause requires that the destruction of the enemies takes place before the event of the first ὅταν clause, which is the delivering of the Kingdom to God at the time of the τέλος. He sees a similar parallel construction in verse 28, where the ὅταν marks the subjugation of the enemies. The τότε of verse 28 brings together the two events: the subjection of all things to Christ, and his handing over of the Kingdom to God. They are two sequential events, but are close together. Cf. W. WALLIS, «Intermediate Kingdom», 230-231.

[102] The destruction of enemies follows the Parousia, and a reign is necessary for that, a reign which extends beyond the parousia into the age to come. He holds that the γάρ clause of v. 25 is tied to the preceding ὅταν clause to give «divine certainty of the fulfillment of the prediction to be introduced from Psalm 110» (W. WALLIS, «Intermediate Kingdom», 232).

In themselves, these terms are neutral, but used in conjunction with one another in a metaphysical sense, they clearly refer to evil spirits or powers[104].

Conzelmann ascribes these three powers to Jewish demonology, and points out that the annihilating of these powers began with the exaltation of Christ which is the purpose of the enthronement[105].

Fee agrees that they represent malevolent evil powers, but downplays the apocalyptic nature of this passage[106].

Macgregor looks to Hellenistic philosophical and religious ideas as the source of this image of the astral deities. Paul, in this and similar passages, admits the existence of these astral forces but denies their divinity, holding that Christ has stripped them of all of their power, thereby freeing Christians from their slavery to elemental forces[107].

Lee investigates the background of this and similar passages from the standpoint of both Jewish apocalyptic ideas and Gnostic astrological religious beliefs, and finds elements of both[108].

---

[103] Macgregor claims that are not the demonic forces interfering in human affairs that we read about in the gospels, but are «*cosmic* spirit forces which possess and control not only individual human lives but the very course of the universe» (19). Quoting from Bultmann's *Theology of the New Testament*, vol. I, 256 on page 18 of his article, Macgregor states that «"kosmos" is an *eschatological concept*. It denotes the world of men and the sphere of human activity as being, on the one hand, a temporary thing hastening towards its end, and on the other hand, the sphere of antigodly power under whose sway the individual who is surrounded by it has fallen. It is the sphere of "the rulers of this age" (I Cor. ii. 6,8) and of "the god of this age" (II Cor. iv. 4)» (G.H.C. MACGREGOR, «Principalities and Powers», 17-28). It is here that Jesus through his word and deeds defeated and subjected the invisible powers. Lietzmann holds that the destruction of the hostile powers, especially death, will bring to an end an in-between kingdom or *zwischenreich* that began with the parousia. Cf. H. LIETZMANN, *An die Korinther*, 81.

[104] Like or similar descriptions of these hostile powers are also found in Rom 8,38; Col 1,16; 2,10.15; Eph 1,21; 3,10; 6,12 and 1 Pet 3,22. In Rom 8,38 and 1 Pet 3,22, ἄγγελοι is used in place of ἐξουσίαν. In addition, the terms κυριότητες (Col 1,16 and Eph 1,21) and θρόνοι (Col 1,16) are used to designate cosmic powers. There are several other terms used very loosely to describe powers, but the difference, if any, between them is almost impossible to determine. See J.Y. LEE, «Demonic Powers», 54-69.

[105] He believes that in Rom 8,38, the terms are used in a non-mythological sense, since they are combined with existential concepts. However, «heights» and «depths» and so on are more than existential concepts, since they are astrological terms and were believed to reflect a cosmological reality. Cf. H. CONZELMANN, *1 Corinthians*, 270-271.

[106] Cf. G. FEE, *Corinthians*, 752.

[107] Cf. G.H.C. MACGREGOR, «Principalities», 22.24.

[108] A prime example of the Jewish apocalyptic worldview that he finds is the dualism between the present age and the age to come, as in 1 Cor 2,6.8; Eph 1,21; Gal

He also points out that some astrological terms are used in the Pauline and deutero-Pauline writings; in particular, κοσμοκράτορες (Eph 6,12) and στοιχεῖα (Gal 4,3.9; Col 2,8.20)[109].

There are similar but not identical parallels in the cosmic angelology of the Qumran community which provide a further background for Paul's ideas[110].

Black observes that among all of the references and allusions to Ps 110,1 in the NT, three occurrences (1 Cor 15,24-7; Eph 1,20-1; and 1 Pet 3,22) associate the ascension and session of Christ at the right hand of God and his victory over his enemies with the destruction of «powers» and «principalities», which function as archenemies. He sees this as an early Christian theologoumenon, the common element in the three passages being the idea of Christ's destruction or subjection of these angelic powers[111].

A pattern based on a connection between Ps 110,1 and Dan 7,26-7 from the OT is the basis of these passages. The τέλος in verse 24 is combined with the destruction of the last of the four kingdoms in the passage from Daniel and developed by a Christian application of the *pesher* exegesis into the destruction of every sort of domination, authority and power[112].

It is interesting that καταργήσῃ is often translated as «destroyed». Lee, along with other scholars, rejects this RSV translation for the following reasons: although the word can mean «annihilate», it can also

---

6,15; 2 Cor 5,17. He sees this «pessimistic dualism» as being Babylonian and Persian in origin, and asserts that the strong Jewish hope for «deliverance from the futility of political and social outcomes consisted in a transformation of the whole cosmos into the kingdom of God» (J.Y. LEE, «Demonic Powers», 56-57).

[109] The first term is used in Hellenistic mystical writings and some Rabbinic works to describe the seven supreme astrological deities which control human fate. It is the invisible world between our world and God. The second term describes elemental spirits which enslave man, but which Paul always insisted were «weak and beggarly». Cf. J.Y. LEE, «Demonic Powers», 60-63.

[110] The Qumran sect's worldview included a cosmos ruled by good and bad angelic powers, such as «sons of heaven», «holy ones», «spirits of eternity», and personalized powers such as Belial, Michael, Mastema, etc. Cf. M. BLACK, «Πᾶσαι,» *Paul and Paulinism*, 74-82.

[111] Cf. M. BLACK, «Πᾶσαι», 74-75.

[112] As a result of the heavenly court's session, the fourth beast is deprived of its sovereignty so that in the end (ἕως τέλους) it may be destroyed and abolished. Power is then given to the saints of the Most High; their power is everlasting, and all sovereignties shall serve and obey them. In the LXX version, it reads πᾶσαι (αἱ) ἐξουσίαι αὐτῷ ὑποταγήσονται, the kingdoms of the world will be subjected to God rather than to the saints of the Most High. It is this version which is used in the Christian *pesher* of the NT, except that «Christ» is substituted for the «Most High» of the book of Daniel. Cf. M. BLACK, «Πᾶσαι», 75.

mean «overthrow», «dethrone», and «devaluate». Its literal meaning is «to make ineffective», or «to disconnect»[113].

Additionally, there are theological reasons for preferring a different translation (such as «dethrone»). It is stated in several passages that the saving action of Christ has redemptive consequences for all of creation, including the cosmos, which in addition to humanity includes στοιχεῖα and κοσμοκράτορες. Ultimately, then, Christ struggles for the sake of the cosmic powers as well, not to destroy them, but restore them to their original nature[114].

This accords well with certain patristic exegetes, most notably Origen, who held that the negative powers, including death, would be made friendly.

2.5.9 Death: The Last Enemy

Verse 26 is the main claim of Paul's argument in vv. 23-28, and states that the last enemy to be destroyed is death. Death is probably not one of the hostile powers listed in v. 24; in Rom 8,38, it is juxtaposed with life, while angels and principalities are listed separately. According to de Boer, Paul wants to make clear to the Corinthians three things: 1) death should be on the list of principalities, authorities and powers that was known to the community; 2) by being on this list, it is also an enemy; and 3) the reigning Christ will destroy death, along with the other powers on the list[115].

It is at this point that the work of Christ is complete, and he can deliver the kingdom – his temporal rule and his reconquest of the cosmos – over to God. By separating it and drawing special attention to it, emphasis is placed on the fact that the reign of Christ is not complete until death is conquered; everything is still in process.

2.6 *Psalms 110 and 8: All of Creation Must Be Subjected to Christ*

It is generally agreed that psalm 110 is a pre-exilic royal psalm composed for a Davidic monarch in Jerusalem. In this psalm, the king reigns

---

[113] J.Y. LEE, «Demonic Powers», 65.

[114] For example: 2 Cor 5,19; Col 1,19.20; Eph 1,10; Heb 1,14. The images used are that Christ reconciles or unites, both on earth and in heaven, in himself. In Col 1,16, it is stated that the cosmic powers owe their very existence to Christ, since all things were created through him and for him. J.Y. LEE, «Demonic Powers», 65-66.

[115] «Verse 26 with its thesis that death is an inimical cosmological power to be destroyed by the reigning Christ in itself represents the crucial modification of the christological traditions known to the Corinthian deniers» (M.C. DE BOER, *Defeat of Death*, 121).

with the power and authority of Yahweh. God promises that he will defeat the king's enemies, and it is clear that as vice regent on earth, the king's throne and power both depend on Yahweh[116].

Allusions to psalm 110 are numerous in Jewish literature of the intertestamental and early Christian periods[117].

The Jews of the NT period applied psalm 110 to several different persons, such as Abraham, David and Hezekiah, and it was not until the third century that consistent rabbinic references were made to the messiah[118].

Of all OT texts, verses 1 and 4 of psalm 110 are the most often quoted or alluded to in the NT, 33 quotations or allusions in the NT and 7 in other Christian writings before the middle of the 2nd century[119].

Early Christians were particularly attracted by the image of someone sitting at the right hand of God, for this seems to be the focus of the references made to Ps 110,1. In most cases, this exaltation is thought to have been the glory enjoyed by Jesus after the resurrection or ascension, although in some cases, it was thought to begin only at the time of the last judgment[120].

An analysis of the references to Ps 110,1 in the NT and early Christian literature indicates that it served a variety of functions. Of the 29 references to Ps 110,1, the vindication or glory of Jesus was illustrated 11 times, the glory or empowerment of Christians 5 times, support for christological titles 10 times, subjection of powers to Jesus 10 times, and intercession or priesthood of Jesus twice[121].

---

[116] See D.M. HAY, *Glory*, 19-20.

[117] TJob 33,3; TLev 18; references to Hasmonean rulers in 1 Macc 14,41, AsMos 6,1, Jub 32,1, TLev 8,3; Dan 7,9-14; Rabbi Akiba; Enoch literature; 11Q Melchizedek (no clear reference to Ps 110 but Melchizedek is central figure). D.M. HAY, *Glory*, 22-27.

[118] There is no clear proof that this psalm was viewed in messianic terms during the NT period, but the assumption is made that there was at least some interpretation in this direction, although its extent is not known. It is of interest that the rabbinic exegesis tended to view the messiah's work and victories as earthly in nature. His session at God's right hand was understood to imply inactivity, and the priesthood in v. 4 was downplayed. Cf. D.M. HAY, *Glory*, 30.33.

[119] See D.M. HAY, *Glory*, 15; T. CALLAN, «Psalm 110:1 and the Origin», 625; J. LAMBRECHT, «Paul's Christological Use», 506.

[120] In this last category are included ApPet 6; Sib Or 2,243; and Mark 14,62. At times believers are thought to share the exaltation in this life by means of baptism (Eph 2,6; Col 3,1) or as a reward after death (Rev 3,21). Cf. D.M. HAY, *Glory*, 45.

[121] Note that in some instances the quotation or allusion served more than one function, and in some cases the function was ambiguous. Cf. D.M. HAY, *Glory*, 45-46.

In this case, Paul utilizes a form of rabbinic exegesis called *gezerah shawah*, or analogy. In this type of exegesis, one OT passage is explained by comparison with another in which identical terminology and analogous traits are found[122].

This type of exegesis is expressed in the combination of psalms 110,1 and 8,6, which is found in Eph 1,20-2,10; 1 Pet 3,21-22; Heb 1 and 2; Phil 3,20-21 and Rom 8,34. The point of interest in these instances is consistent: «the present status or lordly function of the ascended and glorified Christ». These two joined passages, containing similar terms, convey the same meaning: subjection. This is the basic image and term to which Paul or the author of the tradition made additions to express the particular message[123].

It has been noted that three of these citations, Eph 1,22; 1 Pet 3,21b-22 and Heb 2,8, all symbolize the exaltation of Christ over principalities, powers, or angels; additionally, the citations in 1 Pet and Eph also make reference to the resurrection of Christ. This prompts de Boer to claim that rather than quoting the OT to the Corinthians, Paul is referring to a communal tradition describing Christ's exaltation over principalities and powers[124].

There is also a convergence of thought between vv. 25-27 and Heb 2,8ff. The passage in Heb describes the divine glory of the Son and his exaltation over the angels. A special emphasis is placed on the comprehensive and total subjugation of his enemies. In Heb 2:8, «not yet» is used as an amplification of the subjugation, perhaps indicating the future nature of the universal subjugation[125].

The analogous traits under consideration here are: 1) the subjection of all enemies, 2) the continuing reign of God's messianic agent while this is

---

[122] This is the sixth rule of Hillel's system. «Equal ordinance», or «statute» is the meaning of *gezerah shawah*, and parallels the Hellenistic rhetorical term *synkrisis pros ison*, first attested in Hermogenes in the 2nd century B.C. It was supposed to be used with the greatest restraint. Its purpose was to solve a problem by means of comparison with another scriptural passage. See D. COHN-SHERBOK, «Paul and Rabbinic Exegesis», 127-128; H.L. STRACK - G. STEMBERGER, *Introduction to the Talmud and Midrash*, 21.

[123] Cf. C.E. HILL, «Christ's Kingdom», 313; W. WALLIS, «Intermediate Kingdom», 238-239.

[124] «It seems safe to conclude that in *1 Cor 15.20-28 Paul is adapting and reinterpreting christological traditions known to the Corinthians, traditions in which Ps 110.1 and Ps 8.7b had in fact already come to play a fixed role in connection with Christ's resurrection which was understood to entail his exaltation over the principalities and powers* (italics his)» (M.C. DE BOER, *Defeat of Death*, 118).

[125] The defeat of death is also described in Heb 2,9.10.14.15. Cf. M.C. DE BOER, *Defeat of Death*, 238-239.

taking place, 3) the subjugation being accomplished by the power of God. In using these linked texts, the NT writers expressed what 4 Ezra and 2 Bar could not: «an already existing, sovereign kingdom of the son of David, the last Adam Jesus Christ, resultant upon his past resurrection and ascension to heaven»[126].

It is also interesting that v. 2 of psalm 110, which is not quoted, speaks of God telling his anointed to «rule in the midst of your foes» (κατακυρίευε ἐν μέσῳ τῶν ἐχθρῶν σου), implying a period of regal power prior to their final defeat. Additionally, v. 5 says that the Lord will «shatter kings on the day of his wrath», instead of at the coronation when he is enthroned[127].

2.6.1 Paul's Version and Use of Ps 110,1

The early Christians felt entirely free to paraphrase scripture to suit their purpose, and this psalm was no exception[128].

Paul either paraphrased 110,1 or quoted from a pre-Pauline tradition, quoting, rewriting and commenting on these two psalms[129].

Due to consistent similarities of alternate readings which depart from the LXX, it is likely that at least some of the quotations of Ps 110:1 derive from scriptural florilegia, and many allusions to this verse from primitive church confessions and hymns. It may well be that Paul was not citing the psalms directly, but using scriptural ideas to express his ideas rather than presenting proof texts[130].

---

[126] Neither 4 Ezra or 2 Bar refer to these two psalm texts in depicting the messianic kingdom. Cf. C.E. HILL, «Christ's Kingdom», 313.

[127] This entire psalm was utilized for christological reflection and argumentation. Even though not quoted in entirety here, the entire psalm may well have been associated with a few key verses such as v. 1. These two above verses may express additional analogous traits. Cf. C.E. HILL, «Christ's Kingdom», 315.

[128] Several scholars, notably Stendal and Lindars, also suggest that NT writers used the *pesher* method of citing scripture. In this method, a passage is altered to fit a particular situation, and the writer is free to select from several targumic or textual traditions as he sees fit. Although this claim is not widely accepted, it is true that in scriptural allusions there is a reflection of the style and issues of the writer. Cf. D.M. HAY, *Glory*, 36.

[129] This free use of the original text is perfectly permissible in the Jewish midrashic forms of exegesis. With each new translation or paraphrase, the original sense of the text is obscured somewhat as the text is adapted to the particular situation at hand. Cf. J. NEUSNER, *What Is Midrash?* 7-8.

[130] D.M. HAY, *Glory*, 38-39; For example, Rom 8,34, 1 Pet 3,22, and Col 3,1 all have the identical allusion: ὅς ἐστιν ἐν δεξιᾷ τοῦ θεοῦ (J. LAMBRECHT, «Paul's Christological Use», 508). Stanley shows that Paul utilized both the LXX and his own private collection of useful citations, and he departed frequently and freely from both. On numerous occasions he adapts the biblical text for his own purposes,

We saw above that this passage, along with 1 Pet 3,22 and Eph 1,20-1, all quote Ps 110,1 in conjunction with the annihilation of hostile powers, for this was a sort of early Christian theologoumenon. Verses 25-28 are an elaboration and explanation of verse 24, which states that the end will not come before all enemy powers have been destroyed. The verb δεῖ which is found in verse 25 can be either an apocalyptic term meaning the necessity of God's fixed plan and detailed timetable, or of God's plan expressed in the scriptures, especially the prophetic books. There are probably elements of both. This phrase concerning the necessity of Christ's reign is a reworking of the psalm, in which the messianic agent plays a passive role at God's right hand. He is here given an active role on earth[131].

The LXX version of this verse reads, Εἶπεν ὁ κύριος τῷ κυρίῳ μου Κάθου ἐκ δεξιῶν μου, ἕως ἂν θῶ τοὺς ἐχθρούς σου ὑποπόδιον τῶν ποδῶν σου[132].

Paul or an unknown writer vary from this version in several instances. The passivity of sitting at God's right hand is reinterpreted as an active reign on earth by adding αὐτὸν βασιλεύειν to δεῖ; God no longer speaks in direct discourse and this is introduced by γάρ. Due to the influence of verse 27 and Ps 8,7, πάντας is added. Additionally, ὑπο τοὺς πόδας is put in place of the ὑποκάτω + genitive found in Ps. 8,7. Paul wants to emphasize the temporal limitation of Christ's reign, therefore he replaces ἕως with ἄχρι οὗ[133].

In verse 27a, Ps. 8,7 receives a similar treatment. The LXX text, which reads πάντα ὑπέταξας ὑποκάτω τῶν ποδῶν αὐτοῦ is modified in the following ways: γάρ is added as in verse 25 for emphasis, and the third person is used in lieu of the second[134].

---

changing word order, grammar, and making omissions, additions, and substitutions to the text. This was a common practice, utilized to suit the situation, needs, and theology of the author, and was found among all varieties of Jewish theological writings. See C.D. STANLEY, *Paul and the Language of Scripture*, 252-264.

[131] Cf. J. LAMBRECHT, «Paul's Christological Use», 506.

[132] *Septuaginta*, vol. II, 124.

[133] A dependence on conditions is implied by ἕως ἄν. Cf. J. LAMBRECHT, «Paul's Christological Use», 506-507.

[134] A possible explanation for all of this divergence in the text is that Paul is using a version of psalm 110:1 which we do not have. According to Hay, a better explanation is this: Both the reference to 110,1 in v. 25 and to Ps. 8,7 in v. 27 write ὑπὸ τοὺς πόδας αὐτοῦ instead of the original wording. Paul or others may have modified the texts in question because these two verses from Ps 8 and 110 were seen as matching, paired prophecies. The word «all» appears in both; as we saw above, «all» is prominent in verses 20-28 (D.M. HAY, *Glory*, 36-37). It seems that ὑπο instead of ὑποκάτω was Paul's habitual linguistic usage, since the first appears in his writings

Also, the ὑποκάτω + genitive is replaced by ὑπο + accusative, thereby agreeing with verse 25[135].

Paul is hammering home his theme: according to God's plan, Christ is reigning from the time of the resurrection until all enemies are subjugated. The word «all» is very important for Paul's argument in vv. 20-28, being used no less than eleven times. Verse 24 adds «all» twice, to signify the totality of Christ's subjection of inimical powers. In verse 25 πάντας is added, whereas the LXX has only «his enemies»[136].

2.7 Paul's Exegesis in vv. 23-28: Christocentric or Theocentric?

The major difficulty is this: should vv. 23-28 be thought of as Christocentric or theocentric? The form of the problem is manifested in the pronouns that are found in vv. 24-28. A pronoun shift has definitely been carried out, but there is some confusion: it is not always clear who the subject of the pronoun is, due to the substitutions, free treatment of scripture, and the convoluted nature of the argument. Additionally, Kreitzer notes a great fluctuation in Jewish pseudepigraphal literature between God and the Messianic agent, where the distinction between the two roles became blurred. Part of the confusion was resolved by relegating the Messiah to a temporary earthly role. This ambiguity was carried over into the NT, in part because many OT passages which were theocentric were applied by the early church to Christ. This may add to the lack of clarity concerning roles in this passage[137].

It appears that Paul has rewritten Ps 110,1 and 8,7 in a Christocentric way, although with a theocentric goal, as in 28bc. There are those who argue for a theocentric interpretation of the passage, holding that God is already the subject of ὑπέταξεν in 27a[138].

---

often, the latter never. In other NT renderings of Ps 110,1, either the original ὑποπόδιον is used (Luke 20,43; Acts 2,35; Heb 1,13), or it is replaced with ὑποκάτω (Matt 22,44; Mark 12,36) (C.D. STANLEY, Paul and Language of Scripture, 206-207.

[135] Lambrecht points out that many commentators believe that we should assume a double transposition, for while in the psalm it was God who subjected all things under the feet of man in general, in Paul it is probably Christ who subjects all things under his own feet, due to the parallelism with v. 25. This is by no means clear, however. Cf. J. LAMBRECHT, «Paul's Christological Use», 507.

[136] Cf. J. LAMBRECHT, «Paul's Christological Use», 506-507; D.M. HAY, Glory, 36-37.

[137] L.J. KREITZER, Jesus and God, 163-164.

[138] He holds that in v. 25b God is the subject of θῇ. T. Aono claims that in 24c, the second ὅταν clause, God is already the subject. Since the two citations of Ps 110 and 8 are christological proof texts, and are frequently cited in connection with God's exaltation of Christ over the powers and principalities, de Boer views God as the

Lambrecht insists on a Christological interpretation of the passage. He holds to his basic argument: after verse 25a, which contains the «"active Christological" δεῖ [...]αὐτὸν βασιλεύειν» Christ most probably remains the subject of v. 25b, which repeats the idea in v. 24c»[139].

According to Lambrecht, Christ is the subject introduced in v. 23; v. 24, which begins with εἶτα τὸ τέλος, leads into the two related temporal ὅταν clauses, both of which have Christ as the subject. Paul replaces the first person subject of the LXX, θῶ (referring to God), with the third person, θῇ (referring to Christ). Christ is clearly the subject, since he was the subject of the «he must reign», which is a limited temporal period. The subject of αὐτοῦ is not without ambiguity in its immediate context; in the entire argument, however, it becomes clearer that Christ is the subject, since Christ is the subject until the end when he turns the kingdom over to God the Father[140].

In v. 27. we are again faced with a similar question: who is the subject of ὑπέταξεν? There are various possible interpretations, and it is by no means crystal clear[141].

Fee lays out two possible interpretations: in the first, Christ is the subject; it is a further reiteration of vv. 25-26. The next clause is introduced with the same conjunction (ὅταν) as in vv. 24 and 28. The other

---

subject in v. 25 and 27a, in *Defeat of Death*, 116-117. See also F.W. MAIER, «Ps 110,1 (LXX 109,1) im Zusammenhang von 1 Kor 15,24-26», 139-156.

[139] «For Paul, since the resurrection of Christ, actual history means Christ's kingship, Christ's struggle against the evil powers. But this is not the end. The end is decidedly theocentric» (J. LAMBRECHT, «Paul's Christological Use», 508-511).

[140] All agree that Christ is the subject of θῇ for the above reasons. Conzelmann points out that God is the only one who acts. The phrase δεῖ γὰρ αὐτὸν βασιλεύειν fixes Christ as the subject of ἄχρι οὗ θῇ, who then subjects the enemies to himself, annihilating them, making God all in all as the ultimate source. Héring is somewhat ambivalent, stating that it is «perhaps Christ». Based upon v. 25 and v. 27, where it is God who subjects the universe to him, he would hold that God is the subject. However, he points out that the elaborate pains taken in vv. 27 and 28 to subject Christ to God the Father does not make much sense except to preserve the omnipotence and the prerogatives of God the Father. See Lambrecht, p. 521, n. 44 for a more extensive list of those favoring Christ as the subject. Cf. G. FEE, *Corinthians*, 755; J. LAMBRECHT, «Paul's Christological Use», 507; H. CONZELMANN, *1 Corinthians*, 272-273; H. LIETZMANN, *An die Korinther*, 81; J. HÉRING, *First Epistle*, 168; E.B. ALLO, *aux Corinthiens*, 408.

[141] Lietzmann, Conzelmann, Héring (with reservations) choose «Christ»; Weiss and Allo choose «God», while Fee is not sure, but leans towards the second. It gets very confusing here, and there are good arguments for either choice. The ambiguity is clear in the following diversity of translations: «God» (NRSV, RSV); «Scripture says, he has put all things in subjection under his feet» (REB); and «for he has put all things under his feet». In these last two translations, it is not clear who the subject is.

possibility is that this is a sort of a citation of the psalm which anticipates v. 28, where it will be shown that it is God who has subjected all things to Christ. In this case the double ὅταν of v. 24 would be explained by vv. 25-6 and 27-8; v. 24c by 25-6 and 24b by 27-8[142].

Many translations take the second choice, and although the first is tempting, the latter is more likely. In favor of the first, it is unlikely that with a long string of pronouns with Christ as subject, the author would suddenly shift to God as subject and then back again without identifying the subject. Verses 20-28 make claims for the cosmic implications of christological assertions, death being the main object. Additionally, if God were the subject, then the qualifications in 27bc would be unnecessary. Since Christ is the subject, Paul hastens to assure the reader that God cannot be thought of as being subordinated in any way to Christ[143].

Logically, too, Christ is the subject all the way through: v. 24b reflected the sovereignty of God, vv. 24c-28a that of Christ, and 28bc returns that sovereignty again to God. The passage is stressing Christ's active reign, which lasts until the end, when everything is finally turned over to God. In vv. 20-28, the effects of Christ's resurrection are focused first on humanity and then on all of creation. Additionally, God's direct and immediate sovereignty over creation in its entirety is restored[144].

But there are also good arguments for God being the subject. It should be noted first of all that in 27c and 28b, God is the one who subjects all things (τοῦ ὑποτάξαντος and τῷ ὑποτάξαντι). This would be in accordance with the type of exegesis applied here; namely, *gezerah shawah* or analogy. In the original psalm, the messianic agent reigns passively at God's right hand while God crushes and subdues the enemies. God is the source of power and the subjecting agent. With that in mind, we will interpret this difficult passage as follows:

---

[142] It would read, 27 (a) For «he (Christ) has subjected all things under his feet», but (b) whenever (ὅταν) he (Christ) shall have said: «All things have been subjected» (c) (of course excepting Him who subjected to him all things). Fee sees (c) as parenthetical and awkward. Cf. G. FEE, *Corinthians*, 757-758.

[143] Cf. M.C. DE BOER, *Defeat of Death*, 114.

[144] Aletti insists that the emphasis in these verses is on B and B¹: the Lordship of Christ. These verses form a chiasm as follows:

a = 24b reign of God the Father
B = 24b-26 victory of Christ: destruction of enemies.
    ὅταν καταργήσῃ
B¹ = subjection of all of creation to Christ
    ὅταν δὲ ὑποταγῇ
a¹ = subjection of Son to God.
J.-N. ALETTI, «L'Argumentation», 73.

27 πάντα γὰρ ὑπέταξεν (God) ὑπο τοὺς πόδας αὐτοῦ (Christ).
ὅταν δὲ εἴπῃ ὅτι πάντα ὑποτέτακται (God; divine passive)
δῆλον ὅτι ἐκτὸς τοῦ ὑποτάξαντος (God) αὐτῷ (Christ) τὰ πάντα.
28 ὅταν δὲ ὑποταγῇ (God) αὐτῷ (Christ) τὰ πάντα,
τότε καὶ αὐτὸς ὁ υἱὸς ὑποταγήσεται (God as agent; divine passive)
τῷ ὑποτάξαντι (God) αὐτῷ (Christ) τὰ πάντα,
ἵνα ᾖ ὁ θεὸς τὰ πάντα ἐν πᾶσιν.

Working backwards from v. 28, it is God who has subjected all things to Christ in v. 28, and the one to whom Christ must be subjected when all things have been subjected to him (Christ). This shows that αὐτῷ in 28a and 27c refer to Christ. It is noteworthy that the verb in vv. 24-26 that is used in connection with the powers, principalities and death is καταργέω, while in verses 27-28 the verb that is used is ὑποτάσσω, and is used 6 times. God seems to be the agent in these cases. Christ would be the one to whom all things are subjected, but God would be the ultimate agent and source of power, protecting both Christ's status and mission and God's sovereignty. This harmonizes well with apocalyptic theology, which places all ultimate power and interventive force in the hands of God, with the Messiah acting as an agent. It is also reflective of the original intent of the psalm, which places the anointed king at God's right hand while God subdues the king's enemies[145].

Verse 27b, the beginning of this qualification, can be interpreted impersonally. Lietzmann and Conzelmann takes ὅταν δὲ εἴπῃ to be the equivalent of «when it says» or «Scripture says», with God as the subject of the Scripture quote, but without breaking the flow of the argument. This is the choice taken in the RSV, NRSV, and NJB[146].

2.8 All In All: Return of All Sovereignty to God

Verse 28 states that after everything has been subjected, presumably to Christ, then the Son himself will be subjected to the One who subjects all things to him, so that «God will be all in all» ([τὰ] πάντα ἐν πᾶσιν). The exact meaning of this phrase is unclear. It is paralleled directly only in Eph 1,20-23 and Col 3,11. Throughout the Pauline and deutero-Pauline

---

[145] Aletti points out that even if God is chosen as the subject of 27a, the point of the passage is not changed.

[146] It would then read, 27 (a) For «he (God) has subjected all things under his (Christ's) feet». Now (b) When it (scripture) says: «All things have been subjected.» (c) it is clear that «all things» excludes the One who did the subjecting to him. Cf. G. FEE, *Corinthians*, 758-759.

corpus, «all things» usually refers to what God has created, or that over which God rules[147].

Colossians is difficult to date and is of uncertain authorship; some hold that it was written by Paul himself, others by one of his disciples later. Despite who the author may be, however, it represents Pauline style and thought. The texts in question are 1,16.17.20 and 3,11. Paul describes the supremacy of Christ over the church and the universe: «for in him all things in heaven and on earth were created, things visible and invisible, whether thrones or dominions or rulers or powers, all things have been created through him and for him (16). He himself is before all things, and in him all things hold together (17) [...] and through him God was pleased to reconcile to himself all things, whether on earth or in heaven, by making peace through the blood of his cross (20)». Of interest is the fact that the powers discussed in v. 24 appear to have their origin in Christ, whose mission it will be to reconcile the entire cosmos and overcome all division of any sort. In 3:11, Christ overcomes any difference in the human realm between Greek and Jew, slave and free, circumcised and not, etc., by being «all and in all» (ἀλλα τὰ πάντα καὶ ἐν πᾶσιν Χριστός).

In Ephesians, Paul pleads for oneness in 4,5-6 by citing «one Lord, one faith, one baptism, one God and Father of all, who is above all and through all and in all» (εἷς θεὸς καὶ πατὴρ πάντων, ὁ ἐπὶ πάντων καὶ διὰ πάντων καὶ ἐν πᾶσιν). In 1,20-23, Paul explains a cosmic process initiated when God raised Christ and made him sit at his right hand in the heavenly places, far above all rule and authority and power and dominion. God has put all things under his feet, and being above all things, has made him head of the church, which is his Body, the fullness of him who is filled, all in all (τὸ πλήρωμα τοῦ τὰ πάντα ἐν πᾶσιν πληρουμένου).

Both Ephesians and Colossians make it fairly clear that the role of Christ was understood as that of God's instrument (Cf. 2 Cor 5,18-20 and Rom 5,10-11) as reconciler, restorer, and re-creator of the universe, overcoming every split, rupture, division and inimical power, eventually handing over this restored universe to God as in v. 24. Even if these two

---

[147] There are many uses of πᾶς in the NT. Besides the parallel meanings found in Col and Eph, the following examples give some indications of usages which bear some relation to v. 28: Rev 21,5 (I make all things new); 4,11 (you have created all things); 1 Pet 4,7 (the end of all things is near); 2 Pet 3,4 (all things continue as they were from the beginning of creation); 3,11 (all these things are to be dissolved in this way); 1 Tim 6,13 (God gives life to all things); Heb 2,8 (subjecting all things under his feet. Now in subjecting all things to them, God left nothing outside their control); 1,2 (Son heir of all things); Phil 3,21 (Christ makes all things subject to himself); Gal 3,28 (no Jew or Greek, slave or free, male nor female, for you are all one in Christ Jesus).

letters were not written by Paul, they probably give us a reasonable indication of how the «all in all» tradition was understood at that time.

Paul uses this phrase in conjunction with «all things» in v. 27-28 five times, twice without the article. According to de Boer, this is a «summary expression for all the inimical principalities, authorities, and powers that, apart from Christ or God, constitute the *totality* of the world experienced by human beings. These powers are in short «all things» *vis-à-vis the human world*» (italics his)[148].

M. Barth follows a similar line in his explanation of that term[149]. It is not, according to Barth, «the All» of Greek philosophy, but a phrase used in connection with lists of powers, both earthly and heavenly. It is possibly equivalent to a classical Greek adverb (πανταπασιν) meaning «altogether», «wholly», or «all-in-all»[150].

Barrett insists that this must be understood «soteriologicaly, not metaphysically, and that it is a matter of God's sole and unchallenged reign»[151].

The consensus is that it deals chiefly with God's undivided and total power over his creation[152].

---

[148] Christ exalted over these powers becomes «all things» and he is the new universe for human beings instead of death and other powers. Because of this, de Boer opts for a translation of «all things among all people» (see below). M.C. DE BOER, *Defeat of Death*, 126.

[149] As with others, Barth looks to Stoicism to throw light on the origins of the passage. «"All things" does not mean "a haphazard or chaotic conglomeration of objects or events". To the contrary, the term can signify in Pauline writings the world as structured by powerful institutions, forces and constants that may be divided [...] into earthly and heavenly, visible and invisible powers. The technical function of the reference to "all things"[...] is a means of describing the omnipotence exerted by God or conveyed to Christ and exerted by him» (M. BARTH, *Ephesians 1-3*, 176-177.

[150] M. BARTH, *Ephesians*, 156-157.

[151] «It is not the absorption of Christ and mankind, with consequent loss of distinct being into God; but rather the unchallenged reign of God alone, in his pure goodness» (C.K. BARRETT, *Corinthians*, 361). It might be pointed out, however, that Paul would not make such a distinction between soteriology and metaphysics. Human redemption was intimately intertwined (Rom 8,18-25) with the redemption of the entire cosmos and the defeat of unseen powers.

[152] According to Fee, it ties together everything that has preceded it, explaining in the process the statement in v. 24 about handing over the kingdom. The subjection of the powers and the defeat of death was set in motion by Christ's resurrection. The defeat of death heals a rupture in the universe, and restores God as sole ruler over creation. It is God's total rule *through* Christ (G. FEE, *Corinthians*, 759-760). Lietzmann states that during the *Zwischenreich* Christ works at the side of God and *even seems to relegate him to the role of observer; from this point on, however, God* alone reigns (H. LIETZMANN, *An die Korinther*, 81). Héring worries about pantheism. He therefore takes πάντα as an accusative, rendering the phrase «in the whole

There is an interesting problem with the translation. Most versions translate the expression as «all in all», with the exception of the RSV, which opts for «everything to everyone». The translation «everyone» is made possible by the fact that πᾶσιν can be either neuter or masculine plural. This latter option is followed by de Boer, who renders it «all things among all people»[153].

There are more compelling reasons, however, for preferring the traditional translation of «all in all», that is, taking πᾶσιν as a neuter plural. First, there is the witness of the early church, as in Eph and Col. Although we are faced with the same problem in translating πᾶσιν, the expanded cosmological arguments in these two letters make the neuter more likely. Additionally, the patristic fathers understood it in this fashion. The stronger reason is the patently cosmological nature of the argument in this passage. Although soteriological in purpose, it insists that salvation cannot be understood apart from the redemption of the created order and the defeat of inimical powers, especially death. «All things» would include the created order, the world, the heavenly powers, and human beings. In translating these and similar passages throughout the Pauline and deutero-Pauline writings, we must not choose interpretations which are ecclesiastical in a narrow and exclusive sense. The passages were clearly meant to be cosmological and metaphysical in their scope; we must preserve that intent[154].

2.9 *Peroratio: Ad Hominem Arguments*

Verses 29-34 form the *peroratio*, and this has been called the weakest part of Paul's argument. It stands in parallel to vv. 13-19, in that it is an

---

universe and completely», thereby making an «affirmation of the total and visible presence of the Kingdom of God» (J. HÉRING, *Corinthians*, 168-169). Both Allo and Conzelmann agree with the consensus concerning God's undivided power over creation (E.B. ALLO, *Corinthians*, 409; H. CONZELMANN, *1 Corinthians*, 275).

[153] De Boer takes ἐν as distributive and πᾶσιν as masculine plural, and views it as an *inclusio* with v. 22b, where it states that in Christ all (πάντες, masc.) will be made alive. Paul, then, is saying that in the resurrection of the dead, all shall be made alive, since God is all things among all people (M.C. DE BOER, *Defeat of Death*, 125-126). Conzelmann, on the other hand, feels that the emphasis on God's total sovereignty favors πᾶσιν being a neuter plural (H. CONZELMANN, *1 Corinthians*, 275).

[154] In discussing the various English translations of Eph 1,20-23, Barth notes the tendency to obscure the cosmological element and opt for ecclesiastical interpretations. All these choices may be grammatically and linguistically defensible, but we must ask the question: Which best fits the context of this and similar passages and the particular spiritual universe of Paul and his early followers? Cf. M. BARTH, *Ephesians*, 156-157.

affective argument illustrating the negative consequences if indeed there is no resurrection[155].

It is comprised of a series of examples taken from everyday practice, coupled with several rhetorical questions[156].

Paul makes an abrupt change from the lofty cosmological images of vv. 20-28 to these very personal *ad hominem* arguments. Repeating the refrain, «If the dead are not raised» that is, if vv. 20-28 are not true, Paul fires a salvo of several examples and exhortations geared to stir up the emotions, not giving the reader or listener a chance to pause. It seems to fall into three sections: the first is in the third person, addressed to «they», those who practice baptism for the dead (perhaps identical with the τινες of v. 12); the second, the first person, dealing with Paul's own life; while in the third, second person plural imperatives form an exhortation to a better ethical life[157].

Verse 29 is one of the most vigorously disputed passages in the NT. On the surface, it seems rather simple. Using the statement of the opposition as a springboard – there is no resurrection – Paul points to the inconsistency and futility of a practice of the Corinthians, i.e., being baptized on behalf of the dead. Despite the numerous attempts to explain this passage away or get out of the difficulties and discomfort it causes, it seems better to accept the obvious surface meaning of the passage: Some Corinthians practiced a form of vicarious baptism. What is meant exactly

---

[155] Bünker also calls this an argument *ad hominem* (M. BÜNKER, *Briefformular*, 69-70). The purpose of the *peroratio* is to conclude the discourse by either a recapitulation or an arousal of the emotions or affections. The latter concerns us in this passage, and the chief method used is *indignatio*, designed to arouse disgust and hatred towards either an individual or a particular act or form of behavior (B.M.GARAVELLI, *Manuale di Retorica*, 104-105).

[156] Cf. B. MACK, *Rhetoric*, 57; C.K. BARRETT, *Corinthians*, 361. Fee points out that these examples merely come at the same problem again in a new way, offering little in the way of theology (G. FEE, *Corinthians*, 763-764). Conzelmann notes that Paul strings together different thoughts and arguments, and that there is no continuous logical train of thought. The rhetorical questions themselves are for more than rhetorical effect (H. CONZELMANN, *1 Corinthians*, 275-276). They are, according to Wuellner, being used for a definite pastoral purpose. The function of these rhetorical questions in 1 Cor is determined by the techniques of argumentation and the rhetorical genre and situation, as well as the framework and the starting point of Paul's argumentation (W. WUELLNER, «Paul as Pastor», 52-53).

[157] The rhetorical questions of the first two groups Wuellner would see as functioning for a form of praise and shame, which are the two affective themes appropriate for epideictic discourse, which he holds 1 Cor to be. As will be discussed below, certain epideictic elements in a document do not preclude it belonging to another genre, as is the case here. Cf. G. FEE, *Corinthians*, 762.

by that, and when and under what circumstances it was practiced is impossible to answer, and is outside the limits of this study[158].

Paul then focuses attention on himself as an example of the dangers and difficulties faced by Christians. If there is no resurrection of the dead, why risk one's life or suffer? The hope in the resurrection is the only thing that gives this meaning or worth. Even the probably hypothetical or metaphorical example of fighting the wild beasts at Ephesus would be a tragic waste if there is no resurrection from the dead. In other words, the Christian life is a sham and a waste if this life is all that there is[159].

But now the argument moves to a deeper level, and one which perhaps has been at the back of Paul's mind all along; namely, the ethical implications of a denial of the resurrection. He has already shown how this denial renders the Christian life superfluous and useless. Now he will carry it further: hedonism and immorality is the only response to a life without Christian hope. He uses a quote from Isa 22,13, reflecting the contemporary view of Epicurean philosophy, to the effect that eating and drinking is the only sane response to a life that will end completely at death[160]. In v. 33, he uses a proverbial quote from Menander's *Thais* as part of an ethical exhortation: Do not be deceived! Bad company corrupts

---

[158] In A. ROBERTSON – A. PLUMMER, *First Epistle of St. Paul to the Corinthians*, 359, reference is made to an 1890 article which surveys over 36 possible explanations. H. CONZELMANN, reports over 200 in *1 Corinthians*, 276. Both Tertullian (*de resurr* 48 and *adv. Marc.* v.10) and Chrysostom report that certain heretical groups, especially the Marcionites, practiced vicarious baptism for those members of the community who died before being baptized. There is no evidence outside of this passage that the practice existed in the 50's of the first century, but it is not impossible. C.K. BARRETT, notes in *Corinthians*, 361, that Paul merely refers to a known practice; he neither approves or disapproves.

[159] Most agree that the statement about fighting wild beasts cannot be taken literally. Obviously, Paul is still alive to talk about it, but there are other reasons as well. As a Roman citizen, Paul could not have been thrown to the beasts as punishment. Additionally, there is no mention of this in his list of woes in 2 Cor 11,23-29. It perhaps refers metaphorically to his struggle with opponents in Ephesus, or is merely a hypothetical situation. Cf. H. CONZELMANN, *1 Corinthians*, 278; G. FEE, *Corinthians*, 770-771; C.K. BARRETT, *Corinthians*, 365-366.

[160] Bünker calls this (32b) an example of *permissio* (surrender), which is, according to *Rhetorica ad Herennium* IV, XXIX «used when we indicate in speaking that we yield and submit the whole matter to another's will», and is particularly useful for evoking pity. Also present is a touch of irony. This is possible; however, *permissio* usually refers to a surrender to other people, whereas Paul seems to be saying, If this is all that there is, go ahead and live it up! In a sense, he would be surrendering to the dreaded logical consequences of an absence of the resurrection. Cf. M. BÜNKER, *Briefformular*, 70.

good morals! It is unclear who the bad company is; perhaps they are those who say that there is no resurrection. It is a warning not to mix with corrupting influences[161].

Verse 34 ends this section with an outright and blunt command: Come to a sober and right mind, and sin no more; for some people have no knowledge (ἀγνωσίαν) of God! I say this to your shame! Sobriety in contrast to drunkenness is used in eschatological literature as examples of alertness and clearheadedness as contrasted with worldliness and spiritual ignorance[162].

Mistaken ideas and attitudes are often expressed in sinful behavior, and the ἀγνωσίαν experienced by some is manifested in their lives. They claim to have some knowledge, insight and experience of God which puts them in a different ethical class. Paul points out that their lives prove that their so-called knowledge is actually ignorance[163].

The final words of v. 34 – I say this to your shame! – is an example of indignatio, designed to arouse shame and disgust for their behavior and attitudes.

These *ad hominem* arguments are rather incongruous and strange. Hedonism would seem to be a proper response to life only if there were no afterlife, and by verse 29, it does not seem that the Corinthians deny some sort of life after death. There is another possibility: Paul is trying to make the connection between the ethical deeds done while still alive, in the body, and the afterlife itself. It seems that he is saying, «The way you comport yourselves now is related to the type of life you will have in the new age». The body and the spirit are one.

3. Summary and Conclusion

It is clear that Paul appealed to the kerygma which had already been accepted by the Corinthians; this kerygma included the resurrection of Christ, but it is noteworthy that nowhere in that primitive kerygma did Paul mention the resurrection of believers. In a period in which the pa-

---

161 Fee believes that the evil company ὁμιλίαι could also mean disedifying or corrosive conversations, but if it does, it probably does so in the context of interpersonal relationships and friendships. Paul is clearly warning the Corinthians to shun those who hold dangerous ideas. Cf. G. FEE, *Corinthians*, 773.

162 The word ἐκνήψατε reflects the word πίωμεν in 32b. A «standard term of eschatological parenesis», it is found in 1 Thess 5:6ff and Philo's *De ebrietate*. Cf. H. CONZELMANN, *1 Corinthians*, 279.

163 Fee has noticed the strong emphasis on moral exhortation here, and the link between denial of the resurrection and aberrant behavior. The exhortation to righteous living would seem strange and out of place here, unless there were a link with the argument on the resurrection. Cf. G. FEE, *Corinthians*, 773.

rousia was considered to be imminent, there would not have been a need to stress such an idea, although it is also clear from Paul's indignant question in v. 12 that it was part of Christian belief. This kerygma becomes the foundation upon which Paul will base his arguments for the rest of chapter 15.

In answer to criticism and hostility, Paul went to great lengths to protect his reliability as a witness to the Risen Lord, both in vv. 8-11 of this chapter and most of chapter 9. He perhaps anticipated resistance to the message which he was about to deliver.

Paul is going to argue that the resurrection of Christ, which the Corinthians accept, is so inextricably linked with the resurrection of the believer that to deny one is to deny the other. It is extremely difficult to ascertain exactly what was meant by the statement «There is no resurrection», but in the absence of data indicating otherwise, it would be better to take it as much as possible at face value. In the Jewish apocalyptic and pseudepigraphal tradition, denial of the resurrection need not have meant either a denial of the afterlife or a belief in the immortality of the soul, as will be seen in chapter 4.

After carrying the consequences of the denial of the general resurrection of the dead, and thereby that of Christ, to its most radical conclusion, Paul shows that it is an untenable and undesirable position to hold. He asserts that Christ is risen from the dead, but adds that he is the firstfruits of the dead. This is the key concept: that the resurrection of Christ is the first stage in a long apocalyptic event, culminating in the restoration of the universe to God. There must be a set progression and order to events: a destruction of all powers which are hostile to God, including the last enemy, death; the parousia of Christ and the resurrection of those who belong to him; and finally, the culmination, when Christ will hand over the kingdom, or the reconquered universe, to God the Father. He will submit himself to God the Father, thereby ensuring God's complete sovereignty.

Besides the insistence on the link between the resurrection of Christ and the general resurrection, the implicit message of vv. 20-28 is «time and order». Christ will continue to reign (and he can only reign from heaven, when one considers psalm 110) until the conquest is complete. This, coupled with the parenetic exhortations in vv. 29-34 and the whole body of the letter, would indicate that one of the main concerns with the denial of the resurrection was its effects on the ethical behavior of the community. Orthodoxy equals orthopraxis. It is also possible that the denial itself was prompted by frustration and anxiety experienced in the

50's at the delay of the parousia. Again, the message is patience and correct living. Life in the body is important for the afterlife, and the body itself is important: it will take part in the resurrection. This Paul explains in the second half of the chapter, namely, how the body rather than flesh and blood can indeed inherit the kingdom of God.

CHAPTER III

The Last Things In Jewish Apocalyptic Literature

Εἶτα τὸ τέλος, ὅταν παραδιδῷ τὴν βασιλείαν τῷ θεῷ καὶ πατρί, ὅταν
καταργήσῃ πᾶσαν ἀρχὴν καὶ πᾶσαν ἐξουσίαν καὶ δύναμιν ... v.24

ἔσχατος ἐχθρὸς καταργεῖται ὁ θάνατος... v.26

1. The Apocalyptic Genre

From the time of the Enlightenment onwards, apocalyptic literature
began to be viewed in a negative and contemptuous light. Koch states that
in the last century, apocalyptic was in the opinion of many theologians
«the quintessence of what is "eschatologically" improper. Theological eschatology believed that it could best prove its legitimacy by abjuring
apocalyptic as firmly and vocally as possible». In the last century, various
attempts were made to define the apocalyptic genre and to study it scien-
tifically. This attitude has lasted well into this century and still exists in
some quarters[1].

---

[1] K. KOCH, «What is Apocalyptic?», 16-36; J.J. COLLINS, *The Apocalyptic Imagination*, 1-2. German scholars of the 19th century did a fair amount of research on the
apocalyptic genre, although most of them continued to view it as essentially a negative phenomenon: Lücke (1832) described apocalyptic as «degenerate prophecy»;
Schürer (1873); Kautzch (1900); Charles (1913). The latter two aided apocalyptic
research by editing and publishing apocalyptic and pseudepigraphal texts. Hilgenfeld
(1854) was exceptional in being basically positive in his approach: apocalyptic provides the link between OT and NT, prophecy and Christianity (R. STURM, «Defining
the Word "Apocalyptic"», 17-48). Although an adjective, «apocalyptic» will be used
as a substantive referring to literature expressing apocalyptic symbols, ideas or eschatology.

A lack of precision and clarity regarding terms was (and still is in some cases) the cause of much confusion in scholarship. Terms have been and often are still used carelessly and interchangeably. In an attempt to be more clear and precise about what is being discussed, many contemporary scholars make the following distinctions: «apocalypse» defines a particular literary genre; «apocalyptic eschatology» is a particular religious perspective and thought structure; while «apocalypticism» is a sociological ideology. These are closely related to one another, but do not always coincide exactly[2].

Russell makes one of the first modern attempts to define and describe apocalyptic literature and its message. He is reluctant to define it too rigidly, believing it to be a religious mood or temper distinguishable from OT prophecy, although being a development of the latter. The characteristics of apocalyptic literature as opposed to apocalyptic teaching are fourfold: esoteric in nature, literary in form, symbolic in language, and pseudonymous in authorship. This definition is unsatisfactory, since it really says very little and could be applied to other types of literature as well. Russell is much more successful in describing the nature of apocalyptic teaching[3].

In his 1992 work, Russell recognizes the weaknesses of his earlier attempt at definition. After surveying the work of scholars such as Hanson, Koch, Rowland and Collins, he basically opts for the definition of Collins and the SBL Genres Project, with some modifications:

---

[2] For example, a particular work might contain apocalyptic eschatology, but might not be formally an apocalypse. This distinction is important for the study of the possible apocalyptic nature of 1 Cor 15, for there are those like Bultmann who will hold that the passage in question uses apocalyptic language but is not apocalyptic (J.J. COLLINS, ed., «Morphology», 3). See also L. KECK, «Paul and Apocalyptic Theology», 229-241.

[3] Russell describes this religious mood found in apocalyptic by appealing to the descriptions of other scholars, for example J. Lindblom: transcendentalism, mythology, cosmological survey, pessimistic historical surveys, dualism, division of time into periods, teaching of Two Ages, numerology, pseudo-ecstasy, artificial claims to inspiration, pseudonymity, and esotericism. He adds as his own contribution the unity of history, the conception of cosmic history dealing with heaven and earth, primordiality and revelations concerning creation and the fall of men and angels, the source of evil in the universe and the part played by angelic powers, conflict between light and darkness, good and evil, God and Satan; the emergence of the «Son of Man» figure; belief in life after death with an increasing emphasis on individual in resurrection, judgment and eternal bliss. These he sees as «marks» belonging to apocalyptic in that they build an impression which conveys a particular mode of thought and belief. Again, despite the extensive nature of this list, it really says very little, since one could find many of these elements in almost any sort of religious (and much non-religious) literature. Precision is notably lacking (D.S. RUSSELL, *The Method and Message of Jewish Apocalyptic*, 104-106.

apocalypse [...] a literary genre which, though covering a wide range of topics, has a particular interest in details of the heavenly world, the course (if not the content) of Jewish history and the destiny of the world and individuals within it,and claims that this has been given as a direct revelation from God by means of dream or vision or by the agency of angels [...] apocalyptic [...] a certain religious perspective or complex of ideas exemplified by the apocalypse and related literature, a perspective that is wider than that of eschatology but is characterized by a peculiar preoccupation with «the last things» and the coming judgment, and wider too than those books designated «apocalypses», being recognizable also in writings of a related kind [...] apocalyptic eschatology...that expression of belief about «the last things» to be found in those writings that reflect the apocalyptic perspective[4].

Koch makes a distinction between apocalypse as a genre and apocalyptic literature in a survey of the great diversity in opinion concerning the origin, nature and purpose of the latter. He views apocalyptic as a «literary form current round about the turn of the era in the Hebrew-Aramaic linguistic area»[5].

But beyond apocalyptic as a formal literary type, he also uses «apocalyptic» as a descriptor of certain «moods and ideas». Apocalyptic is also an historical and intellectual movement, and these moods and ideas can

---

4 Russell believes that prophetic and apocalyptic eschatology are related to each other with respect to origin but are distinctive from each other in two ways: prophetic eschatology views salvation in communal and national terms, or the righteous remnant of Israel, while the latter views it also in individual terms. Additionally, the former is oriented earthward and towards the restoration of Israel, while the latter is oriented towards the transcendent world, the afterlife, bliss, and the coming judgment (D.S. RUSSELL, *Divine Disclosure*, 8-13). Again, this is an oversimplification: Russell (and others) cannot resist the temptation to present a caricature image of apocalyptic, detaching it almost completely from history, time, earthly categories, etc. Although some of these elements are indeed present in varying degrees, oversimplification must be avoided. The two are not diametrically opposed to each other. History is still the locus of the divine/human drama being played out, but the decisive actions will definitely be from above.

5 His own descriptors for apocalypse as a literary form are as follows: a) discourse cycles, which can take the form of visions or auditions, between the recipient and a heavenly counterpart; b) spiritual turmoils, in which the recipient is often overcome by fright and dismay, sometimes falling to the ground or going into a trance. Stock phraseology is often used; c) parenetic discourses, in which an eschatological ethic unfolds; d) pseudonymity, by which the author usually uses the name of a great biblical figure from the past; e) mythical images rich in symbolism; f) composite character (K. KOCH, «What is Apocalyptic?,» 16-36).

be found in many writings which might not be formally classified as an apocalypse[6].

Hanson concentrates on the sociological aspects of apocalyptic, seeing the crisis engendered by the «collapse of a well-ordered world view which defines values and orders the universe» as the beginnings of apocalyptic. Apocalyptic eschatology is the result of a continuous development from pre-exilic and exilic prophecy, being the new mode that this prophecy assumed in the radically altered post-exilic society. Apocalyptic eschatology is a religious perspective focusing on esoteric disclosure to the elect of the «cosmic vision of Yahweh's sovereignty – especially as it relates to his acting to deliver his faithful». Alienation is the key: pessimism has caused the visionaries to retreat from «plain history, real politics, and human instrumentality»[7].

---

[6] As an intellectual or historical movement, apocalyptic is characterized by writings a) «dominated by an urgent expectation of the impending overthrow of all earthly conditions in the immediate future»; b) the end appearing as a vast cosmic catastrophe; c) the end-time is closely connected with the previous history of mankind and of the cosmos. The time of this world is divided into fixed segments; the content of these segments has been predetermined from the days of creation and can be found alluded to in concealed form in certain sayings of the prophetic books; d) in order to explain the course of historical events and the happenings of the end-time, an army of angels and demons is mustered, divided into a hierarchy of orders; the leading powers even have their own names; e) after the catastrophe there is a new salvation, which is paradisal in nature. This is for that remnant of the people who have been faithful and true to their religion; others will receive this through resurrection. It is interesting in that there is a streak of universalism inherent in this type: salvation is meant for all nations, although Israel remains special; f) transition from disaster to final redemption, with the act issuing from the throne of God. The division between earthly and heavenly history is abolished, divine glory appears, everything hidden is revealed. The Kingdom of God becomes visible on earth. An important element is the concept of the new aeon in radical discontinuity with the preceeding evil age; g) a mediator with royal functions to accomplish and guarantee final redemption, described by various angelic, divine or human terms; h) The catchword «glory» which is used wherever the final state of affairs is set apart from the present and whenever a final amalgamation of the earthly and heavenly spheres is prophesied (K. KOCH, «What is Apocalyptic?», 24-28).

[7] Hanson differentiates apocalyptic eschatology from prophetic eschatology in that the latter affirms that divine activity rightly takes place in the historical realm, the visionary seeking to «translate the vision of divine activity from the cosmic level to the level of the politico-historical realm of every life». The apocalyptic visionaries, on the other hand, are disillusioned with the realm of the historical, and have «disclosed their vision in a manner of growing indifference to and independence from the contingencies of the politico-historical realm, thereby leaving the language increasingly in the idiom of the cosmic realm of the divine warrior and his council». (12) Although Hanson recognizes that the restoration of God's people in a glorified Zion is the goal of both types of eschatology, he still overemphasizes the differences be-

In a later essay, Hanson distinguishes between the genre apocalypse, the perspective of apocalyptic eschatology, and apocalypticism as a religious movement. The first is very loosely defined as a medium for communicating the apocalyptic message, characterized by ecstasy and rapture, angelic guides, and encouragement to those undergoing persecution. The book of Revelation is used as the paradigm. The second is a perspective which «views divine plans in relation to historical realities in a particular way». The third, apocalypticism, is a socio-religious movement which is latent within apocalyptic eschatology, and its generation occurs at the «point where the disappointments of history lead a group to embrace that perspective as an ideology, using it moreover to resolve the contradictions between traditional hopes and frustrating historical realities»[8].

Rowland's approach to apocalyptic differs somewhat in its emphasis. For Rowland, the revelation of divine secrets is the essential element of apocalyptic[9].

Rowland hesitates to define apocalyptic too rigidly, provided that the essential element of the revelation of divine mysteries and heavenly truth

---

tween the two. It is true that the prophetic message calls for the *reform* of the existing order, whereas the apocalyptic visionary usually recognizes that the existing order has degenerated too far, calling for a complete destruction or transformation of the old order. The first emphasizes human initiative; the second, divine. However, God's intervention is called for and history is the battlefield in both approaches, and the message is similar: at this crucial moment, choose whom you will serve, see that your heart and mind is in order, for the time is short. (P.D. HANSON, *The Dawn of Apocalyptic*, 7.11-12.

[8] P.D. HANSON, *Apocalyptic*, 430-433.

[9] Rowland recognizes, of course, that an understanding of the present is the purpose of this genre: «it is hardly surprising that at a later stage of her history the distinctive beliefs about God and history should have demanded an understanding of the Jewish nation's role in history, the relationship of the divine promises to the circumstances of the present, and the conviction that there was a divine dimension to human existence, however obscure it may seem in the present. Jewish apocalyptic sought to provide such an understanding of history and this theological conviction» [p. 9]. «Many would have echoed the cry of the unknown prophet who, in Isaiah 64.1, pleads with God to rend the heavens to solve the many riddles of existence which presented themselves. The answer to this desperate plea is found in apocalyptic. The unveiling of the counsels of God directly to the apocalyptic seer and thence to his readers meant that the latter were being offered an answer directly from the mouth of God himself, apparently without any risk of contradiction. Here was the authoritative pronouncement which claimed to solve the inconclusive debates of man about his world and his destiny. Thus the key to the whole movement is that God reveals his mysteries directly to man and thereby gives them knowledge of the true nature of reality so that they may organize their lives accordingly» (C. ROWLAND, *The Open Heaven*, 9.11).

is present. Although not denying that there are eschatological elements to be found in apocalyptic, he does deny that eschatology must be present[10].

Collins proposes a master paradigm composed of two sections dealing with the framework of the revelation and its content, which in turn is divided into the manner of the revelation's conveyance and the concluding elements. The content includes both historical and eschatological events on a temporal axis and otherworldly beings and places on a spatial one. The main categories are: as regards the manner of revelation: medium, otherworldly mediator, and the human recipient; as regards the temporal axis of the content: protology, history, present salvation through knowledge, eschatological crisis, eschatological judgment and/or destruction, eschatological salvation; as regards the spatial axis of the content: otherworldly elements and parenesis; concluding elements: instructions to the recipient and narrative conclusion. Each of these categories is in turn divided into subcategories for complete description and precision[11].

Collins defines the genre as follows: «"Apocalypse" is a genre of revelatory literature with a narrative framework, in which a revelation is mediated by an otherworldly being to a human recipient, disclosing a transcendent reality which is both temporal, insofar as it envisages eschatological salvation, and spatial, insofar as it involves another, supernatural world»[12].

---

[10] «Although eschatology is an important component of the heavenly mysteries which are revealed in the apocalypses, it is difficult to justify the selection of this particular element as the basis of a definition of apocalyptic. The consequence of this can lead to an indifference to the fact that apocalyptic is concerned with the revelation of a variety of different matters. Any attempt, therefore, to use the term apocalyptic as a synonym of eschatology must be rejected» (C. ROWLAND, *Open Heaven*, 70-71). It is certainly true that apocalyptic must not be used as a synonym for eschatology; however, it must also be recognized that apocalyptic was not just about any heavenly mystery or for the sake of satisfying idle curiosity, but about God's plan for humanity, his justice, vindication of the just, punishment of the wicked, etc. In short, Rowland too easily overlooks the specific conditions that generated apocalyptic literature and the specific nature and purpose of the message.

[11] Not all these elements may be present in a particular work, but in varying degrees and combinations. Neither does the presence of these elements necessarily constitute a completely independent work (J.J. COLLINS, «Morphology», 6-8).

[12] J.J. COLLINS, «Morphology», 9. This makes it possible to distinguish between true apocalyptic material and oracles, dreams and visions that lack these characteristics. According to Collins, this definition «can be shown to apply to various sections of *1 Enoch*, Daniel, 4 Ezra, *2 Baruch, Apocalypse of Abraham, 3 Baruch, 2 Enoch, Testament of Levi 2-5*, the fragmentary *Apocalypse of Zephaniah 1*, and with some qualification to *Jubilees* and the *Testament of Abraham* (both of which also have strong affinities with other genres). It also applies to a fairly wide body of Christian and Gnostic literature and to some Persian and Greco-Roman material» (J.J. COLLINS, *Imagination*, 4).

Collins also finds distinct types of apocalypses that cut across the differences found in various cultural groups, and they are distinguished by manner of revelation and eschatological content[13].

Vielhauer's description of apocalyptic emphasizes its general mindset rather than particular characteristics: 1) the doctrine of the two ages with a dualism that is temporal rather than absolute or metaphysical; 2) a pessimism and otherworldly hope; 3) universalism and individualism. The scale of apocalyptic is cosmic: resurrection, world judgment, world dissolution, and the individual no longer is identified with a collective entity such as race or ethnic group; and 4) determinism and imminent expectation of the kingdom of God. This involves periodization of history and calculations concerning its end[14].

Apocalyptic thought, according to Beker, is characterized by historical dualism, universal cosmic expectation, and the imminent end of the world. These three characteristics comprise a soteriology that includes the human body and the material cosmos as well as spiritual salvation[15].

In positing his eight groups of motifs that are indicative of an apocalyptic attitude of mind, Koch realizes that each of them is distributed throughout various apocalypses, and that many of them can be found outside the genre. It is the way in which they are arranged that is crucial, perhaps being peculiar to apocalyptic alone. Apocalyptic events must be understood as the author's understanding of a definite sequence that runs «like a continuous scarlet thread running through the whole». There are several terms in 1 Cor 15 that express a sequence and a determinism characteristic of apocalyptic[16].

---

[13] The first distinction is between those which do not have an otherworldly journey (type I) and those that do (type II). There are further distinctions within each group according to eschatological content: a) historical type, including a review of history, eschatological crisis and cosmic and/or eschatology; b) those without historical review but which with cosmic and/or political eschatology; c) those without either historical review or cosmic transformation but only personal eschatology. J.J. COLLINS, «Morphology», 13.

[14] Obviously, Vielhauer's definition is not precise enough for evaluating specific works or passages, and is broad enough to encompass many types of literature. P. VIELHAUER, «Introduction to Apocalypses», II, 549-554.

[15] This definition is so general as to be virtually meaningless. It could describe many attitudes and types of literature. Missing is the symbolism, the precise nature of the apocalyptic message, and the parenesis. J.C. BEKER, *Paul the Apostle*, 136.

[16] Koch holds apocalyptic to be «the revelation of a divine revelation,» requiring a *multiplicity of approaches* to express this revelation in a coherent historical pattern rather than a linear logical one. He insists that apocalyptic can be understood not only as a literary genre, but as an «expression of a particular *attitude of mind* (italics his)» (K. KOCH, «What is Apocalyptic?», 29).

1.1 *Excursus: Wisdom and Apocalyptic*

At first, Wisdom and apocalyptic would seem to have little in common with each other. Wisdom is imminent in creation and accessible to all; apocalyptic is absent in the ordinary, being present only in the transcendent, and accessible only to the specially designated seer; wisdom is oriented towards a happy, fruitful and successful life in a world that is well-ordered and harmonious; apocalyptic sees little value in everyday life for its own sake and expresses a lack of confidence in the world and its institutions and relationships, and waits for decisive action from above, through divine agency[17].

On the other hand, there are also similarities and continuities: the apocalyptic seers often refer to themselves as wise men or sages and their works as wisdom books, and both deal with some of the same theological issues. The trend in scholarship has been to recognize many wisdom elements in apocalyptic. Wisdom has been seen by many as influencing both eschatology and apocalyptic, and in many instances being combined with prophetic modes of discourse in one person, who becomes at the same time a sage and apocalyptic prophet. Wisdom is woven from many elements, and there is another view that holds that there is also an aspect of wisdom that is not discernible unless it is revealed from above by God[18].

Wisdom was seen as the one who reveals the secrets of God (Sir 4,18; 14,10) and whose origin itself was a mystery (Wis 6,22). There was a strong element of this mysterious nature of wisdom in the Qumran community, and the job of the sage or holy person was to discern and explain these mysteries (1QH 1,19-20; 12,11-12; CD 9,12.18-19; 1QS 9,17-19; 11,5-8; 11QPsa 18,5-8.12-15). These mysteries contained imminent eschatological events that were predestined by God, reflecting his plan known only to him and to his chosen instruments[19].

---

[17] In her study, Johnson posits a spectrum with wisdom and apocalyptic at opposite poles. Where a written work falls on that spectrum depends on how much or how little of its opposite it contains. Examples of pure wisdom with virtually no apocalyptic: Proverbs; of pure apocalyptic with no wisdom: Apocalypse of Abraham. Many other works fall in between: 1 En, WisSol, 4 Ez, 2 Bar, and the Qumran library. E.E. JOHNSON, *Function of Apocalyptic*, 70-71.

[18] Von Rad posited the derivation of apocalyptic from wisdom, a view that has been for the most part abandoned or radically modified. Hanson allows that wisdom has been «drawn into apocalyptic». Rather than a linear evolution, the confluence model used by Johnson seems to be more apt. B. WITHERINGTON, *Jesus the Sage*, 297-298; E.E. JOHNSON, *Function of Apocalyptic*, 58.70-71.

[19] R. SCROGGS, «Paul: ΣΟΦΟΣ and ΠΝΕΘΜΑΤΙΚΟΣ», 33-55. Johnson cites several examples of the strong confluence of wisdom and apocalyptic at Qumran: «He [that is, the Master] shall conceal the teaching of the Law from men of falsehood, but shall impart true knowledge and righteous judgment to those who have chosen the

Witherington believes that in the NT hymns there is often a «welding together of wisdom ideas and forms with eschatological ideas such as the coming of the Messiah, the vindication of Christ beyond death, and his present lordship». The great volume of recent research on wisdom and Paul indicates that although he emphatically rejects the label «wisdom,» some of his teachings contain sapiential elements as well as eschatological and/or apocalyptic[20].

This confluence of ideas and symbols requires that special care be given to an analysis of a particular word, phrase or passage; one must attempt to determine whether wisdom or apocalyptic ideas predominate in a particular case.

1.2 *Some Difficulties*

A survey of these attempts at defining apocalyptic indicates that when all is said and done, there is still a certain ambiguity and uncertainty among scholars as to the exact nature of apocalyptic. Is a particular word, phrase or symbol apocalyptic in *every* instance? If not, what exactly makes it so in a *particular* instance? It is unlikely that there are many, if any, terms, symbols or phrases that are in themselves apocalyptic. And there is probably no definitive model or explanation that can indicate clearly and infallibly in every situation whether something is apocalyptic or not. There are, however, a number of guidelines and insights that can aid one in analyzing a particular passage or term and arriving at a prudential judgment as to its possible apocalyptic nature. For this purpose, we take insights from the attempts of various scholars to define the genre[21].

Way. He shall guide them in all knowledge according to the spirit of each and according to the rule of the age, and shall thus instruct them in the mysteries of marvelous truth that in the midst of the men of the Community they may walk perfectly together in all that has been revealed to them (1QS 9,17-19a)». Wisdom is also seen as absolutely necessary to interpret the prophetic and apocalyptic tradition properly: «and God told Habakkuk to write down that which would happen to the final generation, but He did not make known to him when time would come to an end. And as for that which He said, "That he who reads may read it speedily" [Hab 2,2], interpreted this concerns the Teacher of Righteousness, to whom God made known all the mysteries of the words of His servants the Prophets (1QpHab 7,1-5)» (E.E. JOHNSON, *Function of Apocalyptic*, 96-97).

[20] He does not believe that the word apocalyptic can be used to describe Paul's theology or world view, although Paul could have used some apocalyptic ideas or expressions in his writings. (B. WITHERINGTON, *Jesus the Sage*, 296). On the relationship of Paul's teaching to wisdom, see also J. MURPHY- O'CONNOR, «I Cor VIII.6: Cosmology or Soteriology?», 253-267 and R.McL. WILSON, «Gnosis at Corinth», 102-114.

[21] For a non-apocalyptic example of this: the word ἀνίστημι in its various verbal and noun forms carries both an eschatological and a mundane meaning. In Matt 9:9,

The first factor to be considered is that of *context*. Hanson draws attention to the conditions which generate an apocalyptic response: acute alienation from the traditional mediators of meaning in a society and the collapse of a well-ordered world view. We might say, then, that crisis of meaning and collapse of confidence in the social, religious and political order is the context in which apocalyptic is generated and in which it thrives. Added to this is the crisis provoked by external pressure such as persecution, especially when this brings to the fore the question of theodicy: why do the faithful suffer unjustly while the wicked and unbelievers thrive?[22].

According to Hanson, the origins of apocalyptic can be found in the later prophetic tradition as expressed in trito-Isaiah. This influence is then found in Zech 9-14; Isa 24-27; and Joel. This is of more than incidental interest, as it explains some of the parallels and similarities in symbolism and language that are present in both. The concept of «newness» and the «Day of the Lord» can be found in both. Are these apocalyptic terms in some, all, or none of their uses?[23].

Jesus sees a man named Matthew, who arose (ἀναστὰς) and followed him. In this and similar cases, the word clearly is not referring to the resurrection. In many other instances, however, the same root, in both its verbal and noun forms, clearly refers to the resurrection from the dead. It is the relationship - in this case to death - that is the deciding factor.

[22] It might appear that this also applies to prophecy. However, it is often the case that the prophet rails against a religious/political establishment *supremely* confident of itself; indeed, it is the job of the prophet to shatter that hubris and warn of impending disaster. P.D. HANSON, *Dawn of Apocalyptic*, 7.

[23] Prophecy preaches against the established religious, social, political and economic order (they are all one in the minds of the prophets and their contemporaries) and predicts a disaster and destruction of this order if the warning is not heeded and correct life and worship reestablished. The message of the prophet is usually public and at times violent in language, often addressed to leaders and at times to the whole nation. In post-exilic prophecy, this is sometimes followed by a renewal and rebuilding, but it is always basically the same order, albeit improved. The later traditions even speak of a time of plenty, peace and tranquility, when the «lion shall lay down with the lamb.» Apocalyptic, on the other hand, is cosmic in its scope, encompassing all of creation. Little attention is paid to reforming the established order, as it is viewed as too corrupt or as having fallen into evil hands. The apocalyptic world view withdraws from the established order and looks for the time when it will be replaced or transformed entirely. In this sense it is not totally negative, for there is hope in the future, but in God's future. With prophecy, judgment and punishment take place on the earth, and consist of the particular military, political and religious disaster and its concomitant consequences. Apocalyptic eschatology again is cosmic in its scope, involving the earth and the heavens. The disaster may well be at the hands of God rather than an earthly or secular agent. The judgment, punishment, reward and so forth are *post-mortem* and involve salvation and some sort of life beyond death: according to Collins, the point of apocalyptic is the transcendence of death.

To answer that question, one must also consider the second factor: *relationship*. Relationship is how the words and symbols are assembled and placed in relationship to one another. Koch has stated that *sequence* runs like a thread through all apocalyptic, expressing a form of determinism. Ordinary terms, symbols etc., can be placed in relationship to one another in order to express a divine plan, order or sequence that culminates in an eschatological event of a cosmic nature and affecting all of humanity. The term firstfruits (ἀπαρχὴ) in vv. 20 and 23 is not in itself an apocalyptic term. Placed within a text in which it is identified with the eschatological event of Christ's resurrection and in which it implies a continuation, culminating in the final judgment, it can be called apocalyptic. Likewise with «trumpet» (σάλπιγξ) in v. 51: this is not apocalyptic unless it indicates the end of the normal earthly existence, the irruption of the divine into history, and the final judgment. Apocalyptic literature is an encoded assemblage of images, words and phrases which are not idiosyncratic but usually common to more than one apocalyptic work (e.g. the beast with the horns in Daniel and Revelation). These encoded symbols usually need an interpreter, often by means of an *angelus interpres*, as they refer in allegorical form to personages, events and institutions.

Barr emphasizes content and outlook in his definition over form alone, and perhaps comes closest to a solution of the problem:

> The wringing of hands over the difficulty of defining a term like apocalyptic seems to me to be misplaced, and to arise from a mistaken preconception of what can constitute a definition in matters of this sort. What we have is bundles of features on various levels; perhaps no work is so perfect and ideal an example of apocalyptic that it embodies all of these features, but substantial clusters of these features normally constitute sufficient reasons to use the term apocalyptic, and still larger groupings of them, under more rigorous criteria, constitute adequate grounds for the use of the term apocalypse. This situation is not substantially more difficult than with other definitions of genres and literary forms[24].

1.3 *Summary and Conclusion*

Obviously, definitions differ in content and emphasis, but there are enough points of similarity to form a working model of the genre apocalypse and apocalyptic eschatology. For the genre apocalypse, the paradigm and definition constructed by Collins for the SBL Genre Project seems to be the clearest and the most comprehensive and scientific. At

---

[24] J. BARR, «Jewish Apocalyptic in Recent Scholarly Study», 18-19.

the same time, there is a degree of flexibility: this is the Platonic ideal of the apocalypse genre; these elements exist in varying degrees – or not at all – in various writings that could be loosely called apocalypses.

Apocalyptic eschatology is somewhat more difficult to define. Keeping in mind that «apocalypse» is a *literary* genre, apocalyptic eschatology can be described as a certain symbolic way of expressing a particular mind set, attitude or world view regarding the eschaton, history, theodicy and ethics. With Koch's definition as a guide, expressions of an «end-time» mentality or concern, an approaching cosmic catastrophe, battles with angelic powers, a new aeon in discontinuity with the past, executed through a Messianic agent with royal functions, a post-crisis paradisal life, and parenetic discourse can all be seen as characteristic of apocalyptic eschatology. When several of these factors are expressed through stereotypical symbols and phrases, and are found together and in relation to one another, it is often possible to say that this is an example of apocalyptic.

2. The Origin and Role of Death

We saw in the previous chapter that in the passage 1 Cor 15,20-28, the defeat of death is the focal point. Of all the enemies of God to be defeated, death is the last and most powerful. Its defeat allows the subjected creation to be restored to God the Father through the agency of the Son.

We are accustomed to think of death as perhaps a natural, unavoidable phenomenon that can be delayed or pushed back, but ultimately accepted. This was the basic attitude of the OT towards death; only a premature death which left the individual bereft of name and progeny was viewed as tragic[25].

To Paul and others with an apocalyptic worldview, death is the enemy, an affront to God and an infringement on his sovereignty[26].

---

[25] Although stressing the naturalness of death in the attitudes of the Hebrews, Barr also introduces some controversial ideas: he denies that the garden of Eden story is primarily a story of the origins of good and evil, and that humans were once immortal. He claims that it describes how humans once had the chance for immortality and lost it. Rather than bringing death into the world, Adam almost brings immortality. J. BARR, *The Garden of Eden*, 4-8.21-23.

[26] According to de Boer, Paul «understands the anthropological reality of death in accordance with the traditions of Jewish cosmological apocalyptic eschatology as an inimical, murderous, quasi-angelic power that has held all Adamic humanity in subjection and enslavement» (M.C. DE BOER, *Defeat of Death*, 182-183). When Paul and others use the language of death, it is to express the discontinuity or disjunction between the two ages: this age is the sphere of death, separation between humanity and God.

An examination of the Jewish pseudepigraphal and apocalyptic literature of the pre-Christian period and the first-century A.D. can give us
some idea of the ideas and images with which Paul was working. The
following questions need to be kept in mind during the survey:

1) What happens to the individual immediately after death?
2) Is there a resurrection, and if so, does it involve the body?
3) Is there an intermediate state before a general resurrection
   and judgment? What is its nature?
4) What is the fate of the wicked? Are all saved? Is there
   destruction or everlasting punishment?
5) What is the nature of the post-resurrection post-judgment
   existence?
6) What is the role of the Messiah figure?
7) What is the role of death? Is it personified and portrayed
   as an enemy of God?

Extensive surveys of Hellenistic Jewish and apocalyptic Jewish literature from the Maccabean period to the end of the first century are inconclusive with respect to the origin of death, the nature of the end times,
post-mortem retribution, and the resurrection of the body. Texts abound,
but often in contradiction to one another, even within the same literary
work. The authors seem unconcerned with vague and contradictory
statements and images that are held loosely together in the same document. Various interpretative models are used to make sense of the mass
of data and explain some of the inconsistencies. The first of these surveys, that of Nickelsburg, uses form criticism as its point of departure[27].

---

[27] Nickelsburg utilizes form criticism for his study: theological concepts are carried in forms; for an analysis of a text, it is enough to ask what particular function it
played at a certain point in time. Basing his analysis on a detailed analysis of certain
texts, Nickelsburg believes that there is a continuous development of these forms towards resurrection as the means for judgment. He puts three basic questions to the
texts: «1) Do different conceptions (e.g. resurrection of the body and immortality of
the soul) ever serve the same function? 2) To what extent do these theological conceptions lose their original functions and assume new ones? 3) Why are these conceptions found in some writings, but not in others?» [10] Form criticism does have its
advantages: it can tell us (sometimes) something about the environment which generated it and those pressures and stimuli that changed it through time. There are difficulties, however. «Function» can be a very arbitrary thing. It is not proven that our
notion of function corresponds to the original. This involves a lot of guess work and
speculation, and a detailed look at individual words does not tell the whole story.
There are also other reservations. First of all, he is selective in the texts that he analyzes. Secondly, many different theologies representing different groups are analyzed
as a whole in arriving at a system or a developmental model. Each theology must

Nickelsburg finds that «in intertestamental Jewish theology the beliefs in resurrection, immortality, and eternal life are carried mainly within the framework of three forms». There can be a mixture of these forms, and the particular form can give a clue as to the function of a specific belief[28].

De Boer, on the other hand, uses a different interpretive model: Jewish apocalyptic eschatology expresses itself in two general, but not mutually exclusive types; namely, the cosmological and the forensic. The first emphasizes the world having been overcome and perverted by evil powers who are responsible for sin and death. These evil powers will be defeated by God working through a faithful remnant. In the second type, the forensic, evil powers are either absent or are not given prominence. Free will and human responsibility are emphasized; adherence to the Law is the normal means of salvation, resulting in a sort of legal piety. The Last

---

speak for itself, and each text must be analyzed as a constituent of the theology which generated it, instead as a mere passage or fragment. Fitting the texts into these three categories automatically excludes many of the differences and subtilties, and renders them less useful for an understanding of the theological landscape of the period in question. Vindication of the righteous was certainly an important issue in these texts, but not the only one. G.W.E. NICKELSBURG, *Resurrection, Immortality, and Eternal Life*.

[28] The first form is that of the righteous man who is persecuted because of his piety and finally vindicated, thus giving a clue as to the conditions which gave rise to this form. As tradition develops, it evolves into a motif of vindication or reward for the righteous and/or condemnation and punishment for the wicked. Gradually, the righteous man disappears altogether or is incorporated as one element of the judgment scene, e.g., Dan 12; AsMos 10; 1 En 104. As in 2 Bar 51 and 2 Macc 7, there is also an increasing emphasis on resurrection of the body. The second form is that of the judgment scene, which is an «ad hoc adjudication» to vindicate those righteous whose piety has led to their death and punish the apostates. What is emphasized is that this judgment is always to adjudicate a specific persecution; it is local and specific. It is to give to each what he really deserves as a result of his behavior during trial or persecution. This tendency is continued in 1 En 94-104. The third form is that of the «two-way» theology, which is a variation on the OT covenant theology. This is an ethical theology, very much concerned with right and wrong behavior and the consequences, which consists of either eternal life or eternal death. According to Nickelsburg, this type of theology tends to be rather vague about the time and the manner of this eternal life and death, and this complicates any attempt to determine with precision what the author of a particular document believed about the afterlife. With this type of theology, the resurrection itself is of minor importance, since death as a physical event which all suffer is not important. True death is the punishment reserved for those who disobey divine commandments. This theology is also very compatible with the eschatologies which stress an immediate assumption, such as TAsh, and the immortality of the soul, such as WisSol. Rather than saying that the resurrection is unimportant, it might be said that its expression is secondary, perhaps being considered a given. There has to be some way of delivering eternal life or death - they are not mere abstractions. G.W.E. NICKELSBURG, *Resurrection*, 170-174.

Judgment resembles a courtroom trial; resurrection in itself does not impart eternal life but is for the sole purpose of judgment[29].

Cavallin provides a detailed and wide survey of the theological texts pertaining to death, judgment and the afterlife. His goal is to understand the background of 1 Cor 15, which is relevant to this study. He recognizes that there is not just one Jewish doctrine of the resurrection of the dead, and he avoids many of the traps into which others fall[30].

It is obvious that consistency is not to be expected in these literary works. Emphasis should instead be given to the symbolic world that is present and the purpose or function of a particular passage within a document. Utilizing de Boer's model, we can see that 1 Cor 15 is in some ways compatible with the cosmological apocalyptic eschatological type. The emphasis is on the cosmos being restored and reconquered from hostile powers. We should not expect a list of punishments for individual sinners, or a detailed description of the afterlife. 1 Cor 15 does not fit perfectly within any of Nickelsburg's categories. It also displays characteristics of the «two-way» theology of the third category. The passage in question presents some very clear choices to the believer: only correct behavior and belief will lead to eternal life.

2.1 Death and the Enemies of God

Death was not God's original intention, it was the fault of man. Within mainstream Judaism, the account of the Fall in Genesis 3 makes this point clear. This idea was developed also in Hellenistic Judaism, as is

---

[29] The forensic type is present more often in 2 Bar and 4 Ez, and there is a corresponding lack of mention of cosmological powers. Many works combine both types: the Qumran Scrolls and the Pseudo-Philo *Liber Antiquitatum Biblicarum (LAB)* are good examples. De Boer is useful in that 1 Cor 15 is the starting point for his study. He seeks to answer the following question through this study: «How does Paul's christologically determined apocalyptic eschatology inform his understanding of death on the one side and how does his understanding of death serve to define his apocalyptic eschatology on the other»? His division of the literature into the two categories is useful as a descriptive tool, but it is questionable whether this indicates two different theologies or types of apocalyptic eschatology. M.C. DE BOER, *Defeat of Death*, 85-89.

[30] There are some reservations concerning his analysis: rather than letting the text speak for itself, he imposes his own questions, phrased according to his own presuppositions. This leads him to deny that certain passages have anything to say, for example, about the resurrection of the body, if they do not describe it explicitly and in the terms which he expects. For the resurrection of the body, he seems to have in mind the very physical and literal descriptions of I and II Macc. At the end of his quasi-statistical analysis, there is a mass of data that is really rather difficult to use. His work is most useful as a collection of texts, although many times one must analyze a particular text for oneself. H.C.C. CAVALLIN, *Life After Death*.

made clear in the Wisdom of Solomon, 1,23-24: «But God created man for immortality, and made him an image of his own proper being; it was through the devil's envy that Death entered into the cosmic order, and they who are his own experience him»[31].

Death is very closely related to the presence of sin and evil in the world. Some works explained the presence of sin and death in the world by an angelic fall which brought the world under the control of evil angelic powers who are the enemies of God. The Jewish apocalyptic background clearly paints a picture of the heavens and the earth teeming with armies of unseen malevolent powers that are hostile to God and humanity[32].

In the NT, ἀρχαί and ἐξουσίαι, (principalities and powers) are found in Rom 8,38; Eph 3,10; 6,12; Col 1,16; 2,15; 1 Cor 15,24; Eph 1,21; Col 2,10. The term δυνάμεις is found in Rom 8,38; 1 Cor 15,24; Eph 1,21. Additionally, there are other terms that are probably synonymous[33].

In Jewish pseudepigraphal and apocalyptic literature, this is expressed most clearly in the vivid account of the descent of the heavenly Watchers, who produced a race of giants through sexual intercourse with earthly women, and who taught humanity forbidden knowledge, especially the sort that was used for warfare and oppression. God will reassert his sov-

---

[31] The envy of the devil is a recurrent theme in pseudepigraphal literature: 2 En 31,3-6; *Vita Adae* 12-17; 3 Bar 4,8; various rabbinical works; and Theophilus *Ad Autolycum* 2,29. Winston sees both this notion and that of death entering thereby into the cosmic order as echoes of Zoroastrian teachings. D. WINSTON, *The Wisdom of Solomon*, 112-3.121-2.

[32] TSol 8,2: «When I, Solomon, saw them, I was amazed and asked them, "Who are you"? They replied, "We are heavenly bodies (στοιχεῖα), rulers of the world of darkness". The first said, "I am Deception". The second said, "I am Strife". The third said, "I am Fate". The fourth said, "I am Distress". The fifth said, "I am Error". The sixth said, "I am Power". The seventh said, "I am The Worst. Our stars in heaven look small, but we are named like gods"». Additionally, there is an extensive list of the thirty-six heavenly bodies (στοιχεῖα) in ch. 18 of TSol. These demonic powers are responsible for diseases, bodily ailments, and human dissension. Dating for this document has varied widely, but since there is a reference to it in the Nag Hammadi documents, and earlier Jewish traditions are probably present within it, it can be treated as coming from the approximate time period under consideration. D.C. DULING, trans., in *OTP* 934-987.

[33] κυριότητες (Col 1,16; Eph 1,21) and θρόνι (Col 1,16) also describe cosmic powers. It is almost impossible to discern any real difference in meaning between the terms. Among other terms are: θεοὶ πολλοί, κύριοι πολλοί (1 Cor 8,5); πᾶν ὄνομα ὀνομαζόμενος (Eph 1,21); ἐπουράνια, ἐπιγεῖα, καταθόνια (Phil 2,10); κοσμοκράτορες τοῦ σκότου τούτου (Eph 6,12); στοιχεῖα (Gal 4,3.9; Col 2,8.20; and ἄρχοντος τοῦ σκότου τούτου (1 Cor 2,6-8). J.Y. LEE, «Demonic Powers», 54-55.

ereignty in the end times through the following: a cosmic war, fought in conjunction with his elect who are the faithful remnant, the overthrow of the wicked angelic powers, and the inauguration of a new age[34].

2.2 Death Personified

Death was sometimes personified as a «quasi-angelic cosmological power that stands opposed to God»[35].

The most important canonical biblical texts with respect to the overthrow and end of death as a force are Isa 25,7-8 and Rev 20,14; 21,4[36].

The pseudepigraphal literature also tied death very closely to Adam's sin[37].

The Testament of Abraham contains probably the most developed example of the personification of death: Death travels to earth at the direction of God to claim the soul of Abraham. Death is horrible to behold; he is the one with the «abominable countenance». He therefore disguises himself with an attractive, angelic appearance so as not to alarm Abraham, for when he displays his true appearance, hundreds of Abraham's servants die at the mere sight of him[38].

---

[34] The specific domination of the angelic powers is found in 1 En 1-36; 37-71; Dan; Jub; Test12P; and various Dead Sea Scrolls. The angelic fall is either referred to directly or alluded to in 1 En 6-19; 64,1-2; 69,4-5; 86,1-6; 106,13-17; Jub 4,15.22; 5,1-8; 10,4-5; TReu 5,6-7; TNaph 3,5; CD 2,17-3,1; 2 Bar 56,12-15; *LAB* 24,1-5; WisSol 2,23-24; Jude 6; 2 Pet 2,4. M.C. DE BOER, *Defeat of Death*, 85. God also has at his disposal for this purpose heavenly armies of angelic powers. For example: 2 En 20:1 describes a trip to the seventh heaven where Enoch sees a «great light, and all the fiery armies of the incorporeal ones, archangels, angels and shining *otanim* stations».

[35] This is expressed primarily in Isa 25,8 and 1 En 69,4-11 (as well as in WisSol 1,14.16; Sir 14,12; and Rev 20,14). Death and Sheol/Hades are personified together, especially in the last judgment of 4 Ez 8,53 and *LAB* 3,10, which may reflect Hos 13,14, quoted by Paul in 1 Cor 15. M.C. DE BOER, *Defeat of Death*, 90.

[36] Isa 15,7-8: «he will swallow up death forever. Then the Lord God will wipe away the tears from all faces, and the disgrace of his people he will take away from all the earth». Rev 20,14: «Then Death and Hades were thrown into the lake of fire». Rev 21,4: «he will wipe every tear from their eyes. Death will be no more; mourning and crying and pain will be no more, for the first things have passed away».

[37] See 4 Ez 3,7; 7,18; 2 Bar 54,15.19. A change in man's nature is described in 4 Ez 3,26; 4,30; 7,92.116-26; as well as in Sir 17,17; 25,24; ApMos 28; 2 Bar 17,3; 19,8; 23,4; 54,15; 56,6. Sir 40,1-11 and ApMos 8,2 describe the distortion of the perfect world intended by God.

[38] The dating for this work (TAb, ch. 16-20) fluctuates wildly: anywhere from 200 B.C. to 200 A.D. Sanders estimates the date to be about 100 A.D. Even if the date is later, earlier traditions were obviously used. E.P SANDERS, trans., in *OTP*, I, 892-895.

The Apocalypse of Elijah (5:36-39) describes an eschatological future similar to that of Rev 20: Christ and the saints will come from heaven, burn the earth, and reign for 1,000 years. Christ will create a new heaven and earth that is purified. No «deadly devil» will exist there; Christ will rule with his saints «ascending and descending for 1,000 years»[39].

Two Baruch contains a prayer by the seer that God reprove the angel of death and that the realm of death be sealed. The time of judgment will also be a time of the passing away of corruption and of everything that dies[40].

Fourth Ezra describes a time when «the root of evil is sealed up from you, illness is banished from you, and death is hidden; hell has fled and corruption has been forgotten; sorrows have passed away, and in the end the treasure of immortality is made manifest»[41].

The Pseudo-Philo looks to the day when death will be no more:

But when the years appointed for the world have been fulfilled, then the light will cease and darkness will fade away. And I will bring the dead to life and raise up those who are sleeping from the earth. And hell will pay back its debt, and the place of perdition will return its deposit so that I may render to each according to his works and according to the fruits of his own devices, until I judge between soul and flesh. And the world will cease, and *death will be abolished, and hell will shut its mouth* [italics mine]. And the earth will not be without progeny or sterile for those inhabiting it; and no one who has been pardoned by me will be tainted. And there will be another earth and another heaven, an everlasting dwelling place[42].

The personification of death as the enemy and the anticipation of the time when death would be overthrown that are found in 1 Cor 15 are paralleled in several Jewish apocalyptic and pseudepigraphal texts of the first two centuries BC and first century AD. Paul was drawing on known symbols for death, its power, and ultimate defeat when he authored this chapter.

2.3 *Beyond Death in Jewish Eschatological and Apocalyptic Texts*

Two major texts rich in background material for comparison with 1 Cor 15 are 4 Ez and 2 Bar. These texts are roughly contemporaneous;

---

[39] ApEl 5,36-39 in *OTP*, I, 721-754. This shows Christian interpolation. The dating is later, possibly between 150-275 A.D. However, it is thought to contain older Jewish traditions.

[40] 2 Bar 21,23-24.

[41] 4 Ez 8,53 in *OTP*, I, 544.

[42] Ps-Philo 3,10, in *OTP*, II, 307. Dating is difficult: although roughly contemporaneous with 2 Bar and 4 Ez, it is perhaps earlier, possibly from around the time of Jesus. There is also a reference to death being sealed up in 33,3.

that is, between approximately 70 and 130 A.D. Both of them deal with theodicy, the destruction of the temple, and the plight of the Jews. There are possible contacts points between 4 Ez and Ps-Philo's *LAB*.

2.3.1 Fourth Ezra

Fourth Ezra is characterized by its insistence on the approaching changing of the ages and a pessimistic view of what this means for humanity. This work is primarily about the reliability of God and what humanity must do to be saved. The present age or world was created for many, the world to come for a few; many have been created but only a few will be saved (8,1.3). Salvation comes only through perfect obedience to the Law, and this is indeed possible[43].

The resurrection comes at the end of history, and is combined with the Last Judgment (7,31-38.113.114)[44].

History is only a sort of interim; at the end time, God's true intention is revealed. Only the righteous will be saved, and God's compassion will play no part[45].

Various texts make it clear that the post resurrection and judgment reality is transformed and glorified, including the bodies of the righteous (7,113.114.125; 8,52-54). There is far less clarity concerning the exact status of the wicked beyond their punishment, or the nature of the post-judgment entity with regard to body and soul[46].

Death is the separation of the body and the soul (7,78.88.100)[47].

---

[43] This makes for what Sanders calls a spirituality of «legalistic perfectionism». Rather than being normative, Sanders holds that the spirituality of 4 Ez is a sort of aberration. This is a pejorative evaluation, and not one that attempts to understand sympathetically the meaning of the spirituality for the community that generated it within its original context. Sanders also is committed to portraying the Judaism of the time in the best possible light and to combating negative stereotypes. This is certainly a desirable goal; however, it also leads him to explain away any contrary evidence as an «aberration». E.P. SANDERS, *Paul and Palestinian Judaism*, 409.

[44] Fourth Ezra follows closely the judgment scene from Dan 12:1. Judgment is not, however, related to suffering or persecution but to obedience or disobedience to the Law. The coming immortal age is one in which the truth appears and corruption passes away. G.W.E. NICKELSBURG, *Resurrection*, 138-139.

[45] A chilling example is 7.60: «I will rejoice over the few that shall be saved and I will not grieve over the multitude of them that perish» (E.P. SANDERS, *Paul and Palestinian Judaism*, 413).

[46] As an example of this transformed and glorified existence, it was said that the faces of those who had practiced self-control would shine more than the stars.

[47] 7,78:«When the decisive decree has gone forth from the Most High that a man shall die, as the soul leaves the body to return again to him who gave it, first of all it adores the glory of the Most High [...] 7,88: But this is the order of those who have

An anticipatory judgment or immediate post mortem retribution takes place at death, separating the wicked from the righteous souls: the wicked are denied access to the «storehouses» or «treasuries» of souls and are made to wander and experience a sevenfold type of despair and sadness, while the righteous receive a sevenfold joy and are admitted to the storehouses (7,75-99) to wait in patience and rest for the day of judgment.

The Day of Judgment is decisive and displays to all the seal of truth (7,104). The time for repentance is past, and no intercession is allowed. The final judgment is expressed in 7,26-38 in a vivid and evocative manner:

> For behold, the time will come, when the signs which I have foretold to you will come, that the city which now is not seen shall appear, and the land which now is hidden shall be disclosed. And everyone who has been delivered from the evils that I have foretold shall see my wonders. For my Messiah shall be revealed with those who are with him, and he shall make rejoice those who remain for four hundred years, And after these years my son (or:servant) the Messiah shall die, and all who draw human breath. And the world shall be turned back to primeval silence for seven days, as it was in the first beginnings; so that no one shall be left. And after seven days the world, which is not yet awake, shall be roused, and that which is corruptible shall perish. And the earth shall give back those who are asleep in it, and the dust those who rest in it; and the treasuries shall give up the souls which have been committed to them. And the Most High shall be revealed upon the seat of judgment, and compassion shall pass away, mercy shall be made distant, and patience shall be withdrawn; but only judgment shall remain, truth shall stand, and faithfulness shall grow strong. And recompense shall follow, and the reward shall be manifested; righteous deeds shall awake, and unrighteous deeds shall not sleep. Then the pit of torment shall appear, and opposite it shall be the place of rest; and the furnace of Gehenna shall be disclosed, and opposite it the paradise of delight. Then the Most High will say to the nations that have been raised, "Look and understand whom you have denied, whom you have not served, whose commandments you have despised! Look opposite you: here are delight and rest, and there are fire and torments"[48]!

The Messianic period is separate from the resurrection and final judgment. There is a type of immediate retribution following death, for those with the Messiah a period of earthly blessedness for 400 years. This is

---

kept the ways of the Most High, when they shall be separated from their mortal vessel [...] 7,100: I answered and said, Will time therefore be given to the souls, after they have been separated from the bodies, to see what you have described to me»?

[48] Translation is from M.E. STONE, *Fourth Ezra*, 202-203.

the traditional view of the Messianic age. This is followed by the annihilation of all living things and a return to the beginning, followed by a strict and uncompromising judgment with appropriate rewards and punishments. Although it is stated that the earth will give up the dead and the treasuries the souls, it does not actually say that this is a resurrection and that the dead shall be reconstituted as they were before; it is implied[49].

As in 1 Cor 15, there is the doctrine of the two ages. The new age is a time of recreation and renewal, but for those who are in correct relationship with God. The destruction or perishing of the corruptible is also present here. Although the wicked are tormented, it does not go into any detail and does not seem overly concerned with their fate. Judgment is based on behavior or deeds which express one's faith or personal relationship with the divine. Contrary to 1 Cor 15, the Messianic figure in this work does not really seem to play much of a role at all in the cosmic destruction and renewal and the subsequent judgment.

2.3.2 Two Baruch

Two Baruch is a closely related work of the same general period, and is seen as the work having closest parallels to 1 Cor 15. For example, in the following passage there is the belief in the two ages, and the notion that the return of the Messiah will initiate the end. There seems to be a doctrine of the resurrection, for it says that those who «sleep in hope of him will rise». There is no explicit mention, however, of the body itself. It seems that souls themselves receive reward and punishment. How this is possible without some sort of body is difficult to say.

30,1 And it will happen after these things when the time of the appearance of the Anointed One has been fulfilled and he returns with glory, that then all who sleep in hope of him will rise. 2 And it will happen at that time that those treasuries will be opened in which the number of the souls of the righteous were kept, and they will go out and the multitudes of the souls will appear together, in one assemblage, of one mind. And the first ones will enjoy themselves and the last ones will not be sad. 3 For they know that the time has come of which it is said that it is the end of times. 4 But the souls of the wicked will the more waste away when they shall see all these

---

[49] Cavallin states that the 400-year Messianic interregnum in between two resurrections serves no real purpose. An attempt has been made to harmonize several traditions in 4 Ez: immediate retribution following death, resurrection and final judgment. This need not necessarily be the case: it is more accurate to state that we do not understand the significance of the Messiah's 400 year reign. Additionally, it is mere assumption to state that this is a device to harmonize several traditions. The apocalyptic authors did not seem to mind having several contradictory eschatologies exist side by side. H.C.C. CAVALLIN, *Life After Death*, 83-84»

things, 5 for they know that their torment has come and that their perditions have arrived[50].

In the following passage, there is again the description of the intermediate state of the dead and their rest in treasuries, which is also found in 2 Bar 21,23; 4 Ez 7,6; and 1 En 22, as well as the destruction of sinners, found also in 4 Ez 7,93; 9,9-12; 1 En 53,2; 56,1-4; 60,6; 69,27; 90,3-10; 102,1-3[51].

50,1 And He answered and said unto me: Hear, Baruch, this word, and write in the remembrance of thy heart all that thou shalt learn. 2 For the earth shall then assuredly restore the dead (which it now receives, in order to preserve them.) It shall make no change in their form, but as it has received, so shall it restore them, and as I delivered them unto it, so also shall it raise them. 3 For then it will be necessary to show to the living that the dead have come to life again, and that those who had departed have returned (again). 4 And it shall come to pass, when they have severally recognized those whom they now know, then judgment shall grow strong, and those things which before were spoken of shall come. 51,1 And it shall come to pass, when that appointed day has gone by, that then shall the aspect of those who are condemned be afterwards changed, and the glory of those who are justified. 2 For the aspect of those who now act wickedly shall become worse than it is, as they shall suffer torment. 3 Also (as for) the glory of those who have now been justified in My law, who have had understanding in their life, and who have planted in their heart the root of wisdom, then their splendour shall be glorified in changes, and the form of their face shall be turned into the light of their beauty, that they may be able to acquit and receive the world which does not die which is then promised to them...5 When therefore they (i.e. the wicked) see those, over whom they are now exalted, (but) who shall then be exalted and glorified more than they, they shall respectively be transformed, the latter into the splendour of angels, and the former shall yet more waste away in wonder at the visions and in the beholding of the forms. 6 For they shall first behold and afterwards depart to be tormented. 7,8 But those who have been saved by their works...shall behold the world which is now invisible to them, and they shall behold the time which is now hidden from them. 9 And time shall no longer age them. 10 For in the heights of that world shall they dwell, and they shall be made like unto the angels, and be made equal to the stars, and they shall be changed into every form they desire, from beauty into loveliness, and from light into the splendour of glory...Moreover there shall then

---

[50] *OTP*, 631. It is unclear, however, from where the Anointed One returns. Is it from heaven? This would make of this a doctrine similar to the parousia.

[51] Perdition does not necessarily mean annihilation, but rather death. There is often a similarity between «corruption», «ways of death», and «paths of perdition», as in 4 Ez 7,48. «Destruction» can be the equivalent of $\dot{\alpha}\pi\omega\lambda\epsilon\dot{\iota}\alpha$ or אבדון, perhaps used as a technical term for the underworld similar to the OT Sheol and Mawet. Stone, *Fourth Ezra*, 322.

be excellency in the righteous surpassing that in the angels. 52,7 (Exhortation to the righteous) Make ready your souls for that which is reserved for you, and prepare your souls for the reward which is laid up for you[52].

Two Baruch comes from the same general milieu as 1 Cor 15, and both contain reflections on the resurrection, although there is probably no direct connection between the two. One Cor 15 contains a more detailed reflection on the role of the Messianic figure in the resurrection, and the nature of the resurrected body. On the other hand, there is a beauty and abundance of images in 2 Bar that express the role of the individual in determining the nature of his afterlife[53].

2.3.3 Pseudo-Philo: Liber Antiquitatum Biblicarum (*LAB*)

Pseudo-Philo's *Liber Antiquitatum Biblicarum (LAB)* is closely related to 4 Ez, 2 Bar and 1 En 51,1. Present is an emphasis on the two ages (3,10; 16,3; 19,7.13; 32,17; 34,3 and 62,9); the raising of the righteous at the turn of the ages at the time of God's visitation (3,9; 16,3; 19,12.15; 26,12; 48,1); and a bitter end for the wicked with no hope of resurrection (16,3; 33,3; 51,5). Death is a separation of the body and soul (43,7; 44,10), after which there is no possibility of repentance (33,2-3). After death, there is an interim state (in storehouses or treasuries) where the righteous souls are at peace or in a sort of sleep, but the

---

[52] Cavallin believes that there is a combination of two views of the resurrection. Perhaps it is better to speak of two images of this same resurrection: a literal restoration of the pre-existing physical state, and a transcendent glorification into an angelic state. The first stage involves a resurrection of the body of some sort for the purpose of recognition and retribution. Following the judgment, the righteous will be transformed into a glorified existence, while the wicked will change into a distorted and loathsome form commensurate with their spiritual state. These are two images to fulfill two different functions in the eyes of the reader: personal accountability and transcendent rewards and punishments. H.C.C. CAVALLIN, *Defeat of Death*, 88-89.

[53] Cavallin finds four similarities with 1 Cor 15: 1) a general background of apology for belief in the resurrection; 2) a consideration of the nature of the resurrected body; 3) the fact that some survive until the resurrection; and 4) the transformation and glorification of the righteous at the resurrection. There are far more dissimilarities. The so-called «body» seems to be a very transient thing, undergoing various metamorphoses until finally achieving the form of the heavenly bodies. Additionally, 1 Cor 15 does not speak about the fate of the wicked, nor about recognition of the risen. Cavallin states that the transformation present in 2 Bar serves no real purpose; again, we can only say that we do not understand that purpose. This purpose would have to be understood in the context of the entire theology of the apocalyptic group that composed it. It is true that this transformation does not take place utilizing Christ or someone else as a model or pattern. But there is really no reason why it should, and this fact does not render it incompatible with 1 Cor 15. H.C.C. CAVALLIN, *Life After Death*, 88-89.

wicked are not (16,3; 23,13; 28,10; 31,7; 32,3; 33,4; 36,4; 38,4; 51,5; 62,9; 63,4). There is a consistent belief in the resurrection of the dead which takes place at the end of the world. Various images are used: the righteous will dwell in heavenly glory or in the promised land[54].

Of particular interest is 3,10, the most important passage bearing similarities to 4 Ez 8,53-54, in which death is personified and its demise foretold: «the world will cease, and death will be abolished, and hell will shut its mouth», and a new creation at the turn of the ages foretold: «And there shall be another heaven, and another earth, even an everlasting habitation».

2.3.4 Book of Jubilees

The Book of Jubilees presents an afterlife whose rewards and punishments are based on observance of the commandments; books are kept in heaven of good and evil deeds (5,13; 28,6; 30,19.22; 36,10; 39,6). A conversion of humanity to righteousness results in a lengthening of days, happiness, and absence of suffering. All Israel is elect and will be saved, but one can cut himself off from Israel (1,18; 15,32-34). The wicked will be driven out with curses, and the just will rejoice in all of this. Absent is a Final Judgment or resurrection, although hints of it may be found in Jub 5,13-16. Bodies are apparently not included: «their (the just) bones shall rest in the earth (23:31)»[55].

2.3.5 Testament of the XII Patriarchs

The Testament of the XII Patriarchs is of special interest for comparison with 1 Cor 15 in that it posits cosmic forces in conflict, especially between God and the evil forces in the world commanded by Beliar. Beliar rules through wicked behavior of all kinds, but especially sexual immorality and the passions, and his rule is called the kingdom (βασιλεία) of the enemy (TDan 6,2.4)[56].

---

[54] *LAB* is filled with passages that seem to contradict each other. Some passages do not seem to be aware of any consciousness between death and final judgment, while others speak of immediate glorification. Cavallin suggests, probably rightly, that rather than interpreting these as factual statements, they should be seen as «motifs for exhortations, reassurances of final rewards» (H.C.C. CAVALLIN, *Life After Death*, 78-80).

[55] H.C.C. CAVALLIN, *Life After Death*, 36-8; E.P. SANDERS, *Paul and Palestinian Judaism*, 366-72. This work, possibly Essene in origin, dates from the second century B.C. Two possible dates have been arrived at: 110-105 or 168-152 B.C.

[56] Beliar is mentioned 29 times and is also called Satan and the devil is the chief of the spirits of Beliar or the spirits of deceit. TGad 4,7; TAsh 6,4; TDan 1,7; 3,6; 5,6;

The defeat of this kingdom is closely connected with hope in the resurrection. Godly behavior and observance of the Law is an effective antidote to the power of Beliar. The individual is exhorted to chose whose side he is on, light or darkness, the Law of the Lord or Beliar, as in TDan 6,2ff:

And now fear the Lord, my children, be on guard against Satan and his spirits. Draw near to God and to the angel who intercedes for you, because he is the mediator between God and men for the peace of Israel. He shall stand in opposition to the kingdom of the enemy. Therefore the enemy is eager to trip up all who call on the Lord, because he knows that on the day in which Israel trusts, the enemy's kingdom will be brought to an end[57].

In language and symbols similar to those found in Rev 20, Is 40, and Dan 12, the author describes the resurrection which will follow the defeat of the kingdom of evil as a time of gladness and transformation. It is not entirely clear whether this includes the body and where exactly this is to take place, i.e., in the heavens or on the earth[58].

Common with 1 Cor 15 is a concern for the defeat of inimical cosmic powers, albeit not death as such but Beliar, and a belief in the coming resurrection and transformation, along with reward and punishment.

6,1; TNap 3,1; 8,4.6; TAsh 3,2; TReu 2,2; TLev 3,3; 18,12; TJud 25,3; TIss 7,7; TZeb 9,8; TBen 3,3; TSim 2,7; TJud 19,4. M.C. DE BOER, *Defeat of Death*, 67-68.

[57] TDan 5,1; TIss 7,7; TSim 3,5; TNap 8,4; TBen 5,2. The wiles and tricks of Beliar in his quest for power over humanity must be resisted until the Day of Judgment, when the malign spirits will be punished: TSim 6,6; TLev 3,3; 18,12; TJud 25,3; TZeb 9,8; TBen 3,8; TDan 4,7; 5,10; TBen 3,3. M.C. DE BOER, *Defeat of Death*, 68-69.

[58] TBen 10,8: «Then shall we also be raised, each of us over our tribe, and we shall prostrate ourselves before the heavenly king. Then all shall be changed, some destined for glory, others for dishonor, for the Lord first judges Israel for the wrong she has committed, and then shall do the same for all the nations». Note the parallel with Dan 12,2 and 1 Cor 15,51. TSim 6,7: «Then I shall arise in gladness and I shall bless the Most High for his marvels». TJud 25,1ff: «And after this Abraham, Isaac and Jacob will be resurrected to life and I and my brothers will be chiefs [...] And you shall be one people of the Lord, with one language. There shall no more be Beliar's spirit of error, because he will be thrown into eternal fire. And those who died in sorrow shall be raised in joy; and those who died in poverty for the Lord's sake shall be made rich; those who died on account of the Lord shall be wakened to life. And the deer of Jacob shall run with gladness; the eagles of Jacob shall fly with joy; the impious shall mourn and sinners shall weep, but all peoples shall glorify the Lord forever». TZeb 10,2: «I will rise again in your midst as a leader among your sons, and I shall be glad in the midst of my tribe [...] but the Lord shall bring down fire on the impious and will destroy them to all generations».

2.3.6 Psalms of Solomon

The Psalms of Solomon make a strong connection between the observance of the Law and the resurrection to eternal life. No clear statement is made concerning the body; rather, the image of light and transformation to a heavenly existence is often used[59].

These psalms have been called an example of «two-way» theology; that is, the way of righteousness leads to eternal life, while that of sin leads to destruction and death (pss 9,13,14,15). Sinners perish forever; darkness and destruction is their lot. Death is personified (7,3-5)[60].

There is only one clear reference to the resurrection, which takes place at the theophany or visitation at the end of the age, and is for the righteous alone (3,10-12). Even here, it is unclear whether the resurrection of the body is referred to or the immortality of the spirit.

> The destruction of the sinner is forever, and he will not be remembered when (God) looks after the righteous. This is the share of sinners forever, but those who fear the Lord shall rise up to eternal life, and their life shall be in the Lord's light, and it shall never end[61].

2.3.7 First Enoch: Book of Watchers

First Enoch is a blend of different eschatologies from different periods and includes apocalyptic material, visions, dreams, speculations concerning the age to come and the inner meaning of history, and astronomical speculations[62].

---

[59] The Psalms of Solomon were written possibly in the mid-first century B.C. They can be called apocalyptic in nature in that there is the presence of the two ages, and it teaches reliance on God's faithfulness in the face of defeat and persecution (2,1.15-18; 13,3-5; 4,8; 8,3.23-26; 9,2). M.C. DE BOER, Defeat of Death, 62-64; H.C.C. CAVALLIN, Life After Death, 57-59.

[60] Destruction (ἀπώλεια) is forever; at times, the violent death of the sinner is itself seen as punishment. God will remember those who fear him at the time of his visitation; the lot of those will be to «rise to eternal life» (ps 3). What is held to be an example of «two-way» theology could apply to almost any type of eschatological or apocalyptic writing: all hold that sin leads to destruction and goodness to reward of some sort. G.W.E. NICKELSBURG, Resurrection, 131-134.

[61] OTP, II, 655. Some receive recompense or judgment on the plane of history, others after death. Psalms 9,13,14,15 suggest some sort of retribution after death; the reference to the resurrection in ps 3 is vague as to whether the body or spirit is meant. G.W.E. NICKELSBURG, Resurrection, 133-134.

[62] A difficulty arises in making general statements about the beliefs expressed in 1 Enoch; that is, not all of the sections come from the same period and the version extant is a composite of several secondary translations such as Old Church Slavonic and Ethiopian. The work is divided into five main sections (chs. 1-36; 37-71; 72-83; 83-

In the Book of Watchers (chs. 1-36), the presence of evil and death in the world is the fault of evil angelic powers, especially the Watchers, or those angels who mated with women and produced giants. These forces perverted the earth and taught man forms of knowledge not meant for him and which he misused. The Final Judgment involves the removal and destruction of these evil forces which are the source of violence and death, as is evident in 1,6-9:

> And great fear and trembling shall seize them unto the ends of the earth. Mountains and high places will fall down and be frightened. And high hills shall be made low; and they shall melt like a honeycomb before the flame. And earth shall be rent asunder; and all that is upon the earth shall perish. And there shall be a judgment upon all, (including) the righteous. And to all the righteous he shall grant peace. He will preserve the elect, and kindness shall be upon them. They shall all belong to God and they shall prosper and be blessed; and the light of God shall shine unto them. Behold, he will arrive with ten million of the holy ones in order to execute judgment upon all. He will destroy the wicked ones and censure all flesh on account of everything that they have done, that which the sinners and the wicked ones committed against him.

In this section, death involves the separation of soul and body, with some sort of continuance. There is no direct mention of the resurrection of a fleshly body. The souls of the dead cry out for vengeance, and 1 En 22 describes «waiting places» for souls between death and final judgment, with some kind of post mortem retribution implied. The righteous are restored to life here on earth (25,1-7; 1,6-9; 10,17)[63].

90; 91-105 [106-108]) and is sometimes referred to as the Enochic Pentateuch. The Parables or Similitudes of Enoch (chs. 37-71) presents a problem: this contains one of the clearest references to the resurrection and judgment. However, these chapters were not found among the others at Qumran; therefore, they may be from a later period and even be influenced by Christian ideas. As a witness to the Jewish background, they must be used with caution. H.C.C. CAVALLIN, *Life After Death*, 40; M.C. DE BOER, *Defeat of Death*, 52.

[63] The spirits are divided according to their conduct on earth: some experience bliss during this waiting period, while the wicked undergo various degrees of punishment. Some have been judged in their lifetimes and punished, but others have not been punished enough; there torment during the waiting period is greater. There is no reason to suppose, as does Cavallin, that the post-mortem existence expressed in this book is probably immortality or resurrection of the soul, since the definition of «body» in much of this apocalyptic literature is very vague and fluid. We might speak of body expressed through various images and symbols. H.C.C. CAVALLIN, *Life After Death*, 40-41; G.W.E. NICKELSBURG, *Resurrection*, 134-137.

2.3.8 First Enoch: Parables or Similitudes

The Parables or Similitudes of Enoch (chs. 37-71) provide the only mention, albeit vague, of the resurrection (ch. 51), which is a vindication of the righteous:

> In those days, Sheol will return all the deposits which she had received and hell give back all that which it owes. And he shall choose the righteous and the holy ones from among (the risen dead), for the day when they shall be selected and saved has arrived. In those days, (the Elect One) shall sit on my throne, and from the conscience of his mouth shall come out all the secrets of wisdom, for the Lord of the Spirits has given them to him and glorified him. In those days, mountains shall dance like rams; and the hills shall leap like kids satiated with milk. And the faces of all the angels in heaven shall glow with joy, because on that day the Elect One has arisen. And the earth shall rejoice, and the righteous ones shall dwell upon her and the elect ones shall walk upon her.

A question arises: What is going to be given back? The consensus is that souls will be restored; however, the life that will be given will be lived out on earth, which is suggestive of bodies. A transformation of light and glory is alluded to in 51,4. This, together with other texts on the post-resurrection life, indicate that it will be a «transformed life on a transformed earth»[64].

Again, there is the personification of death and the notion of an intermediate state. This section refers often to the work of the Elect One, Righteous One, or Messiah. Humanity is on the verge of the changing of the ages, in which there will be a cosmic reversal (38,4-5) in which sinners will be judged (Chs. 38, 45, 48, 51, 53)[65].

Perhaps prefiguring verse 24 of 1 Cor 15, several passages speak of the overthrow, humiliation, and destruction of the kings and powers of

---

«body» in much of this apocalyptic literature is very vague and fluid. We might speak of body expressed through various images and symbols. H.C.C. CAVALLIN, *Life After Death*, 40-41; G.W.E. NICKELSBURG, *Resurrection*, 134-137.

[64] H.C.C. CAVALLIN, *Life After Death*, 45.

[65] 38,3-4: «When the secrets of the Righteous One are revealed, he shall judge the sinners; and the wicked ones will be driven from the presence of the righteous and the elect, and from that time, those who possess the earth will neither be rulers nor princes, they shall not be able to behold the faces of the holy ones, for the light of the Lord of the Spirits has shined upon the face of the holy, the righteous, and the elect.» The fate of sinners and unbelievers is reflected well in ch. 45: «Neither will they ascend into heaven, nor will they reach the ground; such will be the lot of the sinners, who will deny the name of the Lord of the Spirits [...] But sinners have come before me so that by judgment I shall destroy them from before the face of the earth».

the earth because of their oppression, sinfulness, and refusal to recognize and obey God[66].

The fall of the angels was linked to the coming of death (69,4-11). The Son of Man becomes the figure who will judge these angelic powers (55,4; 69,27-29). Purity and righteousness characterized human life before the Fall and will do so again in the New Age, for neither death nor sin were part of God's plan for the human race. Death is a sign of humanity's subjection to the evil powers, and it will cease when God's Elect One overthrows them[67].

Chapters 94-104 of 1 En deal with the oppression of the righteous. These chapters are set in the form of a debate or disputation with the wicked, those who pervert and disobey the Torah and who do not believe that there is retribution or judgment. According to these sinners, there is absolutely no reward for being pious or righteous[68].

Chapter 104 reuses the judgment scene from Dan 12,1-3. It is addressed to the living, and is filled with moral exhortation: the living are told to be hopeful, and not to be afraid, both standard expressions in apocalyptic writings. The author also claims to «know a mystery». This is found in apocalyptic literature, and as we shall see later, in 1 Cor 15. The righteous will be rewarded for having suffered unjustly, not necessarily for the sake of God[69].

2.3.9 Sibylline Oracles

The Sibylline Oracles utilize the pagan prophetic figure of Sibylla for apologetic purposes. The oracles as we have them are Christian, although there are Jewish traditions embedded in them. The passage most applica-

---

[66] 1 En 38,5; 46,4; 48,8; 53,5; 62,1-3.9; 64,1; 67,12; 69,26-29. These various powers control the earth and have become God's enemies.

[67] M.C. DE BOER, *Defeat of Death*, 56.

[68] The most pertinent passages are 102,4 and 104,8, in which both groups are addressed.

[69] «I swear unto you that in heaven the angels will remember you for good before the glory of the Great One; and your names shall be written before the glory of the Great One». 104,1-2. Encouragement and exhortation are found in 4-7: «Be hopeful, and do not abandon your hope, because there shall be a fire for you; you are about to be making a great rejoicing like the angels of heaven. You shall not have to hide on the day of great judgment, and you shall not be found as sinners; but the eternal judgment shall be (far) away from you for all the generations of the world. Now fear not, righteous ones, when you see the sinners waxing strong and flourishing; do not be partners with them, but keep far way from those who lean onto their own injustice; for you are to be partners with the good-hearted people of heaven» (G.W.E. NICKELSBURG, *Resurrection*, 119-20.123).

ble to the judgment and resurrection is IV, 171-190, written in the latter portion of the first century A.D. This passage describes the universal destruction of all life through fire, followed by a re-creation and resurrection in the context of a universal judgment. It is unclear, however, whether this is a general resurrection, or includes only the last generation. The righteous will live their blessed life on earth, while the wicked are sent to Tartarus and Gehenna. There is no mention of a glorified or heavenly state[70].

2.3.10 Qumran Scrolls

The Qumran Scrolls are problematic for the study of apocalyptic and eschatology. According to Nickelsburg, «not a single passage can be interpreted with absolute certainty as a reference to resurrection or immortality». The same might be said, however, of almost any document of this period. Although most of the scrolls are not apocalypses in the technical sense, lacking some of the detailed descriptions of the end and so on, they are filled with apocalyptic terminology and images[71].

---

[70] «But if you do not obey me, evil-minded ones, but love impiety, and receive all these things with evil ears, there will be fire throughout the whole world, and a very great sign with sword and trumpet at the rising sun. The whole world will hear a bellowing noise and mighty sound. He will burn the whole earth, and will destroy the whole race of men and all cities and rivers at once, and the sea. He will destroy everything by fire, and it will be smoking dust. But when everything is already dusty ashes, and God puts to sleep the unspeakable fire, even as he kindled it, God himself will fashion the bones and ashes of men and he will raise up mortals again as they were before. And then there will be a judgment over which God himself will preside, judging the world again. As many as sinned by impiety, these will a mound of earth cover, and broad Tartarus and the repulsive recesses of Gehenna. But as many as are pious, they will live on earth again when God gives spirit and life and favor to these pious ones. Then they will all see themselves beholding the delightful and pleasant light of the sun. Oh most blessed, whatever man will live to that time» (IV 171-90). H.C.C. CAVALLIN, *Life After Death*, 148-150; G.W.E. NICKELSBURG, *Resurrection*, 140-141.

[71] Scholarly opinions are divided: many believe that the Essenes shared the Jewish apocalyptic views of the resurrection of the body, while others deny that they believed in any type of afterlife. Still others make favorable comparisons with Josephus' description of the Essene beliefs in this area. Nickelsburg also describes the scrolls as being prime examples of two-way theology, which by nature is content to describe rewards and punishments for the righteous and wicked in very vague and general terms. It is safe to say that the Essenes believed in some sort of continuation of life following the cataclysmic events of the end time, i.e., the visitation. Not to believe in some sort of afterlife would have belied most of their spirituality and theology. It is also crystal clear that they believed in the punishment of the wicked and rewards for the just. Many of the phrases, words and expressions become problematic only when subjected to tortured or overly subtle analyses. Let us assume that the

One of the clearest witnesses to belief in afterlife, judgment and resurrection is found in 1QS IV, 6b-8, 11b-14:

And as for the visitation of all who walk in this spirit, it shall be healing, great peace in a long life, and fruitfulness, together with every everlasting blessing and eternal joy in life without end, a crown of glory and a garment of majesty in unending light... And the visitation of all who walk in this spirit shall be a multitude of plagues by the hand of all the destroying angels, everlasting damnation by the avenging wrath of the fury of God, eternal torment and endless disgrace together with shameful extinction in the fire of the dark regions. The times of all their generations shall be spent in sorrowful mourning and in bitter misery and in calamities of darkness until they are destroyed without remnant or survivor.

The words and images of the above passage are such, however, that it is not entirely clear whether life after death is physical or consists of a heavenly existence. These occur within a section that consists of a two-way theology; its purpose is ethical exhortation rather than a description of the afterlife[72].

In a detailed study of the Qumran documents, Puech concludes that the Essenes did believe in the afterlife and the resurrection of the body. He emphasizes 4Q Deutero-Ezekiel 2-3 (4Q385); 1QH XIV 37; and most of all, 4Q521. This latter document, called by Puech a «messianic apocalypse», describes the actions of the Messiah:

heaven and earth will obey his messiah. (2) [and all th]at is in them will not turn away from the commandments of holy ones. (3) You who seek the Lord, strengthen yourselves in his service. (4) Is it not in this that you will find the Lord, all who hope in their hearts. (5) For the Lord will seek out the pious and call the righteous by name, (6) and his spirit will hover over the poor and he will renew the faithful by his might. (7) For he will glorify the pious on the throne of an eternal kingdom, (8) releasing captives, giving sight to the blind and raising up those who are bo[wed down]. (9) Forever I will cleave to [those who] hope, and in his kindness... (10) The fru[it of a] good [wor]k will not be delayed for anyone (11) and the glorious things that have not taken place the Lord will do as he s[aid] (12) for he will heal the wounded, give life to the dead and preach good news to the poor (13) and he will [sat]isfy the [weak] ones and lead those who have been cast out and enrich the hungry...(14)...and all of them...[73]

Essenes did share Jewish apocalyptic beliefs concerning the afterlife, that Josephus did describe accurately at least some of their beliefs, and that all of these documents share the ambiguity and apparent contradictions of similar literature of this time and genre. G.W.E. NICKELSBURG, *Resurrection*, 144; H.C.C. CAVALLIN, *Life After Death*, 60.

[72] Other less clear passages in this document are 1QS XI,7b-9a; CD III,20; CD VII,6a and 1QSb III,4-6. H.C.C. CAVALLIN, *Life After Death*, 61.

[73] This text is interesting from several points of view: its parallels with Isa 61 and Luke 4,18-19; 7,22 and the statement in v.12 that God will give life to the dead. Un-

The Hymn Scrolls offer thanks to God for deliverance from enemies and for other divine favors. If the deliverance has not taken place, it is expected imminently. Since death has not occurred and is not expected, there is no mention of retribution or the afterlife. The two-way theology is expressed in the following passages:

1QH IV,21b-22a: Those who are after your mind, will stand before you for ever, and those who walk in the way of your heart will be steadfast forevermore.

1QH VI,29b-30a: All the children of his truth will awake to destroy the children of wickedness and all the children of guilt will be no more... and those who sleep in the dust will raise an ensign and the worm of the dead will lift a banner...in wars with insolent men.

1QH VIII,31: [...] in order to destroy the flesh for many times [...]

1QH XI,10-14: For your glory's sake you have purified man from sin that he may be sanctified before you from all impure abominations and the guilt of transgression that he may be united with the sons of your truth and in a lot with your holy ones, to raise the worm of the dead from the dust to (eternal) council and from a crooked spirit to (your) insight that he may stand in a place of standing before you with an eternal army and spirits (of knowledge) to renew himself with all that there is and with those who know in common exultation[74].

---

fortunately, this document exists only in a single exemplar and it is very fragmentary, so we cannot be sure if this is the work of the Qumran sect or what the entire theology of the work is. The subject of the narrative is probably God, with the Messiah acting merely as an agent. É. PUECH, *La Croyance des Esséniens*, Vol. II, 627-681. English translation taken from J.J. COLLINS, *The Scepter and the Star*, 117.

[74] Nickelsburg claims that all of the above express a two-way theology. It does reflect a moral exhortation, but it is far from clear that it belongs in the two-way category. Two-way theology usually is not explicit in its descriptions of the consequences of walking the wrong way; the above passages are more indicative of apocalyptic exhortation and judgment literature. The second seems to describe a resurrection, although some scholars interpret «awake» as meaning readiness for war and «those who sleep in the dust» and «the worm of the dead» as expressions of lowliness. The third is unclear. The last passage uses resurrection terminology, but seems to describe the present, realized resurrection of one who has entered the community, for they live with angels and experience transcendence now. According to the Essenes, entrance into the community gave one knowledge of God and communion with angels, as one passed from the sphere of death into the realm of life. Some hymns, such as 1QH XI,10-14 above and 1QSb III,4-6, express the belief that community members were already participating in the eschaton. This perhaps would help to explain why there are so few explicit references to the afterlife and resurrection: it is an accomplished fact. G.W.E. NICKELSBURG, *Resurrection*, 144-147; H.C.C. CAVALLIN, *Life After Death*, 63-64.

It also appears that there may have been more than one eschatology in force at Qumran. Mattila contrasts the eschatologies of two key documents, 4Q246 and 1QM (War Scroll) with interesting results. The War Scroll is pitiless: it is about judgment, retribution, and the complete annihilation – without a remnant – of the wicked or lot of Belial. The other document, 4Q246 – offers an eschatology which reflects the peace oracles of Zech 9,10; Hos 2,18; Isa 2,4; and Mic 4,3. The end will herald in a transformation and a period of universal peace, in which «the sword will cease from the land». The wicked are not to be annihilated, but all nations and people will be brought to submission to the people of God, whose everlasting dominion will be sustained by God himself[75].

It is not clear exactly what the Essenes believed concerning the afterlife, and many question whether they believed in a physical resurrection at all, since there is no explicit mention of it in the extant texts. Outside sources, such as Josephus and Hippolytus, can give us additional information, but their reliability is questionable. On the other hand, the documents are filled with descriptions of punishment for the wicked and rewards for the just and pious. Cavallin wisely prefers to use a generalization: the Essenes believed in a «blessed life for the righteous and a punitive death for sinners». Beyond that it is difficult to speculate[76].

2.3.11 Second Maccabees

The literature of the Greek speaking Diaspora provides several examples of belief in the afterlife. Second Maccabees (6,18-31; 7; 12,43-45; 14,37-46; 15,12-16) expresses what Cavallin calls «typical Palestinian Jewish ideas about life after death», even though it is a work of the Greek Diaspora[77].

---

[75] The contrast is so great that Mattila argues that 4Q246 was not authored at Qumran. There is no reason why it could not have been; however, for the sake of this survey it does not matter. It was present among the Essene scrolls, and even if not authored by them, probably reflected at least some aspect of their theology. S.L. MATTILA, «Two Contrasting Eschatologies at Qumran (4Q246 vs 1QM)», 518-538.

[76] Josephus ascribes a belief in the immortality of the soul to the Essenes and a view of the body as a negative encumbrance which is to be left behind (ANT SVIII,18; BJ II,154-7). However, there is no mention of this whatsoever in the scrolls. This description could have been colored by Josephus' conscious efforts to make favorable comparisons between Jewish sectarian doctrines and Greek philosophical schools. In Ref IX,27 Hippolytus repeats some of Josephus' description but adds a belief in the resurrection of the body. H.C.C. CAVALLIN, Defeat of Death, 65.69-70.

[77] 2 Macc is an epitome of a five volume work by Jason of Cyrene; it is unclear whether the above passages are the work of Jason or the epitomist. By «typical Pal-

Verses 6,18-31 describe the martyrdom of Eleazar and the seven brothers. No details are given about rewards and punishments after death, or when it will take place, but there is an emphatic affirmation of the existence of justice after death for both the righteous and the sinners:

v. 26: Even if for the present I would avoid the punishment of mortals, yet whether I live or die I shall not escape the hands of the Almighty (NRSV).

Chapter 7 is particularly rich. The second brother expresses his faith in the resurrection in the following fashion:

v. 9: ...you dismiss us from this present life, but the King of the universe will raise us up (ἀναστήσει) to an everlasting renewal of life (αἰώνιον ἀναβίωσιν ζωῆς), because we have died for his laws (NRSV).

vv. 10-11: After him the third was a victim of their sport. When it was demanded, he quickly put out his tongue and courageously stretched forth his hands, and said nobly, «I got these from Heaven, and because of his laws I disdain them, and from him I hope to get them back again» (NRSV).

v. 14: One cannot but choose to die at the hands of mortals and to cherish the hope God gives of being raised again (ἀναστήσεσθαι) by him. But for you there will be no resurrection to life (ἀνάστασις εἰς ζωήν) (NRSV)!

v. 22-23: I do not know how you came into being in my womb. It was not I who gave you life and breath, nor I who set in order the elements within each of you. Therefore the Creator of the world, who shaped the beginning of humankind and devised the origin of all things, will in his mercy give life and breath back to you again, since you now forget yourselves for the sake of his laws (NRSV).

v. 36: For our brothers after enduring a brief suffering have drunk of ever-flowing life, under God's covenant; but you, by the judgment of God, will receive just punishment for your arrogance. My brothers have now fallen in loyalty to God's covenant, after brief pain leading to eternal life (NRSV).

See also 14:45-46: Still alive and aflame with anger, he rose, and though his blood gushed forth and his wounds were severe he ran through the crowd; and standing upon a steep rock, with his blood now completely drained from him, he tore out his entrails, took them in both hands and hurled them at the crowd, calling upon the Lord of life and spirit to give them back to him again. This was the manner of his death[78].

---

estinian Jewish ideas about life after death», Cavallin probably means an emphasis on the physical rather than the spiritual aspects of the human person. It should be clear from a study of the sources that there is no «typical» Palestinian Jewish ideas about life after death. Generalities such as this one are not helpful in analysis. H.C.C. CAVALLIN, *Life After Death*, 111-115.

[78] The NRSV translation is used for these quotes which are taken from H.C.C. CAVALLIN, *Life After Death*, 112-113.

Several points are noteworthy concerning these passages: 1) God is looked upon as the Lord of life and breath and the giver of life, and the resurrection is based upon this aspect of God; 2) there is a literal belief in a very physical resurrection; 3) there is a strong sense of vindication of the righteous; 4) there is no date or description of the end or the judgment. It must also be noted that the extreme emphasis on the physical and literal nature of the resurrection could in part be due to its function: to encourage those undergoing persecution and to show that those who die a martyr's death will be vindicated. Having one's fleshly body restored is the form that this vindication takes.

The following passage (12,43-45) implies that resurrection could include punishment for sins. Some of the Jewish fallen were wearing pagan amulets, so Judas makes a sin-offering on their behalf. There is no explicit mention of the body sharing in the resurrection.

> So they all blessed the ways of the Lord, the righteous judge, who reveals the things that are hidden; and they turned to supplication, praying that the sin that had been committed might be wholly blotted out. The noble Judas exhorted the people to keep themselves free from sin, for they had seen with their own eyes what had happened as the result of the sin of those who had fallen. He also took up a collection and sent it to Jerusalem to provide for a sin offering. In doing this he acted very well and honorably, taking account of the resurrection (ὑπὲρ ἀναστάσεως). For if he were not expecting that those who had fallen would rise again (ἀναστῆναι), it would have been superfluous and foolish to pray for the dead. But if he was looking to the splendid reward that is laid up for those who fall asleep in godliness, it was a holy and pious thought. Therefore he made atonement for the dead, so that they might be delivered from their sin (NRSV).

According to Cavallin, this passage is similar to 1 Cor 15 in several respects: 1) both defend the resurrection against deniers; 2) both describe a «liturgical, vicarious action on behalf of dead people» as in 1 Cor 15,29; 3) both consider this action to be foolish unless there is a resurrection of the dead. On the other hand, there is no fixed point or time for this resurrection such as the parousia; there is no reference to cosmological powers or God's all-encompassing conquest; and there is no messianic agent or transformation of the body[79].

---

[79] Cavallin states that in this pericope ἀνάστασις is the single term used for the afterlife, and the alternative to this is no life at all. Judas' vicarious action would be compatible with almost any sort of belief in the afterlife. H.C.C. CAVALLIN, *Life After Death*, 113-114.

2.3.12 Fourth Maccabees

Fourth Maccabees was written approximately a century later than 2 Macc. It too is concerned with the martyrdom of Eleazar, the seven brothers and their mother, but the emphasis and the theology is very different than 2 Macc. In 4 Macc, the characters in the martyrdom account display the «superiority and sovereignty of religious reason over the passions and emotions.» The statements from 2 Macc which expressed a literal conception of the resurrection were replaced with expressions describing a spiritual type of immortality[80].

This belief in the necessity of mastering the passions (παθῶν) is expressed in 7,18-19 and 16,16-23. Those who are faithful and successful in this will prove that to God they do not die and they will «live to God» (ζῶσιν τῷ θεῷ) as do all of the patriarchs such as Abraham, Isaac and Jacob. The present tense of «to live» probably indicates that the patriarchs were already experiencing this life and that those who die a martyr's death will achieve this immediately after death. A fine example is the reply of the seven brothers to the tyrant in 9,7-9:

> If you take our lives and inflict upon us a death (τὰς ἡμῶν ψυχὰς εἰ θανατώσεις) for religion's sake, do not think that you are injuring us by your torments. We, by our suffering and endurance, shall obtain the prize of virtue; and we shall be with God (παρὰ θεῷ), on Whose account we suffer; but you, for our foul murder, will endure at the hand of divine justice the condign punishment of eternal torment (αἰώνιον βάσανον)[81].

In several instances, the life after death gained by martyrdom is referred to as immortality (ἀθάνατος or ἀθανασία) and is illustrated in 14,45-6: This and other passages such as 16,13 and 18,23 suggest that immortality was not an inherent quality of the soul but was something granted by God after death, especially death by martyrdom.

> All as if running the course to immortality, sped onward to death by torture. Just as hands and feet move in harmony with the promptings of the soul, so did those holy youths, as if prompted by the immortal soul of religion, harmoniously accept death on its behalf[82].

Special attention is given in 18,23 to the status of the martyrs as children of Abraham, who will receive pure and immortal souls upon death. The death of the martyrs is seen as the gateway to the form of life described by that term, a life that is transcendent. Being a son of Abraham

---

[80] 4 Macc draws heavily on 2 Macc 6-7. The author is probably an orthodox Jew from the Greek Diaspora. H.C.C. CAVALLIN, *Life After Death*, 116.

[81] H.C.C. CAVALLIN, *Life After Death*, 117.

[82] H.C.C. CAVALLIN, *Life After Death*, 118.

means displaying some of the same qualities, i.e., walking in faith and trust and enduring hardships. This «way» is described in the death of one of the brothers in 9,21:

> Even when the frame of his body was already dissevered, the great-spirited youth, a true son of Abraham, uttered no groan. As though he were being transformed into incorruption by the fire, he nobly endured the torments[83].

A reference to a «divine portion» in 18,3 also describes the blessings of the afterlife and the immortality received immediately after death by the martyrs:

> Those men who yielded up their bodies to suffering for the sake of religion were in recompense not only admired by mankind, but were also deemed worthy of a divine portion (θεία μέρις).

Verse 17,18 goes on to explain that the life of eternal blessedness is lived in the presence of God[84].

The future life is very much a concern of 4 Macc, and this includes not only the reward for the righteous who have suffered for their faith and remained faithful during persecution, but also punishment for those who oppressed them. Reference is not made to resurrection of the body, but neither is it denied. The souls of the just are not inherently immortal, but this is received from God in recompense for their faithful suffering. Of particular interest is the fact that the moment of decisive change in other works is the «last day» of the «end time», while in 4 Macc, it is the moment of the death of the individual[85].

2.3.13 Testament of Job

The Testament of Job is probably a pre-Christian work of the Hellenistic Jewish Diaspora, written about 40 B.C. It promises salvation through resurrection to those who convert from idolatry, although the mode of resurrection is not well developed. Job is told, after having decided to destroy idols and worship the true God:

---

[83] This has very close parallels with the Martyrdom of Polycarp 15, which in turn draws inspiration from WisSol 3,6. Cavallin believes that 4 Macc 9,21 and WisSol 3,6 form the background of early Christian martyrologies. Fourth Macc 9,22 uses ἀφθαρσία instead of ἀθάνασια; in the LXX this is used only in 4 Macc and Wis. In 1 Cor 15,50-54, this term is used to describe the form of life which will inherit the kingdom of God, and which is obtained only by death and resurrection or by transformation. In 1 Cor 15 and 2 Bar 51, this is obtained on the day of the resurrection, while it is obtained in the act of dying in 4 Macc 9,22. H.C.C. CAVALLIN, *Life After Death*, 119-120.

[84] H.C.C. CAVALLIN, *Life After Death*, 121.

[85] H.C.C. CAVALLIN, *Life After Death*, 123.

4,9 You shall be raised (ἐγέρθησῃ) at the resurrection (ἀνάστασει).

Again, in 40,4, Job's wife proclaims the following. Noteworthy is the language describing a slumber or intermediate state.

Now I know that my memory remains with the Lord. I shall then rise and I shall enter the city, and I will slumber a little. Then I shall receive the reward for my slavery.

Several passages use assumption language in describing the post-mortem state (39,12; 40,3 and 52,2). In the first passage, the bodies of Job's children were taken up along with their souls immediately after death. This assumption is followed by divine glorification in 40,3.

39,12: since they have been taken up (ἀνελήφθησαν) into the heavens by the King, their Maker [...] My children have been taken up (ἀνελήφθη) into heaven.

40,3: crowned near the glory of Him who is in heaven.

Upon Job's death, angels come for him, and after a kiss from God, his soul is taken up into heaven while his body remains on earth:

52,2: he took the soul of Job and He soared upward taking her by the arm and carrying her upon the chariot, and He went towards the East. His body, however, was brought to the grave.

Three different descriptions of the life immediately after death are given in the same document: resurrection in the eschatological future; assumption of the whole person, body and soul; and assumption of the soul, with the body remaining in the grave. Cavallin notes that these three contradictory views exist simultaneously in the same document, with no real attempt to harmonize the contradictions[86].

2.3.14 Rabbinic Tradition

The rabbinic tradition contains some vague statements concerning the resurrection and afterlife. Dating and authenticity of these traditions is very problematic, limiting the sort of use that can be made of them. The discussions between followers of Shammai and Hillel provide some references to the resurrection, albeit of a very literal sort. There is an interesting debate between the two parties over the question of what happens to «mediocre» souls who are neither evil enough for hell nor good enough for the resurrected life. The party of Hillel believed that if the good deeds outweighed the evil, then they would prevail; the party of Shammai be-

---

[86] H.C.C. CAVALLIN, *Life After Death*, 160-162.

lieved in a sort of purgatorial state: «the last of them descend to Gehenna and squeal and rise again and are healed (TSanh 13,3)»[87].

The Mishnah Sanhedrin provides an interesting parallel to v. 12 of 1 Cor 15: «All Israelites have a share in the world to come... And these are they that have no share in the world to come: he that says that there is no resurrection of the dead prescribed in the Law, and he that says that the Law is not from Heaven, and an Epicurean (MSanh 10.1a)»[88].

It appears that the rabbinic sources express a rather imprecise belief in a resurrection or new life.

2.3.15 Josephus

The works of Josephus in the later part of the first century reflected a strong Hellenizing influence, especially with regard to the afterlife. He is a source of information about the beliefs of different Jewish groups of the time, but the veracity of his statements are questionable at times, being tinged with many of his apologetic and Hellenizing concerns. Of the beliefs of the Essenes, he said the following:

Every soul, they maintain, is imperishable (ψυχὴν δὲ πᾶσαν ἄφθαρτον) but the soul of the good alone passes into another body (μεταβαίνειν δὲ εἰς ἕτερον σῶμα) while the souls of the wicked suffer eternal punishment (BJ 11,163)[89].

It is not entirely clear what is meant by passing into a new body. It most likely refers to the new body given at the resurrection, for there are several other references to «new life» being given at the resurrection, especially for martyrs and for good souls. ANT XVIII,14 describes his eschatology: reward and punishment; passage to a new life for the good souls and eternal punishment for the wicked. Although not explicitly stated, the term ἀναβίουν perhaps alludes to the resurrection of the body[90].

---

[87] GnR 14,5 and LvR 14,9 discuss the order of corporeal formation in the world to come: sinews and bones first, then skin and flesh, the opposite of this age. The followers of Hillel considered that the resurrected body was re-created *ex nihilo*. Both schools believed that resurrected life was in an earthly rather than a transformed body, and that this took place at some indefinite future time. H.C.C. CAVALLIN, *Life After Death*, 171-172.175.

[88] H.C.C. CAVALLIN, *Life After Death*, 183.

[89] He indicates that immortality is inherent in the soul. There is nothing about when this is to happen or the nature of the new body. H.C.C. CAVALLIN, *Life After Death*, 141.

[90] H.C.C. CAVALLIN, *Life After Death*, 142-142.

The posthumous state of the martyrs is described in *BJ* I, 647-664 as being particularly happy, while an anthropology of the unity of soul and body is described in *BJ* III, 362-382, although in 372 of this same section, it is stated that the body perishes, and the soul lives forever, since it is a portion of the Deity[91].

Josephus is very concerned with life after death, especially for the purpose of reward and punishment. His belief in the nature of this postmortem state is characterized chiefly by the immortality of the soul, and is somewhat dualistic. There are some statements regarding a resurrection at the change of the ages, but these are not clear or well formulated, and little is said about the nature of the new life that is given.

2.3.16 Philo of Alexandria

Philo of Alexandria represents a more Hellenistic tradition concerning the human person and life after death. Philo's human being is composed of both an earthly substance (χοῦς) and the divine spirit, the latter being uncreated and breathed into the person by the Father and Ruler of the universe. The mind is of supreme importance for Philo, being called the «soul of the soul». Immortality is an inherent quality of the mind, the body alone being mortal by nature. The body is looked upon rather negatively, as being that which is mortal and opposed to wisdom and virtue. A realized eschatology of sorts is possible for humans, for man can become immortal during his life corresponding to how much his body is dominated and controlled by the mind (*SpecLeg I* 345). Immortality itself is knowledge of God who is being and life (based upon Deut 4,4) or communion on a deep personal level[92].

Death is the gateway to a life that is immortal and blessed and in a sense more real. There is a form of spiritual death, and the godless are seen as already dead in the soul[93].

Rather than a corporeal state after death, Philo builds on the belief that the soul is composed of the same matter as the stars and heavenly bodies:

---

[91] According to 374, only the soul survives death, since this is seen as God reclaiming his «loan». The souls of the just are glorified and elevated to high heavenly positions. Eventually, these souls then return to «chaste bodies» or «new habitations». This is the resurrection, and takes place at the «revolution of the ages». Apparently there is no continuity with the earthly body. H.C.C. CAVALLIN, *Life After Death*, 142-143.

[92] H.C.C. CAVALLIN, *Life After Death*, 135.

[93] The first view is expressed in the *Vita Contemplativa 13*, while the notion that the godless are dead in the soul is found in *SpecLeg I 345*. One who is enslaved to passions and to evil is viewed as existing in Hell, even while still living. It is not clear whether the wicked are annihilated by death or whether they undergo eternal torments. H.C.C. CAVALLIN, *Life After Death*, 136.

ether. After death, then, the just are transformed and glorified into the likeness of stars and angels (*Sacr* 5)[94].

Two contradictory views are held in tension: on the one hand, death is seen as the moment of change and liberation of the soul from the body; on the other hand, traditional Jewish eschatology with an End time and a restoration of Israel is still hoped for. Although there are no polemics against the resurrection of the body, neither is there any real evidence of belief. It appears that the immortality of the soul is something taken for granted[95].

2.3.17 Wisdom of Solomon

The Wisdom of Solomon, coming from a Hellenistic milieu, does not provide much on the nature of the resurrection, but is rich in the life-giving power of the ethical life and communion with God. According to Cavallin, 1,15 is the guiding principle in WisSol's doctrine of the im-mortality of the soul: «Justice (δικαιοσύνη) is immortal (ἀθάνατος)». Righteousness has a life-giving power of its own, and is almost the same as communion with God: «To know thee is perfect righteousness, and to acknowledge thy power is the root of immortality» (15:3). This knowl-edge of the true God is always contrasted with wickedness and idolatry. Eternal life, then, begins in this life with justice, righteousness and com-munion with God. Immortality is not an inherent quality of the soul, but something given as a reward for righteousness. The identification of righteousness with immortality is made in several places (1,15; 3,4; 3,7). Immortality begins during the life of the righteous, and their death is not really death, since their relationship with God is never broken. It is inter-esting that wisdom and righteousness are nearly identical. It states in 6,18-19, that «To keep her laws is a warrant of immortality (ἀφθαρσία) and immortality brings a man near to God»[96].

---

[94] This identification of immortal souls with heavenly bodies is a theme found in several of Philo's texts. This casts some doubts on whether Philo held personal im-mortality: other places speak of leaving or getting out of oneself, and the analogy of music is used in such a way as to suggest a more impersonal form of immortality (Gig. 61; Exsecr 158). Cavallin believes these terms «probably cannot be taken univocally and literally, but should rather be understood as metaphorical language of the mystic». There is no reason why these terms cannot be taken literally; astral im-mortality was very much part of Hellenistic religiosity. H.C.C. CAVALLIN, *Life After Death*, 138.

[95] H.C.C. CAVALLIN, *Life After Death*, 139.

[96] H.C.C. CAVALLIN, *Life After Death*, 130. ἀφθαρσία corresponds to the He-brew חיים and is a result of obeying divine law.

The soul alone continues to exist after death. The foolish think that the death of the body is the total reality, and that there is no reward and punishment. Immediately after death, the souls are «in God's hand» and «at peace». Immortality and glorification remain a hope for the time of the visitation, but still there is no real mention of the resurrection:

> But the souls of the just are in God's hand, and torment shall not touch them. In the eyes of the foolish men they seemed to be dead [...] But they are at peace [...] they have a sure hope of immortality. (3,1-4)

> In the moment of their visitation they will kindle into flame, like sparks that sweep through stubble, they will be judges and rulers over the nations of the world [...][97]

The eschatology represented by WisSol seems to be comprised of two stages: for the righteous, there is a period of peace in God's hands immediately following death, followed by the glorified state after the visitation (ἐπισκοπή) which consists of judgment, reward and punishment[98].

The punishment of the wicked and ungodly is described in 4,17ff in a way that implies a resurrection for judgment and a continued existence for both good and wicked, as well as an eschatological confrontation between the two groups:

> Then the righteous man shall take his stand, full of assurance, to confront those who oppressed him...at the sight of him there will be terror and confusion, and they will be beside themselves to see him so unexpectedly safe home...they will say among themselves: This is he whom once we held as a laughingstock. To think that he is now counted one of the sons of God and his portion is among the saints[99].

A passage in 8,19-21 asserts that wisdom is a gift from God, as is immortality, for those who are willing to receive it:

> As a child I was born to excellence, and a noble soul fell to my lot; or rather, I myself was noble, and I entered into an unblemished body but I

---

[97] This scene of future glorification of the righteous may reflect Jewish apocalyptic thought, with the fire being associated with judgment. H.C.C. CAVALLIN, *Life After Death*, 127.

[98] This represents the end of human history and is when the resurrection of the dead is expected to take place, although it is not mentioned. It seems to suggest an intermediate state for the dead, but the idea is not developed. There are, however, other models in use in WisSol. A passage in 4,7 alludes to the assumption of Enoch in Gen 5,24, and compares the death of a righteous man to this assumption. H.C.C. CAVALLIN, *Life After Death*, 127-128.

[99] The importance in this scene is not the restoration of the body, but vindication of the righteous. H.C.C. CAVALLIN, *Life After Death*, 129.

saw that there was no way to gain possession of her except by gift of God.[100]

The Wisdom of Solomon teaches unequivocally life after death and reward and punishment. It is completely silent on the issue of the resurrection. Immortality is given after death to the righteous; their lives are preserved by God. They are glorified, transformed, and given angelic glory, after which they will live in close union with God. The book teaches some sort of future eschatological confrontation between the righteous and their oppressors, but it is not clear whether the wicked are living or dead[101].

2.3.18 Joseph and Asenath

The story of Joseph and Asenath makes novel use of resurrection terminology, in that salvation from death rather than after death is meant. All of the language normally used of life after death or resurrection is used in connection with the reception of a proselyte into the community and his participation in the sacred meal. Real death and eternal life in the usual sense are not mentioned. This is the same sort of realized eschatology held in the Qumran community, and is of interest in a study of 1 Cor, since it appears, according to several scholars, that the Corinthians were guilty of living out a realized eschatology connected with baptism. The meal is described in 15,3-4[102].

Of interest in the above passage is that the resurrection language is used «from this day» signifying entrance into the community and partici-

---

[100] This passage seems to suggest Platonic influences in the form of a doctrine of the preexistence of the soul. Most modern scholars disagree, pointing out that this would conflict with the principle that immortality is not an inherent quality of the soul but is a reward for righteousness. This analysis, however, imposes a modern structure on the text. We have seen that many contradictory ideas are held in tension with one another in the same work. Given the Hellenistic background of Wisdom, it is perfectly possible that preexistence of the soul is signified. Other passages, such as 9,15, also seem to reflect a Platonic influence. H.C.C. CAVALLIN, *Defeat of Death*, 131.

[101] H.C.C. CAVALLIN, *Life After Death*, 132-133.

[102] «Your name has been written in the book of life and shall not be blotted out forever. But from this day you will be renewed and refashioned and requickened, and you will eat the bread of life and drink the cup of immortality and be anointed with the unction of incorruption». This is a Jewish legend that has been extensively reworked. Due to the description of ritual sacred meals, this work was thought to be Christian, although the tendency now is to see it in light of the Jewish sacred meal and the Hellenistic mystery religions, with perhaps some Christian interpolations. Given the time and milieu, it might be rather difficult to draw definitive lines between Jewish, Christian and mystery religion elements (the same difficulty with the Psalms of Solomon). H.C.C. CAVALLIN, *Defeat of Death*, 155-158.

pation in its common rituals. It is not clear whether this is a Christian interpolation. However, many of these terms, such as ἀνακαινίζειν (renew) and ζωοποιῆσαι (quicken) were used both in mystery cults and in
early Christian baptismal liturgies.

The role of quickening is given to the God of Israel, as in 27,8 and
8,10:

> Lord, my God, who quickened me and delivered me from death, you who
> said to me: «Your soul shall live for ever», save me from these men. Lord
> God of my father Israel, the Most High and the Mighty, who quickened all
> things and called them from the darkness to the light and from error to truth
> and from death to life, may you yourself, O Lord, quicken and bless this
> virgin. And renew with your holy spirit, and reform her with your hidden
> arm, and quicken her with your life that she may eat the bread of your life
> and drink the cup of your blessing. Let her whom you chose enter the rest
> which you have prepared for your elect[103].

3. The Role of the Messiah in Jewish Apocalyptic

Schürer represents the classic synthetic and developmental approach to
the study of the Messiah. According to this approach, the concept of the
Messiah underwent a long period of development which continued
through the NT period[104].

By the time of Christ, there were several expectations concerning the
coming of the Messiah involving the end of the age, cosmic upheavals,
and judgment[105].

This will be followed by the destruction of hostile powers and more
specifically, the gentile world powers[106].

---

[103] H.C.C. CAVALLIN, *Defeat of Death*, 157.

[104] In pre-exilic Israel, the Messiah was thought to be the just king who would pu-
rify the nation and society of all evil elements. As the concept developed, his role
became more universal and transcendent: he would be the judge and ruler of Israel
and would usher in a new world or age completely different from the present one, an
age completely under the dominion of God. E. SCHÜRER, *Jewish People*, 488-544.

[105] The expectations varied: a final ordeal and confusion or birth pangs (Hos
13,13; Dan 12,1 Matt 24,8; Mark 13,8; Sibyl 3,795-807; 2 Macc 5,2-3; 1QM 12,9;
19,1-2; *BJ* VI,5; 4 Ez 5,1-13; 4 Ez 6,17-28; Bar 70,2-8; 4 Ez 6,24; 9,1-12; 13,29-
31); the coming of Elijah as a precursor (Mal 3,23-4; Eccl 43,10-11; Matt 17,10;
Mark 9,11; Matt 11,14; 16,14; Mark 6,15; 8,28; Luke 9,8.19; John 1,21); and the
last attack by the hostile powers (4 Ez 13,33; 1 En 90,16; 1QM 15-19; Sibyl 663 ff).
This assault by hostile powers is sometimes led by an adversary or antitype of the
Messiah, who is represented in the NT literature as the antichrist and as a satanic antitype of Melchizedek in the Qumran literature (1 John 2,18.22; 4,3; 2 John 7; 2 Bar
40; 2 Thess 2; Rev 13; 11QMelech). E. SCHÜRER, *Jewish People*, II, 514-516.525.

Based upon the promise of a new heaven on earth in Isa 65,17 and Isa 66,22, messianism of this period expected that the coming of the age would renew the world (Matt 19,28; Rev 21,1; 2 Pet 3,13). There was a distinction made between the present world העולם הזה and the world to come העולם הבא in much of Jewish literature, and this is reflected in the NT (Matt 12,32; Mark 10,30; Luke 18,30; Eph 1,21)[107].

But the role of the Messiah is hard to define and is by no means consistent and unequivocal. In the Jewish apocalyptic tradition, the Messiah played an ambiguous and at times minor role in the actual events taking place at the change of the ages, especially the final judgment. Rather than a mediator of salvation, he was a Messianic agent of God, exercising judgment or authority on God's behalf, at times exercising an active role in the final judgment, while at other times taking a seemingly passive one[108].

It is important to avoid preconceptions concerning the Messiah, and to distinguish carefully between the Messiah of different time periods, messianic movements, and genres of literature. According to Charlesworth, most of our conceptions concerning the Messiah, both in the Jewish tradition and in early Christianity, crumble and fall under the scrutiny of modern scholarship. We must beware of making any facile statement

---

[106] The destruction of the hostile powers is described in Sibyl 3,622; PssSol 17,27,39; Isa 11,4 and Philo *Praem* 16; the destruction of the gentile world powers in 4 Ez 12,32-3; 35-38; ApocBar 39,7-40,2; 70,2-6; 1 En 46,4-6; 52,4-9; 49,3-4; 45,3; 55,4; 61,8-10; 62; 69. E. SCHÜRER, *Jewish People*, 526-527.

[107] There was some confusion concerning the messianic age: in some literature it is seen as belonging to the future world, while other sources depict it as already existing. Some rabbinic literature places it between this world and the next; this tendency is reflected in Bar 74,2-3. E. SCHÜRER, *Jewish People*, 537-538.

[108] Kreitzer notes repeatedly the blurring of roles or the «referential confusion» between God and his messianic agent, especially with regard to judgment. He states that the functional overlap between God and his Messianic agent become so blurred that the boundaries separating the two are no longer clear. Examples of the passive role: 4 Ez 7,26-30; the active: 12,31-34 and 12,21-49. Even when a role is given to the Messiah, however, it is «always within the context of God's ultimate judgment and authority» (L.J. KREITZER, *Paul's Eschatology*, 60.80.90). This is corroborated by Schürer's observation that the Messiah is absent from the AsMoses, and in 1 En 90,37 he appears after the judgment. In these two cases, God himself pronounces judgment (E. SCHÜRER, *Jewish People*, II, 526); Although important, the figure of the Messiah is not a *sine qua non* for apocalyptic works: «But just as in the Old Testament the ideal leader is not necessarily or always associated with the Golden Age, so in the apocalyptic literature the Messiah is not indispensable to the eschatological kingdom. Indeed, in a fairly considerable number of writings of the period (apocalyptic and otherwise) in which the messianic hope is in the forefront, the figure of the Messiah is not even mentioned» (D.S. RUSSELL, *Method and Message*, 309).

concerning the Messiah, especially when it seems to represent conventional wisdom[109].

A survey of Jewish apocalyptic literature reveals that there are a variety of images and ideas concerning the Messiah or a messianic figure, and many of them are contradictory. A study of the Jewish intertestamental documents that actually contain the word «Messiah» discloses that on all of the crucial question concerning the role of the Messiah, there is a lack of uniformity and much contradiction[110].

---

[109] Charlesworth summarizes the results of modern scholarship as follows: The term «the Messiah» does not appear in the Old Testament. In the OT, «the Anointed One» denotes a prophet, a priest, and especially a king. There are some very important passages in the OT that are implicitly messianic, such as Ps 2, 2 Sam 7, Isa 7, 9, and 11, Zech 9, and Dan 9,26. He adds a caution, however: these passages may only be defined as «messianic» as long as this does not mean the prediction of an apocalyptic, eschatological «Messiah». These passages were, however, interpreted in this messianic fashion for approximately two centuries before the destruction of the temple. The term «the Messiah» is rare in the Jewish literature from roughly 250 B.C.E. to 200 C.E., but it does appear more often during this period than in any other. The preaching of Jesus focuses on the coming of God's kingdom rather than on the coming of the Messiah. Jesus never proclaimed himself to be the Messiah, and seems to have rejected Peter's confession that he was the Christ as satanic, fearing that his mission and message might be judged according to human ideas and preconceptions of the Messiah. A closer reading, however, shows that Jesus reacted against Peter's denial of the Messiah's mission to suffer and die. The disciples do not appear to have been interested in the Messiah as they are depicted in the gospels. According to Acts 3,20 and Paul's letters, «Christ» was a proper name for Jesus of Nazareth. In the gospels it is a proper name or title (Matt 1,1, Mark 1,1, Luke 2,11, John 1,17). (pp. 11-12) All of this can of course be argued, and the debate continues, but at least this should prevent us from making casual statements about the Messiah or Jewish messianic expectations (J.H. CHARLESWORTH, ed., The Messiah, 9-35). This caution is echoed by Collins in his study of the messianic imagery of Qumran. J.J. COLLINS, The Scepter and the Star, 3.

[110] The documents in question are four, the Psalms of Solomon, the Parables of Enoch, 4 Ez and 2 Bar, which date roughly from the period 50 B.C. to 100 A.D. Several questions are addressed to these documents: 1) Is it possible to discern the ancestry of the Messiah? Only PssSol 17,21-34 and 4 Ez 12,31-34 answer in an affirmative manner. Messianic ideas are not necessarily Davidic. There are also groups who linked the Messiah with Enoch or Moses. 2) Is the Messiah a militant warrior? This widespread assumption finds support in 2 Bar 72,6, but is negated by PssSol 17,21-33 and 4 Ez 13,4-11, which stress the non-military nature of his intervention. 3) Will the Messiah purge Jerusalem? Definitely, says PssSol 17,21-33, but not so according to 4 Ez 7,28-29. 4) Why will the Messiah destroy the nations? The Parables of Enoch insist that this will be because they are full of sinners who deny God (1 En 45,2), while other writings claim that it is because they are «unlawful nations» ruled by «unrighteous rulers» or because they rule Jerusalem (PssSol 17,21-24; 2 Bar 72). 5) Will the Messiah condemn sinners? Yes, according to PssSol 17 and 4 Ez 12,32, but not even mentioned in 4 Ez 7,28-29. 6) Is the Messiah always portrayed as a king? PssSol 17,21-33 portrays him as Israel's king, and yet the beginning and

In fact, the startling conclusion is that there is «no single, discernible role description for a "Messiah" into which a historical figure like Jesus could be fit. Rather, each group which entertained a messianic hope interpreted "Messiah" in light of its historical experiences and reinterpreted Scripture accordingly». Rather than imposing a modern precision, he feels that we should respect the ambiguity, as it represents richness and vitality rather than weakness or chaos[111].

4. Summary

Although there is great diversity in these texts, there are some general points of similarity. Death is not part of God's plan: it is the result of

---

end of this psalm insists that God alone is king. 7) Will the Messiah be the eschatological judge? Most of the texts, such as PssSol 17,21-33; 4 Ez 12,31-34 and 2 Bar 40,1-2 hold that he certainly will be the judge, but 4 Ez 7,31-44 and 7,113-14 state that it is only *after* the death of the Messiah and the primeval silence that the judgment will take place. 8) Will the Messiah gather a holy people? There are varied answers: he does in PssSol 17,21-23, and 2 Bar 40, 4 Ez 7,140 and 8,3 give us the chilling news that there will be only a very few people in the new age. In many passages, however, the Messiah performs no functions at all, especially in 4 Ez 7,28-29 and 2 Bar 30,1-4. 9) Will the Messiah inaugurate a new age? This is the case in PssSol 17, but in 4 Ez 7, the Messiah comes between these two ages, and his death appears to have no redemptive value. Charlesworth suggests that we must get over our reluctance to speak of a Messiah that is relatively functionless. 10) Will the Messiah assist in the resurrection of the dead? The Enoch tradition is very ambiguous: 1 En 51,1 says that Sheol and Hell will give back the dead, without mentioning the Messiah. In other places in 1 En, there is reference to «he» who will choose righteous ones. It is unclear whether this refers to the Messiah or the Lord of the Spirits. Both 2 Bar 30 and 4 Ez 7,28-29 hold that both the righteous and unrighteous will be resurrected *after* the Messiah dies; the Messiah is not the one who will raise the dead. 11) Will the Messiah establish a permanent kingdom? This idea derives from some interpretations of Isa 7, 9, and 11; and Isa 42-45, and this is reflected in PssSol 17,21-32. In 2 Bar 36-40 and 4 Ez 7, however, the messianic kingdom will be finite, being part of the limited messianic kingdom preceding the eschaton. Contrary to this, the kingdom will be eschatological and eternal according to 1 En 38, 48-52 and 2 Bar 73-74. 12) Will the Messiah be human? Again, there are varying views: 4 Ez 12,31-34 and 2 Bar both portray the Messiah as a king who embodies all of the peoples' hopes and dreams, while 4 Ez 13,3-14,9 describes him as one who rises from the depths of the sea. As is obvious from this summary, it is difficult if not impossible to make any absolute statement concerning the role or nature of the Messiah. J.H. CHARLESWORTH, *Messiah*, 19-24.

111 «We must not claim as clear what is intentionally imprecise. We must heed the words of the discerning philosophical mathematician, F.P. Ramsey, when he warns that the "chief danger" of the scholar is to treat "what is vague as if it were precise" [...] Krister Stendahl [...] recently cautioned against the ancient and modern "authority figures [...] who claim more precision in their definitions than is good for theology"» (J.H. CHARLESWORTH, *Messiah*, xv, 9).

human sin and is opposed to God. This age is rapidly drawing to a cli-
mactic end. The new age will be a radical break from the past, with a
commensurate change in human existence. Although some texts speak of
only rewards for the righteous, rewards for them and punishment for the
wicked is usually in order in most of the texts. Many texts speak of an
immediate post-mortem retribution, an intermediate state, followed by
universal judgment later on. The texts are silent on the fate of the wicked
or non-believers[112].

One of the most persistent and dominant symbols in Jewish apocalyptic
literature is that of the two ages or the approaching change of ages. The
present age is rapidly coming to a close, and the coming of the new age
will have drastic cosmic consequences. In many instances, this means the
destruction of the old physical order: fiery conflagration, return to primeval silence, etc. The new age means a created order that is transformed and renewed[113].

This change of ages also has very strong ethical and spiritual consequences. The new order is not for all: it is for the righteous. The cosmic
reversal or change of ages is the time for the rendering of accounts, for
reward and punishment. Vindication of the righteous is at the very core
of Jewish apocalyptic. Righteousness means fidelity to God, especially in
the form of obedience to the Law, in the face of suffering and persecution. In some cases, especially in the two-way theology, fidelity to the
Law while living in a sinful milieu is the mark of righteousness. At
times, this vindication means a destruction of evil or opposing cosmic
forces. In others, the punishment of the wicked is called for, although
many written works don't mention the fate of the wicked. In nearly all of
the works, however, there is the promise of rewards for the righteous. At

---

[112] De Boer finds in all of the Jewish apocalyptic literature three notions of death,
all united by the concept of relationship of humans to God: «Death characterizes this
relationship as one of *separation*. By definition, death (physical, moral and eschatological) is not remediable through human effort». The term «perish» does not mean
total annihilation, but exclusion from the eschatological life. Physical death is the
first category; this causes separation from God and the cessation of life with all of its
possibilities. All views of the resurrection begin with this basic OT understanding of
death. The second category is the application of physical death to the ethical realm:
sinful or unrighteous behavior is the cause of spiritual or moral death, and can apply
to people who are still physically alive. This is also found in the OT, especially in
the wisdom literature. The third type of death is the eschatological death associated
with perdition: exclusion from God's presence in the age to come, following the final
judgment. This meaning of death is found only in Jewish apocalyptic eschatology.
M.C. DE BOER, *Defeat of Death*, 83-85.

[113] Vielhauer states that the eschatological dualism of the two-ages is essential to
apocalyptic. P. VIELHAUER, «Apocalyptic in Early Christianity», 542-569.

times, a glorified life on a transformed earth is implied, while at other times, a glorified life with God or the angels is described. Ethical decision is in order: the individual is challenged to choose which side he wishes to be on, light or darkness[114].

It is somewhat surprising that the resurrection of the physical body in the later Christian sense does not seem to have been widely held. Even life after death itself was not always a central theme in every Jewish theological text from Paul's time. In fact, many texts are completely silent on this matter. Perhaps one of the reasons for this is a different focus or emphasis. Instead of individual salvation or the afterlife being the issue at stake, it was most often the justice and faithfulness of God and the vindication of the believer and his fidelity to the Law or to godly ways. If these values were affirmed, and the believer was assured that in some way good would be rewarded and evil punished, the exact means and details were perhaps of secondary importance[115].

Their are certain texts which hold this belief in a clear and literal manner; e.g., 2 Macc. Many are the implicit claims for the resurrection of the body: in order to be punished or tormented, it would seem that a body is necessary, unless there is another way of undergoing this experience. By far the most common beliefs are the immortality of the soul (4 Macc) and a sort of glorification and transformation of the human person either upon death or at the judgment. In the case of Maccabees, it is interesting that both deal with the time of persecution, but reassure the reader in different ways: in the first, martyrs are assured of the literal restoration of their physical bodies; while in the second, the body is not held to be important and the importance of rising above pain and emotions is stressed.

In 1 Cor 15, Paul appears to be in the Jewish apocalyptic tradition when he balances or reconciles two traditions: he on the one hand defends the resurrection of the body at the parousia, while on the other hand insists that it is not a mere resuscitation of a corpse, but involves transformation and a new order of physical existence. This is not carelessness or lack of rigor, but the way of expressing theology common to

---

[114] Although the new age often involves the destruction of hostile powers, which is part of what de Boer calls the «track one» or cosmological-apocalyptic eschatology, there is a very strong tendency to stress the second type, or forensic, type of eschatology. People will be judged for their deeds and rewarded or punished accordingly; fidelity to the Law or the ways of God is of paramount importance. M.C. DE BOER, «Paul and Jewish Apocalyptic», 169-190.

[115] Silent texts include Sir, Tob, Aristeas, 1 Bar, 1 Macc, 2 Macc, 3 Ezra, AssMos, and MartIs. H.C.C. CAVALLIN, *Life After Death*, 193.

that milieu. In fact, Cavallin finds no single Jewish doctrine about the afterlife or the resurrection in the texts of this period. A skillful mixture of symbols and languages were used in these texts to convey various messages: the vindication of the martyred dead; individual ethical responsibility; the importance of obeying the commandments; God's victory over evil and injustice.

There can be found in the Pauline and deutero-Pauline writings the same juxtaposition of images and symbols, and as will be shown in the following chapter, trying to define what Paul held on the resurrection, final judgment or salvation is not much easier than trying to do so for the authors of the intertestamental period. Studying 1 Cor 15 against the backdrop of Jewish apocalyptic literature will help us to understand what the defeat of the inimical powers and death and the fullness of God's conquest might have meant for Paul. Apocalyptic literature and eschatology is uniquely suited to a cosmological interpretation of the Christ event and a communal salvation for believers that depends on God's initiative and intervention in Christ.

CHAPTER IV

The Apocalyptic Nature of 1 Cor 15

A comparison with the material drawn from the survey in the last chapter indicates that Paul inherited a great deal from the apocalyptic tradition. But it may be asked: Which symbols does Paul use and how does he hold all of these various images and symbols together? Are these concepts, images and symbols taken directly into the NT, or are they modified in any way? What is Paul's unique contribution to the apocalyptic eschatology of the NT? And more specifically, is there evidence of this apocalyptic inheritance in 1 Cor 15, and if so, how is it presented[1]?

1. Paul's Use of Intertestamental Apocalyptic Images

In the NT itself, there are relatively few descriptions of the eschaton. The eschaton is expressed in terms of the parousia, being taken up with the Lord, judgment, retribution, eschatological fire. These eschatological symbols and expressions are not necessarily inherently «apocalyptic», but as we saw, they can be considered apocalyptic when they are linked together with the characteristics discussed in the last chapter. Some of these eschatological and apocalyptic characteristics include the concept of the two ages, the parousia, the Day of the Lord and the wrath of God, revelations of God's hidden plan, determinism, and angelology.

In the synoptics, there is the well-known apocalyptic passage in Mark 13 (= Matt 24, Luke 21). In the Pauline letters, there are descriptions of judgment, retribution, eschatological fire, or the return of Christ with the rising of Christians found in 1 Cor 3,10-15, 2 Cor 5,10, 1 Thess 4,13-18, 2 Thess 1,5-10, Gal 6,7-9, and Rom 2. In the catholic epistles, 1 Pet 4 and 2 Pet 3,10-13 provide vivid descriptions of the approaching end

---

[1] According to Beker, Paul's apocalyptic outlook derives from his Pharisaic background rather than his conversion. J.C. BEKER, *Paul the Apostle*, 144.

and the dissolution of the elements and fire that will accompany it. Probably the most detailed and uncompromising description is in Rev 20. It is of interest that in every case, there is mention of judgment and punishment for sinners[2].

One of the most persistent and dominant symbols in Jewish apocalyptic literature is that of the two ages or the approaching change of ages. The present age is rapidly coming to a close, and the coming of the new age will have drastic cosmic consequences. In many instances, this means the destruction of the old physical order: fiery conflagration, return to primeval silence, etc. The new age means a created order that is transformed and renewed. It derives its apocalyptic slant from the urgency and imminence of the expiration of the old age and the birth of the new and its being linked with other eschatological symbols in an apocalyptic cluster. Paul makes extensive use of what Vielhauer calls eschatological dualism: there are references to «this age» (ὁ αἰὼν οὗτος) in Rom 12,2; 2 Cor 4,4; Gal 1,4 (present evil age). De Boer also notes the following: although Paul does not use the phrase «the age to come» (ὁ αἰὼν ὁ μέλλων or ἐρχόμενος) as in Matt 12,32; Mark 10,30; Luke 18,30; Eph 1,21; Heb 6,5, his constant references to «this age» imply a new one to come. Additionally, phrases such as «Kingdom of God» (Rom 14,7; Gal 5,21; 1 Thess 2,12); «eternal life» (Rom 2,7; 5,21; 6,22.23; Gal 6,8) and «new creation» (2 Cor 5,17; Gal 6,15) are all indicative of the same sort of eschatological dualism. First Corinthians is well represented in both categories. «This age» is referred to in 1 Cor 1,20; 2,6.8; 3,18, while the «Kingdom of God» is found in 1 Cor 4,20; 6,9; 15,24.50. In the first instance, «this age» is used as a pejorative reference to worldly wisdom, the same wisdom that is foolishness in the eyes of God and which he has ne-

---

[2] The first chapter of 2 Thess echoes some of the classical passages from intertestamental literature. Written to strengthen and encourage those under persecution, it assures them in vivid and uncompromising terms that God will vindicate them, «when the Lord Jesus is revealed from heaven with his mighty angels in flaming fire, inflicting vengeance upon those who do not know God and upon those who do not obey the gospel of our Lord Jesus. They shall suffer the punishment of eternal destruction and exclusion from the presence of the Lord and from the glory of his might» (1,7-9). In speculating about the time of the coming of the Lord, chapter 2 warns enigmatically of the mystery of lawlessness, a time of delusion and deception permitted by God in which many will turn from the truth. This will be led by one who opposes himself to God and claims worship for himself, a true Antichrist figure. He will be slain by the breath of the mouth of Jesus at his coming, and those who followed him will be condemned. It is the very starkness of this passage that has led many to question the authenticity of this letter, since Paul tempered and reinterpreted the apocalyptic tradition in various ways. We examine this passage because it represents a reflection of one of the Pauline communities.

gated through the cross. The Kingdom of God is something that is denied to sinners guilty of a long list of sins listed in 1 Cor 6,9, as well as to «flesh and blood» as stated in 15,50. This is the same kingdom handed over to God the Father in 15,24[3].

Beker states that one of the ways in which Paul differs from traditional Jewish apocalyptic is his lack of emphasis on the doctrine of the two ways and his belief that the end time has already begun, having been initiated with the resurrection of Christ, which has «strongly modified the dualistic structure of normal apocalyptic thought». The tension of the «already» and «not yet» present in much of Paul's writings stems from this belief. The «age to come» is already present; the «new age» is present in the old. Christ is the «firstfruits», and the Spirit has been given as an earnest or down payment (2 Cor 1,22) of what will be experienced in the future at the time of the resurrection[4].

In the Pauline and deutero-Pauline literature, the wrath of God is another link in the apocalyptic chain. This wrath is the expression of God's justice in the face of human sin and it must be discharged or vindicated. The background of this concept is found in passages such as Isa 13,9; Zeph 1,15; 2,2; Dan 8,19; Jub 24,28; 1 En 62,12; 1QH 15,17; 1QS 4,12-13; 1QM 3,9. The terms for anger, ὀργή and θυμός are often used in the NT to express divine anger, especially when referring to the eschatological day of judgment which will bring about the destruction of evil. It expresses God's judgment both within history and at the final judgment. This concept is used extensively in 1 Thess to encourage the community and foster vigilance and fidelity. Christ, as the Son from heaven, delivers believers from the wrath to come (1,10); God's wrath has come upon the Jews (2,16); and although the day of the Lord comes like a thief in the night (5,2), God has not destined believers for wrath (5,9)[5].

---

[3] Vielhauer states that the eschatological dualism of the two-ages is essential to apocalyptic (P. VIELHAUER, «Apocalyptic in Early Christianity», 549-550); M.C. DE BOER, *Defeat of Death*, 22-23.

[4] More particularly, he does not use the traditional apocalyptic terminology «this age» in conjunction with the «age to come.» Beker notes that Paul «does not engage in apocalyptic timetables, descriptions of the architecture of heaven, or accounts of demons and angels. He does not relish the rewards of the blessed or delight in the torture of the wicked» (J.C. BEKER, *Paul the Apostle*, 145). Branick draws attention to these tensions and is of the opinion that Paul is not totally apocalyptic, and that the transition to a realized eschatology is already present in Paul as in other NT writings such as John and Luke-Acts. V. BRANICK, «Apocalyptic Paul?», 664-675.

[5] S.H. TRAVIS, «Wrath of God». The concept is seldom used in this sense in the Synoptics, appearing only in passages such as Matt 3,7-10; Luke 21,23; and Mark 13. In the Pauline tradition the term is used 18 times: as occurring at the final judgment, Rom 2,5; 2,8; 5,9; 1 Thess 1,10; 5,9; already experienced by sinners, 1 Thess

Part of the inheritance from intertestamental apocalyptic literature and another link in the apocalyptic chain are the terms «day of Yahweh» (from the OT) and «day of the Messiah». The day is heralded by supernatural portents and «tribulations». At times God himself intervenes on the day, while at other times his Messiah establishes a kingdom on earth. The kingdom of God and the kingdom of the Messiah are at times identified with each other, while at other times the earthly kingdom of the Messiah is followed by a transcendental one of God. Again, there is this ambiguity between God and his Messianic agent. In the NT, several analogous terms are used: «day of Christ» (Phil 1,10; 2,16); «day of Jesus Christ» (Phil 1,6); «day of Our Lord Jesus Christ» (1 Cor 1,8); «day of the Lord Jesus» (1 Cor 5,5; 2 Cor 1,14). Additionally, there are uses of similar expressions such as «day of the Lord» (1 Thess 5,2; 2 Thess 2,2) in a context which makes it clear that it refers to Jesus[6].

Angelology, which is very characteristic of Jewish apocalyptic eschatology, is also found in the Pauline writings, although without descriptions or reports of any verbal revelations from them. This includes both angelic beings laboring on the side of God, and those demonic forces intent on controlling creation and subjugating humanity. Paul refers to Sa-

---

2,16; Rom 1,18-32; as the wrath *of God*, Rom 1,18; Eph 5,6; Col 3,6; Rom 3,5; 9,22; 12,19. Some scholars (notably Hanson and Dodd) have spoken of wrath as something impersonal, a law of cause and effect, an idea with which Travis and Best take issue. The term, rather than describing a «feeling» on the part of God, signifies a «justifiable reaction of a loving and faithful God toward his disobedient people [...] it denotes God's steadfast attitude as a judge of Israel's breach of the covenant», Paul takes this concept and associates it with the cosmic judgment of God of the cosmos and humanity as a whole, against every sort of idolatry and sinfulness. The term θυμός is used in the ordinary sense throughout the NT; the apocalyptic use of this term is limited to the Book of Revelation 12,12; 14,8; 14,10; 14,19; 15,1; 15,7; 16,1; 16,19; 18,3; 19,15, and describes either the wrath of God or the wrath built up as a result of human sin. J. FITZMYER, *Romans*, 107-108; E. BEST, *Thessalonians*, 84-85.

6 R.H. HIERS, «Day of Christ». Paul and deutero-Pauline authors use the term «that day» (1 Thess 5,4; 2 Thess 1,10; 2,3; 2 Tim 1,12,18; 4,8) and «the day» (Rom 2,16 and 1 Cor 3,13) in conjunction with other phrases that make it clear that Jesus is intended. In the two Thessalonian letters, the opening address refers to God the Father and the Lord Jesus Christ. In the rest of the two letters, «Lord» is used of Christ, while «Father» or «God» is used to refer to God the Father. Additionally, passages such as 2 Thess 2,1-2 make it even more clear: 2,1 refers to the «coming of our Lord Jesus Christ», while v. 2 speaks of those who claim that the «day of the Lord» has come. The concept of the Day of the Lord is seen by von Rad as the «very heart of the prophetic eschatology», being based upon passages such as Amos 5,18-20; Isa 13,6-8; 34,8; Ez 7,7-10; Joel 1,1-11 and Zeph 1,7-18 (G. VON RAD, *Old Testament Theology*, II, 119). This older prophetic tradition is adapted for the new eschatology of the writers of apocalyptic literature. D.S. RUSSELL, *Method and Message*, 92.272.

tan as the adversary of God and Christ in Rom 16,20; 7,5; 2 Cor 2,11; 11,14; 12,7; 1 Thess 2,18; 2 Cor 6,14; 1 Thess 3,5; and to angels in Rom 8,38; 2 Cor 11,14; 12,7; Gal 1,8; 3,19; 4,14; 1 Thess 4,16; «of God» Gal 4:14 or «of Satan» 2 Cor 12,7. Paul speaks of Satan as an adversary in 1 Cor 5,5; 7,5, while speaking of angels in a positive sense in 1 Cor 4,9; 6,3; 11,10; 13,1. As discussed in the last chapter, the NT contains many terms such as ἀρχαί and ἐξουσίαι (Rom 8,38; Eph 3,10; 6,12; Col 1,16; 2,15; 1 Cor 15,24; Eph 1,21; Col 2,10); δυνάμεις (Rom 8,38; 1 Cor 15,24; Eph 1,21); and many other terms that are probably synonymous. These terms are usually negative and hostile in nature. For Paul and many of his contemporaries, the heavens were teeming with supernatural enemies or friends, and vv. 24 and 26 of 1 Cor 15 may be read against this background. According to Beker, Paul believes that the principle apocalyptic forces at work are «those ontological powers that determine the human situation within the context of God's created order and comprise the "field" of death, sin, the law and the flesh»[7].

Paul utilizes the concept of the disintegration of the world and change of the ages in his theology. As in the Jewish apocalyptic tradition, he emphasizes the ethical aspects of the change of the ages: to encourage the community in the face of suffering and persecution (Rom 8,18-25); to encourage the practice of celibacy so that the believer can prepare himself for the coming changes (1 Cor 7,25-35; and as a sanction for certain unacceptable ethical behavior (1 Cor 6,9-10 and Gal 5,21). According to Beker, Paul again modifies traditional apocalyptic thought by recasting the view of the escalation of evil the last times. This is particularly evident in the way the so-called «messianic woes» are portrayed; they are not merely endured, but gloried in, since they show God's power already evident amidst suffering[8].

As in much of apocalyptic, hope is an essential part of Paul's theology – not just hope in general, for this is scarcely apocalyptic, but hope in the blessings inherent in the kingdom of God. This would be centered on the glory of the coming new age (Rom 5,2; 8,18); the redemption of the

---

[7] Referring to page 269 of Russell's *Method and Message*, de Boer concludes that Jewish apocalyptic eschatology is reflected in Paul, and it involves a «cosmic drama in which divine and cosmic forces are at war» (M.C. DE BOER, *Defeat of Death*, 23). Cf. also J.C. BEKER, *Paul the Apostle*, 145.

[8] In his attempt to transcend the deadlocked debate on the apocalyptic nature of Paul's theology, Gager analyzes the *functional* nature rather than the content of Paul's «end-time» language. Although this results in some interesting observations on the nature of Paul's theology, it seems to dodge the question of whether these same functional uses could just as well be called apocalyptic. In his emphasis on this rather modern functional category, he does not ask what larger purpose or theology the functions serve. Merely avoiding the term does not solve the problem. J.G. GAGER, «Functional Diversity», 325-337.

body (Rom 8,23; the parousia (1 Thess 1,10); cosmic peace (Rom 5,1; Gal 5,5). Hope is very specific: it is centered on a spatial and temporal event; namely, the victory over evil and death in the parousia of Christ, as in 1 Cor 15,24[9].

To counter the negativity of the present age and the destructive effects of its disintegration, and to make the transition to the age to come, a symbol or concept is needed. How does the new age come into being, and how is the world transformed[10]?

It is, in fact, this concept of «newness» (καινός) that provides Paul with the apocalyptic image needed to transcend the destructive aspects of the passing away of the former age. «Newness» itself is not necessarily an apocalyptic concept, but may be considered so when placed in very sharp juxtaposition and contrast with the old, which is considered in an extremely negative light. It is also this newness which transcends and reconciles opposites. The theological and apocalyptic sense of the term is used in the NT to express «God's ultimate and definitive action in history», expressing such symbols as the new commandment (John 13,34; 1 John 2,7,8; 2 John 1,5), the new covenant (Luke 22,20; 1 Cor 11,25; 2 Cor 3,6; Heb 8,8,13; 9,15; 12,24), new creation (2 Cor 5,17; Gal 6,15), new earth (2 Pet 3,13; Rev 21,1), new Jerusalem (Rev 3,12; 21,2), new heavens (2 Pet 3,13 Rev 21,1), new hymn (Rev 5,9; 14,3), new name (Rev 2,17; 3,12), new person (Eph 2,15; 4,24; Col 3,10), new teaching (Mark 1,27), new tongues Mark 16,17). It is meant to contrast sharply with the old order, and to show the qualitative difference accomplished by God's intervention. Of particular interest for the individual believer

---

[9] Beker denies that Paul's apocalyptic dualism displays contempt for the world or otherworldliness; rather, it is determined by the Christ event. This Christ event did more than negate the old order. It initiated the hope for the transformation of a fallen creation that longs for redemption from its error and decay. J.C. BEKER, *Paul the Apostle*, 149.

[10] According to Martyn, Paul sometimes speaks by means of «apocalyptic antinomies», the prime examples being Gal 6,13ff and Gal 5,16-17. Paul transcends conflicting opposites by moving to a new level of reality, or «new creation». This new creation is marked by an «anthropological unity» in Christ, and does not have warring opposites. Martyn is seeking to prove that apocalyptic theology is found even in Galatians, which at first glance seems to be totally lacking this type of theology. The antinomy itself becomes an expression of apocalyptic, as it presupposes an imminent end to this world and a new creation. In the old world Jew and Greek, slave and freeman, male and female, etc., were opposites. In the new world, these opposites do not dissolve into a unity, but continue to exist, although rearranged into new patterns and relationships. Martyn's analysis is not universally accepted. These antinomies are not normally thought to be apocalyptic categories, and it remains to be proven if these examples given from Gal are such. J.L. MARTYN, «Apocalyptic Antinomies», 410-424.

and his salvation is its use to describe a new creation (καινὴ κτίσις; 2 Cor 5,17; Gal 6,15) and a new man or person (καινὸν ἄνθρωπον; Eph 2,15; 4,24). In this new creation, all enmity with God is abolished as well as the requirements of the law: it is in Christ that two are made one[11].

In chapter 3 it was stated that in the Jewish apocalyptic tradition, the Messiah was a very ambiguous, and at times rather passive figure. He was more of an agent than a mediator, and he was not the author of these eschatological events. Paul gives a particular twist to the existing ideas concerning the Messiah. It is in Christ that all contradictions and tensions are reconciled, and the limitations of the present age transcended. One participates in and becomes a new creation by being «in Christ» (ἐν Χριστῷ); this is the focal point of Paul's theology[12].

The destruction of enemies, the new age, the new creation, the judgment, and cosmic reconciliation are all embodied in the person of the Messiah himself. Christ becomes a representative of humanity rather than a substitute, and through what Hooker refers to as «interchange», humanity is identified with what Christ is and is saved from the wrath to come[13].

---

[11] There are also other instances in which the stark contrast of the message of Jesus with that of the old order is stressed by referring to new wine, new wineskins, new teaching, new cloth, etc.: Matt 9,17; 26,29; Mark 2,21,22; Luke 5,36-39. The compound word ἀνακαινόω is also used in the LXX to signify a renewing or regenerating action on the part of God (Ps 102,5; 103,30; Lam 5,21). In the first and last instance, the action describes a restoration of youthful strength and status before God. In Ps 103,30 it is God's spirit that creates and renews the face of the earth; Ps 104,30, «When thou sendest forth thy Spirit, they are created, and thou renewest the face of the ground»; Ps 103,5, «Who satisfies you with good as long as you live so that your youth is renewed like the eagle's». R.F. COLLINS, «New», in ABD, IV:1086-1088.

[12] These uses of the phrase «in Christ» fall into several categories: (a) salvation and redemption and transformation: Rom 3,24; 6,23; 1 Cor 1,30; 15,18.19.22; 2 Cor 5,17; Col 2,20; 3,1; 3,3; 1 Thess 4,16; Eph 1,12.20; 2,6.7.10.13; Eph 3,11; (b) revelation and mystical experience: 2 Cor 12,2; 3,14; (c) reconciliation between God and man: Rom 6,11; 8,1.2; 8,39; 2 Cor 2,14; Eph 1,1.3.10; Eph 3,6; 4,32; Gal 2,17; 3,14; 3,26.28; 5,6 (d) Christian life, growth, and living the truth: 1 Cor 3,1; 4,10; 4,15; 4,17; 15,31; 2 Cor 2,17; 12,19; Col 1,2.4.28; Phil 1,1.13.26; 2,1.5; 3,3.14; 4,7.19.21; 1 Thess 5,18; Rom 9,1; (e) community: Rom 12,5; 16,3.7.9.10; 1 Cor 1,2.4; 16,24; 1 Thess 1,1; 2,14; 2 Thess 1,1; 2 Thess 3,12; Eph 3,21; Gal 1,22.

[13] Several images are used: Christ became a curse or was made sin (Gal 3,13; 2 Cor 5,21); we are transferred into Christ's image, thereby restoring the glory of God (2 Cor 3,18; 4,4; Col 3,10; Rom 5,12-19; Rom 1,3). M.D. HOOKER, From Adam to Christ, 22.37. Many adjectival and adverbial phrases use ἐν, and the exact meaning in the NT usages of this phrase is elusive, and most grammatical studies inconclu-

Christ, as the Messiah, becomes the gateway to the new age, it is in him that a person is defined and is given eschatological status. It is in Christ that the two are made one, polarization overcome, and participation in the reality of the new creation achieved. As we can see from the various greetings in the letters, being *in Christ* defined one as a member of the Christian community, but also as a member of the new spiritual and cosmological order, and it is only in Christ that one could share in the benefits of that new order[14].

2. 1 Cor 15 and the Apocalyptic Pattern

Utilizing the paradigm of the SBL Genres project and the general characteristics of apocalyptic eschatology, a comparison can be made with 1 Cor 15 to determine possible points of similarity and whether the passage can be legitimately called an *apocalypse* or an example of apocalyptic eschatology[15].

As regards the manner of revelation, there is no direct reference to a heavenly revelation in this passage. There is evidence elsewhere in the NT that Paul in fact did have revelatory experiences, especially as expressed in 2 Cor 12,1-4. There is the possibility, impossible to prove, that in the above passage Paul was referring to the «mystery» explained in 1 Cor 15,12-58. If that is so, visions and auditory experiences would be the means of revelation, as described in 2 Cor 12,1-4. If not, than the means of revelation itself must remain a mystery[16].

---

sive. Wedderburn draws attention to instances in which the phrase is used in an instrumental or causal sense; God or his messengers do something to those who are «in Christ» (or something is done to them with the use of a divine passive): Rom 8,2; 12,5; 1 Cor 1,2; 1,4; 1,5; 15,22; 2 Cor 5,19; Gal 2,4; 2,17; 3,28; Phil 3,14; 4,7; 4,13; 4,19. Other prepositions are also used: σύν and δία. These have similar but not identical meanings; ἐν seems to suggest a sense of togetherness. A.J.M. WEDDERBURN, «Paul's Use of the Phrases», 83-97. See also J. FITZMYER, *Romans*, 141.

[14] There are several instances of the use of this expression in the non-Pauline letters expressing grace, peace, glory, spiritual refreshment, boldness, a holy and godly life, and wisdom (1 Tim 1,14; 3,13; 2 Tim 1,1; 1,9; 1,13; 2,1; 2,10; 3,12; 3,15; Philemon 1.8; 1,20; 1,23; 1 Pet 3,16; 5,10; 5,14; 5,20; Jude 1,1).

[15] According to the SBL model, the category of medium concerns the manner in which the revelation was made, and can be by visual means, visions, epiphanies, auditory means, discourse, dialogue, otherworldly journey, or writing. J.J. COLLINS, «Morphology», 6-7.

[16] «It is necessary to boast; nothing is to be gained by it, but I will go on to visions and revelations of the Lord. I know a person in Christ who fourteen years ago was caught up to the third heaven – whether in the body or out of the body I do not know; God knows. And I know that such a person – whether in the body or out of the body I do not know; God knows – was caught up into Paradise and heard things

The term «mystery» itself is open to various interpretations. The word is used 28 times in the NT: Matt 13,11; Mark 4,11; Luke 8,10; Rom 11,25; 16,25; 1 Cor 2,1; 2,7; 4,11; 13,2; 14,2; 15,51; Eph 1,9; 3,3; 3,4; 3,9; 5,32; 6,19; Col 1,26; 1,27; 2,2; 4,3; 2 Thess 2,7; 1 Tim 3,9; 3,16; Rev 1,20; 10,7; 17,5; 17,7. This word is a translation of the Persian loan word *raz* (רז), which is used extensively in the Qumran literature. It is used to describe God's hidden plan of salvation which is revealed only to a select few. As was shown above, it was also a word that came to be used in the late wisdom literature of the turn of the era. Within 1 Corinthians itself, it describes God's hidden plan, «God's wisdom, secret and hidden, which God decreed before the ages for our glory» (1 Cor 2,7). This reflects the revelatory nature of apocalyptic, the revelation of heavenly mysteries and of God's hidden plan. But even knowing or interpreting mysteries is of dubious value unless accomplished with love and with the goal of building up the Christian community (13,2; 14,2)[17].

An otherworldly mediator of the revelation is lacking in the passage in question. The closest example in the NT is the appearance of Christ to Paul on the road to Damascus (Acts 9,22.26). The possible apocalyptic nature of these passages in Acts remains a topic for further research. In the apocalypse genre, the human recipient is often described in pseudonymous terms, along with an account of his disposition and reactions at the time of the revelation. If 2 Cor 12,1-4 is indicative of apocalyptic revelation, then it could possibly be an example of pseudonymity, although there is no attempt to ascribe it to a noted biblical or religious figure from the past. The manner of revelation, so very important in defining the apocalypse genre, is very poorly developed or represented in this passage. Within 1 Cor 15 itself, the only indication of the revelatory nature is the use of the term «mystery» in v. 51[18].

---

that are not to be told, that no mortal is permitted to repeat. On behalf of such a one I will boast, but on my own behalf I will not boast, except of my weaknesses (2 Cor 12,1-4)». It is widely believed that Paul was referring to himself in this passage, although that cannot be proven. This passage is a classic description of a revelation of the type found in an apocalypse. It is possible that this also is a parallel to Gal 1,16 and 1 Cor 15,8, but this is conjecture. It is fairly obvious, however, that Paul had had some of the experiences described in apocalyptic literature.

[17] R.E. BROWN, «The Pre-Christian Concept of Mystery», 417-443; ID., «The Semitic Background of the New Testament *mysterion*», (1958) 426-448 (1959) 70-87; J. COPPENS, «"Mystery" in the Theology of Saint Paul», 132-158.

[18] In the rubric of «manner of revelation», there are two further categories: «otherworldly mediator» and «human recipient». The latter is broken down into three subcategories of pseudonymity, disposition and reaction of the recipient, none of which

2.1 *Content: Temporal Axis*

This passage contains a clear but very basic protological statement which describes «primordial events, which have paradigmatic significance for the remainder of history». This is the Old Adam-New Adam parallel in 1 Cor 15,21-22, which is similar to that found in chapter 5 of Romans. The origins of sin and death are described, the consequences for all humanity throughout history, and the consequences of the imminent reversal. History is not reviewed either in the form of explicit recollection of the past or *ex eventu* prophecy, nor is it found elsewhere in the Pauline corpus (except for passing references to past events by Paul during his argumentation)[19].

2.1.1 Eschatology

The usual sort of eschatological crisis, often in the form of persecution or cosmic upheavals, is not present in this passage but is well represented in other parts of the Pauline literature[20].

For Paul, the resurrection of Christ has inaugurated the end time. Christ is the firstfruits of all those that will follow. The rather ordinary word ἀπαρχή, used in vv. 20 and 23, is the term that initiates the sequence of events. This word in the OT always referred to the firstfruits; the part was always the guarantee of the whole. In the NT, the term is used of the Holy Spirit (Rom 8,23) and of Israel (Rom 11,16). It is the beginning of a process that guarantees that which follows; it cannot be understood outside of a context that includes that which follows[21].

---

are developed in the passage in question or in most of the pertinent NT passages. J.J. COLLINS, «Morphology», 6.

[19] According to the SBL model, the temporal axis can be described in terms of protology, history, present salvation through knowledge, eschatological crisis, eschatological judgment and/or destruction, eschatological salvation. J.J. COLLINS, «Morphology», 6-7.

[20] Often the tribulations or sufferings (θλίψις) herald the approach of the final eschatological crisis, usually the destruction or transformation of the cosmos and the judgment with its accompanying rewards and punishments. The concept and term are found in the apocalyptic synoptic passages of Mark 13 and Matt 24, as well as in Rom, 1 and 2 Thess, and Rev. Of the 43 occurrences in the NT, θλίψις is used 16 times in a manner which suggests meaningful suffering or suffering that is a presage of something greater. The eschatological crisis brought about by supernatural intervention is coming upon sinners, the world (natural elements), and otherworldly beings. For apocalyptic usage, see: Matt 24,9.21.29; Mark 13,19.24; Rom 2,9; 2 Cor 4,17; 1 Thess 1,6; 3,3.7; 2 Thess 1,4.6; Rev 1,9; 2,9.10; 7,14. J.J. COLLINS, «Morphology», 7.

[21] G. DELLING, «ἀπαρχή»; C.E. HILL, «Christ's Kingdom», 299.

Between the two instances of ἀπαρχή there is a parallelism in vv. 21–22 in which it is stated that death came through a man and so did resurrection from the dead; just as in Adam *all* died, so in Christ *all* will be made alive. Among the verses in 1 Cor 15,20-28 reflecting a concern with salvation or resurrection, the parallel text of v. 22 provides the most fuel for speculation: «For as in Adam all die, so also in Christ all shall be made alive». Does «all» include all of humanity, or is it restricted to Christians[22]?

The term ζῳοποιέω – to make alive – is a word that was often used with an eschatological and apocalyptic meaning, being used in vv. 22, 36 and 45. It is present in the Corpus Hermeticum, where it refers to the godhead: he it is who κινεῖ τὰ πάντα and through whom ζῳοποιεῖται τὰ πάντα. This association with τὰ πάντα is interesting in that it is also found in vv. 25-8 of 1 Cor 15. Outside the NT, the term is used in Ezra 9,8.9, Neh 9,6, 2 Kgs 5,7 and Qoh 7,12, as well as in the TGad 4,6. The gift of eternal ζωή is given in the new age from the source of life itself[23].

In each of the 11 times in the NT that the term is used, the subject is God, Christ, or the Spirit, and the life given is soteriological. At times the term is contrasted with the flesh or the law. It is used in John 5,21; 6,63; Rom 4,17; 8,11; 1 Cor 15,22.36.45; 2 Cor 3,6; Gal 3,21; and 1 Pet 3,18. Used in the future as it is in v. 22 – ζῳοποιηθήσονται – it refers to the eschatological raising of the dead, and referring as it does to God's definitive intervention in history and the fulfillment of his plan, it is apocalyptic. It appears that this term in v. 22b is explicated in all that follows, ending only with the «all in all» statement of v. 28. The subsequent verses discuss the manner and order in which all will be made alive. In v. 45 it refers to the life-giving action of the last Adam, who is Christ. In both cases, it expresses God's salvific action at the end of time[24].

The second «sequential» term in this sequence, τάγμα, is of military origin, denoting a rank, order, and what is ordered or fixed. It is used in

---

[22] Crockett concentrates his study on the two parallel occurrences of πάντες and the question of whether the «all» in Christ are identical with the «all» in Adam. This Adamic symbol is not in itself apocalyptic; Paul has taken a common anthropological symbol from the Jewish exegetical tradition and put it to apocalyptic eschatological use in that it signifies the ontological status of humanity as a whole, both after a primeval catastrophe and after the parousia of the Risen Christ. W. CROCKETT, «Ultimate Restoration», 83.

[23] The term appears in IX.6; XI.4; XII.22; XI.117 of the Corp. Herm. In Judg 21,14 and Job 36,6, it is used in the sense of «to keep alive». R. BULTMANN, «ζῳοποιέω».

[24] M.C. DE BOER, *Defeat of Death*, 113; A. LINDEMANN, «Parusie Christi und Herrschaft Gottes», 87-107.

the LXX (Num 2,2ff; 10,14ff; 1 Sam 4,10) to describe units or divisions of the Israelite camp. Its use in v. 23 is a *hapax* in the NT; its position following and preceding the word ἀπαρχὴ, indicates that this is to be understood in the sense of position or rank. It is of interest that the phrase in v. 23, ἐν τῷ ἰδίῳ τάγματι, corresponds exactly to איש בתכונו in 1QS 6,8, which refers to the Qumran community's division into ranks or orders. There is the important exegetical question, dealt with in chapter 3, of whether there are two or three orders or ranks[25].

It is clear that for Paul the resurrection of Christ is an eschatological event that has initiated the time of the end. The end itself with its attendant events, especially the resurrection of the dead, is triggered by the παρουσία or the coming of Christ. This term is used both in an ordinary secular and an apocalyptic sense in the NT. In the latter sense, it refers to the coming of the Lord, probably the equivalent of Day of the Lord: Matt 24,3; 24,7; 24,37; 24,39; 1 Cor 15,23; 1 Thess 2,19; 3,13; 4,15; 5,23; 2 Thess 2,1.8.9; James 5,7.8; 2 Pet 1,16; 3,4; 3,12; 1 John 2,28. In the synoptics the sudden and unexpected nature of the parousia is stressed, while in the Pauline and Catholic epistles the occasion is the counseling of patience in awaiting the coming of the Lord. Paul's technical use is found in 1 Cor 1,8; 15,23; 1 Thess 2,19; 3,13; 4,15; 5,23 and 2 Thess 2,1; 2,8. It is particularly linked with the resurrection in 1 Thess 4,13-17. It is also only at the παρουσία that the rulership of Christ becomes apparent: there is no explanation as to its exact nature or origin. This kingdom must be handed back to the Father; it is evident that the parousia and its attendant events bring it to an end[26].

We saw in chapter 3 the important but ambiguous nature of the term τὸ τέλος in v. 24, the word which seems to signal the end and the handing of the kingdom over to God the Father. The term is often used in an

---

[25] G. DELLING, «τάγμα»; C.E. HILL, «Christ's Kingdom», 307-308.

[26] A. OEPKE, «παρουσία». The term itself is used widely in the LXX, and Hellenistic literature, and even in the NT without technical meaning. It is used often of men, especially important personages and kings. Paul begins to use it in a technical sense, perhaps replacing the phrase ἡμέρα τοῦ κυρίου from the Synoptics and John. Later Christian literature and the pastorals moves towards the use of ἐπιφάνεια. One must distinguish between the term παρουσία and the concept of the visitation of God's eschatological agent. Koester denies that παρουσία is a technical term, noting its frequent and varied use. In 1 and 2 Thessalonians, Paul uses the term in a political and social sense, stressing the need to be prepared for the arrival of the personage, and for correct behavior. In this functional sense, it can be apocalyptic in its application (H. KOESTER, «Paul's Eschatology», 440). According to Lindemann, it is used here with a similar meaning to the term «day of the Lord» in 1 Cor 1,8, but without connotations of judgment (A. LINDEMANN, «Parusie», 90-93).

apocalyptic sense, and several times it refers to the end of a period of endurance or testing or the end of an age[27].

Of interest for the analysis of the term τὸ τέλος is a corresponding term used extensively in Daniel: the masculine noun קץ, which means the end of a period of time. It is used in Daniel and in other pasages of the OT in a strict eschatological sense[28].

Daniel 12,2-3 appears to have inspired much of the apocalyptic imagery later associated with the resurrection in the NT. It is clear that a resurrection is being described, although there is much ambiguity over several points[29].

The passage which is most clearly of an apocalyptic nature is Matt 24,6 (= Mark 13,7 and Luke 21,9): Jesus, in his eschatological discourse, narrates the events that will presage the end, i.e., wars, rumors of wars etc. He insists, however, that «the end is not yet». This will be followed by great tribulations: persecutions, apostasy, and confusion, and then «the end will come». The common thread that runs throughout the passages with the eschatological slant is that they describe a period of testing and perseverance followed by the end. The end is not, however, merely the cessation of activity, but a denouement and completion of a cosmic and salvific process. In this context, the «end» means something closer to the goal towards which salvation history has been moving, and

---

[27] Matt 10,22 «he who endures till the end will be saved»; Luke 1,33 «and His kingdom will have no end»; John 13,1 «he loved them till the end»; 1 Cor 1,8 «Christ will sustain you to the end»; 10,11 «end of the ages has come»; Hebrews 3,6 «until the end»; 6,8 «till the ultimate fulfillment of your hope»; 1 Pet 4,7 «the end of all things is at hand»; Rev 2,26 «keeps my words until the end»; Rev 21,6 and 22,13 «I am the Alpha and Omega, beginning and the end».

[28] For example: Ezek 21,30-34; 35,5; Heb 2,3; Dan 8,17.19; 9,26; 11,27.35.40; 12,4.6.9.

[29] Cavallin points out that there is disagreement over whether the resurrection depicted is only for the just, or also for the wicked; for Israel only, or for gentiles; for only the exceptionally good or evil, or for everyone; etc (H.C.C. CAVALLIN, *Life After Death*, 26-27). There appears to be the same ambiguity present in other eschatological texts in the OT and NT. In several places in Daniel it clearly denotes the end of a period of great tribulation, a time in which final judgment and punishment is accomplished. This term is translated in the LXX as συντέλεια, a term which appears in several places in the pseudepigrapha and NT, although it seems to have been synonymous with τὸ τέλος (TBen 11,3; TLevi 10,2; TZeb 9,9; Matt 13,39ff.49; 24,3; 28,20; Heb 9,26). It is used in a formal sense in the phrase «consummation of the ages», or «end of the age». The preferred term in the NT seems to be τὸ τέλος, although Matt 24 is of special interest, in that the passage begins with a question about the end directed to Jesus using συντελείας in v. 3. Jesus replies with a long description of the end in which he does not use that term, but instead, τὸ τέλος, three times in vv. 6,13.14. There appears to be little if any difference in meaning.

could possibly include a general resurrection of all humanity, both good and wicked[30].

In addition to sequence, determinism is an essential element in apocalyptic thought. This is expressed in this passage by the term δεῖ, the third person neuter singular, used to express «the character of necessity or compulsion». The authority behind this power is not stated; it only becomes evident in context[31].

The term has a wide eschatological use, expressing the necessity of an eschatological event, as an expression of the hidden will of God and his mysterious plan for humanity. The necessity in any event is the expression and revelation of the hidden plan of God. This is shown in LXX Dan 2,28; Rev 1,1; 4,1; 22,6. In the synoptic gospels, Matt 24,6; Mark 13,10; Matt 17,10; Mark 9,11 all express the concept that certain things must take place before the new age begins. The suffering, death and resurrection of Christ were seen as an expression of this δεῖ, the eschatological action of God in Christ. This is expressed as being a fulfillment of prophecy and scripture[32].

Here δεῖ is linked with the term βασιλεύειν in v. 25, stating not only the divine necessity for Christ to reign until all the enemies have been defeated, but also implying that it is at that point that the reign must end (ἄχρι οὗ). This concept is used of Jesus mostly as a noun in the NT, and in a threefold manner: a) to describe his status as King of Israel, usually in fulfillment of prophecies (Matt 2,2; Matt 21,5; Luke 1,33; 19,38; John 1,49; 12,13; 12,15); b) in an ironic or mocking sense (Matt 27,11; 27,29; 27,37; 27,42; Mark 15,2; 15,18; 15,26; 15,32; Luke 23,3; 23,37; 23,38; John 18,33; 18,37; 19,3; 19,14; 19,19; 19,21); and c) in a spiritual, universal and transcendent sense (Matt 25,34; 25,40; Rom 5,17;

---

[30] According to Wallis, Arndt and Gingrich note two nuances of *telos*: 1) an «end period» and 2) «end point» or goal. Paul focuses on a goal beyond the Parousia, and this harmonizes well with the more general meaning of the word. W. WALLIS, «Intermediate Kingdom», 231.

[31] In Luke/Acts Luke 2,49; 4,43; 9,22; 11,42; 12,12; 13,14.16; 13,33; 15,32; 18,1; 19,5; 17,25; 22,7; 22,37; 24,7.26; 24,44; Acts 15,5; 5,29; 20,35; 1,16; 3,21; 17,3; 9,6.16; 14,22; 19,22; 23,11; 27,24. It was taken to mean logical and scientific necessities in the philosophical realm, as well as ethical and religious obligations. It is found quite often in the Lucan works, being found there 41 of the 102 occurrences, and was used as a general expression for the will of God for humanity and for Christ, as it most often expressed the will of God with which Christ lived and acted in complete conformity. W. GRUNDMANN, «δεῖ».

[32] Ibid., 24. Matt 16,21; Luke 17,25; 24,7.26; Acts 3,21; 17,3; Matt 26,54; Luke 22,37; 24,25; John 3,14; 20,9; 1 Cor 8,2; 15,25; 15,53; 2 Cor 5,10. God expresses his saving action towards humanity; the demands that this imposes are expressed in passages such as John 3,7; Acts 4,12; 16,30. The term is also applied to the necessity of human behavior to conform to the will of God, e.g., Rev 12,3; 1 Thess 4,1; 2 Thess 3,7; 1 Tim 3,2.7; 3,7.

5,21; 1 Cor 15,25; 1 Titus 6,15; Rev 11,15; 15,3; 17,4; 19,16; 20,6).
Of special interest is the latter category: Matt 25,34 and 40 speak crypti-
cally of the king at the final judgment – obviously Christ – who will pro-
nounce judgment and award salvation or eternal punishment. This would
seem to suggest that the coming of Christ involved a universal judgment
and punishment for sinners. Rom 5,17 and 21 speak of righteousness
reigning through Jesus Christ in contradistinction to the sin which has
reigned before. First Titus 6,15 proclaims Christ the King of Kings, and
Lord of Lords, a title which is also present in Rev 17,14 and 19,16. Finally Rev 11,15 states that the kingdoms of the world have become the
kingdom of Our Lord, and His Christ, and he shall reign for ever and
ever. It seems as if the earthly kingdoms must be conquered and returned
to the reign of God, as in 1 Cor 15.

The otherworldly elements found in vv. 24-26 are basically hostile.
These powers – rulers, authorities, and powers, in addition to death – are
responsible for the enslavement of humanity and the cosmos. It is only
after they are all destroyed or subjected to Christ that God's sovereignty
– temporarily challenged or weakened and with God's forbearance – will
be completely restored. The destruction of demonic or carnal powers at
the time of the parousia is described in 1 Cor 15,24.26; 2 Thess 2,8; and
1 Cor 6,13 utilizing the word καταργέω. The religious use of the word
καταργέω is found mostly in the Pauline literature. The term means «to
render inactive, to put out of use, and sometimes, to destroy.» For Paul,
it signifies the new order, in that it renders inactive or ineffective the
wisdom and ways of the world (1 Cor 1,28), the Law (Eph 2,15), the
rulers of this world (1 Cor 2,6), and death itself (2 Tim 1,10; Heb
2,14)[33].

In verses 27-8, the hierarchical term ὑποτάσσω is used 6 times. In the
Greek world and in the LXX, it had always meant «to place under» or «to
subordinate». In the NT, it is used to express relationship to hierarchical
superiors; but most importantly, it is used in conjunction with the verb
βασιλεύειν and Ps. 8,6 and 110,1 in v. 25 as a christological statement
(Heb 2; Eph 1; 1 Cor 15). De Boer demonstrated the likelihood that these
two psalms were often quoted together to describe Christ's exaltation
over principalities and powers (Eph 1,22; 1 Pet 3,21b-22 and Heb 2,8).
The use of these two royal psalms also reflects the apocalyptic practice of

---

[33] The term is used in the LXX 2 Esdras four times with the sense of «to destroy».
It is also found in the Corp. Herm., XIII,7. The term is also found in Luke 13,7;
Rom 3,3; 3,31; 6,6; 1 Cor 1,28; 1 Cor 6,13; 1 Cor 13,8; 13,10; 15,24.26; 2 Cor
3,7; 3,11; 3,13; 3,14; Gal 3,17; Eph 2,15; 2 Thess 2,8; 2 Tim 1,10. G. DELLING,
«καταργέω».

placing the end-time events in the hands of a mediator with royal functions[34].

The trumpet or σάλπιγξ is used many times in the OT to assemble the Israelites or to engage in battle. In a few instances, it is also an eschatological symbol: Joel 2,1; Zeph 1,16; Zech 9,14 and Isa 27,13 all speak of the trumpet as announcing the Day of the Lord or judgment. This word is used several times in the NT, but only three times in a distinctly apocalyptic eschatological sense: Matt 24,31; 1 Thess 4:16; and 1 Cor 15,52. Additionally, 4 Ez 6,23 uses this symbol in the same manner[35].

The entire passage – vv. 12-58 – is about eschatological salvation in the form of the resurrection of the dead. In this it differs from much of Jewish apocalyptic literature in that it discusses the resurrection at length and even describes the manner of the resurrection of the body. Even so, many questions remain unanswered: there is still that vagueness and reluctance to be too exact and precise. Verses 51-52 describe the resurrection in terms of a cosmic transformation brought about by supernatural means, i.e., «We will all be changed in the twinkling of an eye». In the putting on of imperishability, there is still an element of exaltation; the exact nature of the resurrected body is not disclosed. This exaltation is also reflected in the «resurrection» passage of 1 Thess 5,4-17. It is clear in other passages in the Pauline and deutero-Pauline writings that this eschatological salvation also includes the cosmos.

2.2 *The Ethical Aspect of Apocalyptic Literature*

The eschatology of apocalyptic works differs from prophetic eschatology in that the former always expects a retribution after death instead of in the land of the living. Towards this end, apocalyptic literature is often hortatory in nature, generating, as Keck states, an «intense ethical concern», not with a definite ethic oriented towards fashioning the world, but an ethic of a minority that is struggling to be faithful in opposition to the world[36].

This literature, written in «end-time» language, seeks to reinforce the solidarity of the Christian community and to encourage or discourage

---

[34] G. DELLING, «ὑποτάσσω».

[35] In the NT, the word also appears in 1 Cor 14,8; Heb 12,19; Rev 1,10; 4,1; 8,2ff; and 9,14. In many of these instances, it is used in a metaphorical sense; in the passages from Rev, it is used to describe the sound of the voice speaking to the seer, and the seven trumpets of judgment of the angels. The latter might fall into the apocalyptic category described above; they do not, however, signify the Day of the Lord or the universal judgment. G. FRIEDRICH, «σάλπιγξ».

[36] J.J. COLLINS, *Imagination*, 5; L. KECK, «Paul and Apocalyptic», 234.

certain forms of behavior. Contrary to common belief, it emphasizes rather than explains away dissonance and suffering, and the frequent judgment theophanies emphasize vindication for the persecuted and punishment for the oppressors. Literature such as 1 Thess is parenetic, showing that the community of Christians crosses the boundary of death[37].

The true nature of reality is disclosed to the believer; he is situated in history and is asked to make a simple but momentous decision: on whose side does he stand, that of God or the earthly powers[38]?

Apocalyptic imagery and schemata also have political and social applications: of special note is the use of apocalyptic sequences and timetables to either proclaim the nearness of certain events or to put them at a distance and counteract speculation and hysteria[39].

Lebram, on the other hand, views apocalyptic literature as being for the purpose of provoking religious reaction and encouraging piety or a living relationship with God. Along with Nickelsburg, it is seen as providing a window into the world as the author perceives it. Most of the literature with which we are dealing looks for a divine intervention at the end of history. The present age is seen as evil; salvation consists in belonging to the correct group and/or living one's life in the correct way. Usually the parenesis is rather vague; the law is general, not specific. Purification and cleansing must be performed, and the pious man must live in accordance with the cosmic order[40].

Keck sees Jewish apocalyptic theology or eschatology as the first radical theology to emerge from covenental theology. Whereas before it was

---

[37] On page 698, Meeks lists several passages of 1 Cor in which apocalyptic and eschatological language is found: 1,7; 2,6-10; 3,13 cf vv. 10-15; 3,17; 4,5; 5,5; 6,2.3; 6,9.13; 7,26-31; 11,32; 15,24; 15,54ff; 16,22. W. MEEKS, «Social Functions of Apocalyptic Language», 687-706.

[38] As Collins states, «even parenesis, when it occurs, only makes explicit what is implied elsewhere: the apocalyptic revelation provides a framework in which humans can decide their commitments in the full knowledge of the nature of reality present and future» (J.J. COLLINS, «Morphology», 12).

[39] Koester believes that much of Paul's apocalyptic imagery in Thessalonians is political and social in its concern, the apocalyptic schemata being used to dampen and contain enthusiasm and to allow for the building up of the community. H. KOESTER, «From Paul's Eschatology», 441-458.

[40] The emphasis is different for various works; for example, 1 En 1-5 deals with the relationship with the wicked. There is a conflict: two groups,the pious and the godless. The believer must be preserved from the temptation of evil. The author of 4 Ez emphasizes concern for belief in and respect for the law. The work is open to the future, as the believer is encouraged to turn from earthly things towards the hereafter, for the present is finished and there is no hope for the many who are going to be lost. J.C.H. LEBRAM, «The Piety of Jewish Apocalyptists», 171-210.

thought that fidelity to God and the Law brought prosperity, now it seemed as if the wicked prosper and the faithful suffer. In order to resolve the question of theodicy, which Keck believes to be the fundamental question of apocalyptic, a clear break must be made with the present world and time. According to Keck, «the heart of apocalyptic theology is the doctrine of a radically discontinuous future, made necessary by the undeniable scope of evil and made possible by the unquestionable sovereignty of a righteous God»[41].

Parenetic elements are present in the greater part of 1 Cor, and this passage is no exception. The Christian community is exhorted to lead an upright life in liturgical, sexual, marital, and communal matters. The apocalyptic events described in ch. 15 have ethical consequences: the believer must live correctly. Negating the apocalyptic event of the resurrection of the dead means draining the life of the believer of all meaning and purpose, and rendering futile the act of martyrdom. The message is clear in vv. 29-34: «Come to a sober and right mind, and sin no more», and v. 58 «Therefore, my beloved, be steadfast, immovable, always excelling in the work of the Lord, because you know that in the Lord your labor is not in vain».

2.3 Conclusion

Many of the elements of the apocalypse genre are found in 1 Cor 15,12-34 and the second half of the passage in vv. 35-58. Protology, eschatology, and parenesis are represented. It is weak in the area of transcendent revelation of heavenly mysteries. Additionally, the revelation is not made in heaven to a seer called there for that purpose, but is instead made openly and to all. This passage cannot be called an apocalypse in its fullest sense, since it is underdeveloped and is not in the same category as a full-fledged work in the apocalypse genre such as the Book of Revelation. It is skeletal and fragmentary in nature, and is probably more accurately described by Schüssler-Fiorenza as one of many «smaller early Christian apocalyptic text units» in which the apocalyptic pattern of eschatological events is combined with parenesis to form «motif clusters»[42].

---

[41] L. KECK, «Paul and Apocalyptic», 234.

[42] Schüssler-Fiorenza views the resurrection of Christ plus the general resurrection as a tensive symbol, which is supposed to evoke a wide response. Christian apocalyptic is in continuity with the Jewish; its newness lies in Christ as Lord in the center of the community. With Jewish apocalyptic, there is hope for the imminent intervention of God, while in Christian apocalyptic, the end events have already been inaugurated in the person of Christ. E. SCHÜSSLER-FIORENZA, «The Phenomenon of Early Christian Apocalyptic», 295-316.

3. Wisdom and 1 Corinthians

It is fairly clear in chapters 1-4 of 1 Corinthians that Paul does not want his message to be confused with wisdom. He uses some wisdom terminology, but in a disparaging sense, seeking to show that the wisdom of the world is folly and that the Corinthians are wrong in their high opinion of their own wisdom. But we may ask: for all of Paul's protestations about wisdom, could it be that he uses some of the same ideas and symbols? Should 1 Cor be read against a background of Hellenistic Jewish wisdom thought? Is it possible that 1 Cor 15 reflects more of wisdom imagery than that of apocalyptic[43]?

Although in the past it has been fashionable to turn to gnosticism to explain Paul's use of *gnosis* terminology and the presence of spiritual elitism and distinctions between *pneumatikos*, *psychikos*, *teleioi*, etc., there is now general agreement that analogous if not always identical terminology and concepts discussed in 1 Corinthians can be found in Philo. In both Wisdom and Philo, *sophia* is seen to be an integral part of mystical piety and ascent to God. In Corinthians, *gnosis* can be said to be an expression of *sophia*[44].

---

[43] Witherington points out that of all the extra canonical literature that Paul alludes to, Sirach and Wisdom are the most frequent. There is clearly sapiential teaching in 2 Cor 11; Phil 2,6-11; Rom 10,6-8; Rom 11,33-36; and Col 1,15ff. Additionally, of the 17 times that *sophia* is used in 1 Cor, 16 of these occur in chapters 1-3; the word is used 11 times elsewhere in his letters. B. WITHERINGTON, *Jesus the Sage*, 307; R.A. HORSLEY, «Gnosis in Corinth», 32-51.

[44] This in fact may be part of the problem present in the Corinthian community. Taking very seriously some of the implications read from Wis 10,10 and Philo *de Somm* 2:243-244, many were seeing themselves as already reigning and sharing in the glory of Christ, being already *teleioi*. Their spiritual arrogance was reflected perhaps in their pride over their eloquence, seen as itself a sign of perfection. B. WITHERINGTON, *Jesus the Sage*, 303. Horsley determines that there were three types of knowledge in Philo and Wisdom: 1) knowledge is always directly or indirectly a knowledge of God (Wis 15,2-3; *Virt.* 178f., 213-16; *Leg. All.* III. 46-8, 100,126f); 2) parallel or similar to *sophia* (Wis 9,10-11; 10,10; *Leg. All.* 95; *Quod Deus* 143; *Fug.* 76; *Mos.* II 98); 3) knowledge is «the particular religious and theological content of *sophia*, i.e., the ontological and especially soteriological knowledge of divine teaching supposedly derived from Scripture» (Wis 10,10; IV Macc 1,16-17; *Quod Deus* 92; *Cong* 79; *Spec. Leg.* 1:30, 50, 269). It is this third type, according to Horsley, that is especially applicable to the Corinthian situation: the *gnosis* mentioned in 1 Cor is related closely to, but not identical with, the *sophia* rejected by Paul in chapters 1-4 (R.A. HORSLEY, «Gnosis in Corinth», 32-51). Parallels for the terminology of spiritual distinction and perfection such as powerful, noble birth, wealthy, reigning like kings, babes and so on are to be found in Philo: *Agr.* 8-9; *Leg. All.* 1.90-94; *Mig.* 28-40; *Sob.* 55-57; *Virt.* 174; *Her.* 313-315. R.A. HORSLEY, «Wisdom of Word», 224-239; ID., «Pneumatikos vs. Psychikos», 269-288.

One can also see the parallels between the holy spirit in chapters 1-4 and wisdom as expressed in Wis 1,6; 7,7.23.24. Scroggs sees a very close connection (but not total identification) between σοφία and πνεῦμα and the «absolute revelatory quality of God's wisdom». This makes it rather unlikely that Paul was heavily influenced by pagan, Jewish or Christian gnosticism. Some of the images and symbols for the expression of Paul's theology were readily available in the Hellenistic wisdom tradition; there was no need to turn to gnosticism (if indeed there was a pre-Christian gnosticism)[45].

Utilizing Job 28-42; Wis 7,27; 9,17; Sir 24,33, all of which stress the revelatory nature of Wisdom, Paul negates wisdom on the human level, giving credence only to that form of wisdom revealed by God in the cross of Christ. In response to the obsessive and exaggerated emphasis on wisdom found in chapters 1-2 of Corinthians, Paul substitutes his own wisdom: Christ crucified. The wisdom of God becomes an apocalyptic mystery – the crucifixion of the Lord of glory – revealed by God through the Holy Spirit (2,6.10). Paul counters the Hellenistic Jewish wisdom theology of the Corinthians with an apocalyptic theology that presupposes an eschatological judgment of the world, especially of demonic powers, idolatry, etc. This last move, according to Horsley, shifts the image of Christ from the crucified to the exalted Lord, as in 1 Thess 1,10 and 1 Cor 15,20-5. It is Paul's goal to insist on the Lordship of Christ (1 Cor 3,21-3; 10,4; 15,25.27), since perhaps some viewed him as merely a revealer or spokesman for Sophia[46].

The mysteries mentioned in Corinthians, especially 15,51, can possibly be read in this light, and may be, according to Scroggs, fragments of Paul's «esoteric apocalyptic-wisdom» teaching. Having shown that human wisdom is not adequate for *salvific* purposes, Paul proposes his own apocalyptic discernment with regard to the resurrection. The fact that this mystery is a detailed description of the nature of the resurrection suggests that it went beyond the usual apocalyptic revelation and contained in fact elements of wisdom teaching[47].

Additionally, some of the terminology present in 1 Cor 15,47-50 is perhaps a reflection of Philo *Quod Deus* 120-61. In that passage, those who possess *sophia* are said to renounce wealth, nobility and glory for what is heavenly (οὐράνιος) and incorruptible (ἄφθαρτος). Philo also

---

[45] R. SCROGGS, «ΣΟΦΟΣ», 54.

[46] R.A. HORSLEY, «Gnosis in Corinth», 48-51; ID., «Wisdom of Word», 237.

[47] Scroggs holds that Paul had knowledge of an esoteric Christian apocalyptic-wisdom teaching which he withheld from all but the spiritually mature. R. SCROGGS, «ΣΟΦΟΣ», 46.54; R.A. HORSLEY, «Gnosis in Corinth», 51.

teaches a dualistic view of humanity, with a contrast between earthly-heavenly, mortal-immortal, body-soul etc[48].

It has been said that «Wisdom theology is creation theology». Wisdom is seen as flowing from the mouth of God, of being present as God's helper before creation, and as constantly continuing the creative work (Prov 8; Job 38-41; Wis 6-9; Sir 24,1-12). The book of Wisdom states that death was not God's intention, but the work of the devil. Death and Wisdom are seen as opposite and incompatible. In a passage describing the hidden nature and profundity of Wisdom (Job 28,22), Abaddan and Death do not know wisdom, they have heard only vague rumors of her. In 1 Cor 15,26, death is presented as the last enemy to be overcome and destroyed in God's reconquest of the cosmos.

One opinion has it that there is a confluence of wisdom and apocalyptic, and that this is sometimes reflected in the NT. This «apocalyptic-wisdom» theology was well suited for negating human and earthly claims and stresses the transcendence of God and the need for divine intervention for salvation and life beyond the grave. Foremost in the apocalyptic message of this passage is that of the impending divine intervention in the form of the parousia. Throughout the entire letter there is a depreciation of human values and modes of thinking and the concomitant forms of behavior, and these are sharply contrasted with the way of life that shows that one is in Christ. Clearly, only God's action in the form of the Holy Spirit can give true wisdom and lead people to correct behavior, and it is only God's action that can raise and transform the dead.

Although there are perhaps echoes of wisdom theology in 1 Cor, it is totally absent in 1 Cor 15, except for some of the general images and language noted above that would have been part of the intellectual background of anyone educated in a Hellenistic culture at this time. For this reason and because Paul is anxious to negate rather than exalt wisdom, we may conclude that 1 Cor 15 is apocalyptic rather than sapiential in nature.

4. Universal Or Particular Salvation (1 Cor 15)?

With its emphasis on the defeat of death and on the resurrection, 1 Cor 15 has been a source of speculation for the doctrine of universal salvation[49].

---

[48] Examples of this dualism can be found in Philo's *Her.* 55-56; *Op.* 135; *Leg. All.* 3.161; and in Wisdom 2,23-3,4; 9,15; 15,11. Most of this is based on an interpretation of Gen 2:7. The actual terms *pneumatikos* and *psychikos* are not found in Philo, but these many contrasts provide us with a parallel. R.A. HORSLEY, «Gnosis in Corinth», 45; ID., «Pneumatikos vs. Psychikos», 269-288.

[49] M.E. BORING, «Universal Salvation», 269-292; W.V. CROCKETT, «Ultimate Restoration», 83-87.

Conzelmann observes that this chapter is only concerned with the fate of Christians. There are, however, several ambiguities in the text. It is clear that Paul held for punishment of some sort for the wicked. Is some form of a resurrection required for this, as some Jewish apocalyptic literature seems to indicate? Or is there another way in which the elect can be saved and the wicked punished[50]?

There are many attempts to deal with the ambiguity and inconsistency issue. For example, the heart of J. Beker's extensive reflection on the problem is a denial of the logical and systematic nature of Paul's thought concerning salvation[51].

Some have seen a definite development in Paul's theology of salvation. C.H. Dodd, for example, makes a sharp distinction between the early Paul who teaches a «day of wrath» eschatology and the later Paul who teaches universal salvation[52].

---

[50] H. CONZELMANN, *1 Corinthians*, 268, note 49; A. ROBERTSON – A. PLUMMER, *First Corinthians*, 353, quoted in W.V. CROCKETT, «Ultimate Restoration», 83-87. Crockett points out that the resurrection of all does not necessarily mean the salvation of all; however, in Paul's theology, the resurrection entails sharing in Christ's glory, so this would probably not be the case.

[51] In particular, J.C. BEKER, in *Paul the Apostle*. On page 270 of his article, Boring notes several points from pp. 193-4 of Beker's work that deal with the inconsistency issue. Beker says that Paul's contextual arguments cannot be systematized or molded into dogma; ontological statements must be distinguished from the anthropological, especially concerning the destiny of individuals; Paul's thought is corporate and universalistic, but since every argument is contextual, it cannot be pressed. Sometimes the universal reign of grace is stressed, other times the conditions for participating in it. Probably one of the strongest arguments for the totality of salvation or resurrection is the following: «The final apocalyptic triumph of God does not permit a permanent pocket of evil or resistance to God in his creation [...] everything that opposes God will be overcome or taken up in God's glory» (M.E. BORING, «Universal Salvation», 272-273). Beker also holds that Paul's thought has a deep structure or coherent core which is the apocalyptic victory of God. It is expressed in a surface structure which is comprised of symbols that cannot be reconciled on this level, making them seem vague and contradictory. We have access to the deep structure only in its surface manifestations. In essence, Beker denies that all of these inconsistencies can be or should be reconciled.

[52] Drawing from a number of Dodd's works, Boring shows that he held that Paul's thought underwent an evolution, beginning with the typical idea of God's wrath and punishment for the sinner inherited from Jewish apocalyptic and ending with a universalist view of salvation in Romans, Colossians and Ephesians. This is a rather satisfying view, except that Boring claims that the Pauline texts cannot be placed in a chronological order that leaves all of the particularist passages before the universalist ones. Other modern studies support this criticism, and have shown that there is no clear and definitive linear development in Paul's salvation theology. M.E. BORING, 271. See B.F. MEYER, «Paul's View of the Resurrection», 363-387.

Others have maintained that Paul was a universalist, basing their views on 1 Cor 15,21-28, Rom 11,36, Col 1,16, and Phil 2,9-10. Foremost among these are M. Rissi and E. Best[53].

Boring observes, however, that the differing views of Pauline scholars on this issue often result from subordinating either the particularist passages to the universalist or vice versa, according to the views of the author[54].

4.1 *Pauline View of Salvation*

For Paul, the resurrection of Christ was his glorification, and for the individual, the resurrection means to be with Christ and to share in that glory (2 Cor 4,17; Rom 8,17; 1 Cor 15,43-44; Phil 3,20; 2 Thess 1,9). To be cut off from this creative power of God is destruction and death itself (2 Thess 1,9). This would indicate that a resurrection for the wicked is unlikely, as that would imply their glorification[55].

The main difficulty is the number of apparently contradictory Pauline statements concerning salvation. Some seem to say that only those who have faith in Christ will be saved, while others imply salvation for all of humanity. This ambiguity makes more sense, however, when we remember what Nickelsburg observed concerning the apocalyptic language of intertestamental literature; namely, that the images, symbols, and words used were greatly influenced by the situation which generated their composition. A detailed examination of the pertinent passages in Paul's letters will clarify the various stresses, emphases and omissions concerning judgment, salvation, resurrection and so on[56].

---

[53] Rissi holds that the «whole of mankind will become the body of Christ» and that all of creation will be redeemed in God's kingdom. M. RISSI, *Time and History*, 124-128. E. BEST, *The First and Second Epistles to the Thessalonians*, 208.261-263. In Best's work, he argues that ὄλεθρος (disaster) does not necessarily mean complete destruction or annihilation.

[54] Examples of this trend are E. Best and M. Rissi, both of whom argue for universalism on the basis of their own hermeneutical schemes and subordination of particularist texts. M.E. BORING, «Universal Salvation», 272.

[55] God's glory was seen in the OT as an expression of his grandeur and power as creator and redeemer. As an eschatological term, it signified a final transforming revelation of the power of God (Hab 2,14; Isa 40,5; 58,8; 62,1-2).

[56] Boring gives 1 Cor 1,18 as an example of the first category «For the word of the cross is folly to those who are perishing, but to us who are being saved it is the power of God», while Rom 5,18 illustrates the second «Then as one man's trespass led to condemnation for all men, so one man's act of righteousness leads to acquittal and life for all men». Other illustrative texts include: for limited salvation, 1 Thess 1,10; 4,13-17; 5,3-9; 1 Cor 1,21-31; 3,16-17; 9,22; 11,32; 15,18; 2 Cor 2,15-16; 4,3; 5,10; Gal 3,10.23.29; 5,19-21; Rom 1,16-17; 2,1-16; 3,21-25; 8,5-8; 9,2; 10,1;

4.1.1 The Corinthian Tradition: 1 Corinthians

One Corinthians was written to encourage the unity of the community, adherence to the apostolic teaching, and the following of the Christian life so as to be guiltless on the Day of the Lord. A transition from one state to another is imminent for the world: the two-ages symbol insists that time is short, the former world is passing away or the end of the ages is near (2,6; 7,29; 10,11) The Day of the Lord is approaching, a day on which the world will be judged and treated accordingly (1,8; 3,10) and a day on which one must be found guiltless. No one may claim to be holy before God (1,29-30); the only way to be saved is in Christ who is the source of life (1,29-30), and the gospel, which are folly to those who are perishing.

The Corinthian tradition also seems to favor limited salvation: 1 Cor 1,21-31 proclaims that the world does not know God, and that it pleases him to save *those who believe*, those who are called, through the folly of what Paul preaches. Most striking is Paul's statement that he becomes all things to all men, so that he might save *some* (9,22). Christians are chastened so that they may not be condemned along with the world (11,32). From the passage under discussion, 15,18, we are told that if there is no resurrection, then those who have fallen asleep *in Christ* have perished.

4.1.2 2 Corinthians

Two Corinthians is also rather explicit: 2 Cor 2,15-16 identifies believers as the «aroma of Christ to God among those who are being saved and among those who are perishing, to one a fragrance from death to death, to the other a fragrance from life to life». The gospel is veiled «only to those who are perishing» (4,3) and «we must all appear before the judgment seat of Christ, so that each one may receive good or evil, according to what he has done in the body» (5,10). Second Corinthians 5,19 teaches that «in Christ God was reconciling the world to himself, not counting their trespasses against them, and entrusting to us the message of reconciliation». Of interest is the fact that the Law is consigned to the dispensation of death (3,7), indicating that it is in Christ rather than in observance of the Law that one is saved.

---

universal salvation is seen in 1 Cor 15,22-28; 2 Cor 5,19; Rom 5,12-21; 11,26-36; Phil 2,6-11. M.E. BORING, «Universal Salvation», 209.

4.2 *The Totality of God's Power: All*

The use of «all» is crucial in this entire passage; indeed, Wallis sees the «all» in Ps 8,7 as the key to the whole section. This mundane word is adopted by Paul as a symbol of comprehensiveness and completeness. With its universalist and cosmic eschatological orientation and use in this passage, it can be seen as serving an apocalyptic function[57].

In the OT and LXX, πᾶς was used extensively to express the universality and sovereign power of God, who is the Creator and Ruler of all things. Because of this role, the word is often used in a universalist sense tied to Zion and Israel.

In the NT, it is used to express totality, especially with regard to creation and redemption, e.g., 1 Cor 8,6 «Yet for us there is one God, the Father, from whom are all things and for whom we exist, and one Lord, Jesus Christ, through whom are all things and through whom we exist», and Rom 11,36 «For from him and through him and to him are all things», as well as Eph 3,9; Rom 9,5; 1 Tim 6,13; Acts 17,25; John 1,3; Col 1,15-18. This is perhaps linked with Isa 44,24, «I am the Lord who has made all things».

The refusal of the created universe to recognize its creator has universal negative effects: Rom 1,18-25; 3,19; 8,20.22; Gal 3,22. With his crucifixion and resurrection, Christ has all power (Matt 28,18) and is the Risen Lord exalted above all angelic beings (Rom 8,38; Eph 1,21; Phil 2,9ff; Col 2,10.15; 1 Pet 3,22). In Eph and Col, cosmological reconciliation is illustrated by combining the term with the words «fullness» (πλήρωμα) and «recapitulation» (ἀνακεφαλαιόομαι).

Further instances state that «all flesh will see salvation» (Luke 3,6); «whole world, all creation» (Mark 16,15; Col 1,6.23); «all in all» (Eph 1,22ff; 3,19; 4,16; Col 1,19ff; 2,9.19; 3,11); «all creatures do Him homage» (Rev 5,13); «all things made new» (Rev 21,5); «after destroying every rule and every authority and power» (1 Cor 15,24). The term appears to express God's action at the end of the ages when he reasserts his authority over all creation[58].

But the question arises: is the «all» in 22b as inclusive as that in 22a? It certainly is indicative of the universal role of Christ. There are two schools of thought: one believes in a universal salvation or at least resur-

---

[57] Wallis notes that Paul sees fit to add «all» to the corresponding psalm 110,1 in v. 25a. «All» is used 12 times in vv. 20-28; as will be shown, this is important as a symbol of comprehensiveness in Paul's argument. It would seem to imply that the life giving effects of the resurrection are for all, just as death was the common lot of all. W. WALLIS, «Intermediate Kingdom», 233.

[58] B. REICKE, «πᾶς».

rection, while the other holds that the resurrection involves only believers. It seems that the «all» in Ps 8,7 quoted in 27a should interpret both uses of «all» in verse 22[59].

The logic of the two parallels in vv. 21-22 would also seem to indicate that something much greater is intended. Paul takes great pains to fill this entire passage with «all»; the conclusion in v. 28 is that nothing is outside of or alienated from God. Those who die do so involuntarily as a result of Adam's sin and their common humanity; in a similar fashion, all humanity will be brought to life by their commonality with Christ[60].

Adam is the collective symbol which epitomizes the complete and all-encompassing hold which death has on humanity. Adam stands in relation to all those who die, while Christ stands in relation to all those who will be made alive. Some interpret this to mean that only those who are in Christ will be made alive. However, the condition of humanity with respect to death does not involve choice: all die, even those who lead good lives. Death is the uncompromising result of primordial disobedience. The symbol of Christ as the second Adam would seem to demand that the effects of Christ's resurrection and victory over death also be given to the entire human race[61].

Militating against this view of the Adam symbolism, however, are the observations of Wright; namely, that within Jewish theology, Adam speculation was about Israel – the people of God – rather than about humanity in general. The second Adam is the whole eschatological people of God. This is basically Paul's theology with one important difference: the role assigned to Israel was now applicable to Jesus Christ instead of Israel; Jesus was the new Israel and God's true humanity[62].

---

[59] «The comprehensiveness of the "all" of Psalm 8,7 must decide the interpretation of "all" in verse 22b: In Christ all will be made alive» (W. WALLIS, «Intermediate Kingdom», 234).

[60] «The concept of totality and completeness in the pervasive "all" provides an answer to the often-repeated idea that Paul is only concerned with the resurrection of the righteous» (W. WALLIS, «Intermediate Kingdom», 234).

[61] Boring holds that the parallel nature of the text requires that ἐν τῷ 'Αδάμ be balanced by those who are ἐν τῷ Χριστῷ. This reasoning is faulty, however. No one doubts that it is only through Christ that all will be made alive; he is certainly the unique source of this life-giving power. The question is, however, whether one must have explicitly expressed faith in Christ to receive this new life, and this is not clear in the parallel symbols of v.22 (M.E. BORING, «Universal Salvation», 279). M.C. DE BOER, *Defeat of Death*, 112, points out that if the strict parallel were adhered to, it would imply that there were some who were not in Adam and did not die. Universality is the theme of this passage: Rom 14,9 speaks of Christ's Lordship over the living and the dead; Rom 11,32 states that «God consigned all to disobedience that he might have mercy on all»; 2 Cor 5,14 states that Christ «died for all, therefore all died».

[62] N.T. WRIGHT, «Adam in Pauline Christology», 359-389.

On the question of whether the second πάντες refers to all of humanity or only those who are in Christ in the sense of being believers, the dominant opinion seems to be the latter[63].

This same parallel symbolism is developed further in Romans 5, but again there is ambiguity. Verse 1 states that we are justified by faith, and that it is through Jesus Christ that we have our peace with God. But verse 12 goes on to say that «sin came into the world through one man, and death came through sin, and so death spread to all because all have sinned». Death reigned from Adam to Moses even over those whose sins were not like the transgressions of Adam[64].

The intent of Rom 5 is to show the universality of effects radiating from one agent: just as negative consequences for humanity resulted from the actions of one man, i.e., sin and death, so now does life and justification before God come through the action of one man. Verse 18 states that «just as one man's trespass led to condemnation for all, so one man's act of righteousness leads to justification and life for all»[65].

---

[63] M.C. DE BOER, in *Defeat of Death*, 221 n. 81, states that Wilcke lists 26 interpreters, in addition to himself, who deny the inclusive nature of the second «all». Sixteen hold that it is inclusive and means exactly what it says: all. Among those in the first group are A. ROBERTSON – A. PLUMMER, *First Corinthians*, 353. They hold that the notion that πάντες in the second clause has the same meaning as in the first is «precarious». They believe that the sense may be «As it is in Adam that all who die die, so it is in Christ that all who are made alive are made alive». This seems like a very convoluted and tortuous way to explain something which seems rather straightforward. Crockett points out that this tautology still does not resolve the question of what «all» means; Fee is adamant in his insistence that the second «all» means only those who are «in Christ». He correctly observes, although perhaps overstated, that the fate of non-believers or a general resurrection is simply not Paul's concern. Just as all die as a member of Adam's race, so all who become a member of the new race by faith in Jesus will be made alive (G. FEE, *Corinthians*, 749-51); H. CONZELMANN, *1 Corinthians*, 268-269, also denies a general sense of the second all; B. SPÖRLEIN, *Leugnung*, 74 and C.K. BARRETT, *Corinthians*, 352 insist that the concern of Paul is with the futurity of the resurrection; H. LIETZMANN, *An die Korinther I/II*, 79-80 merely raises the question without answering it, but his exegesis of v. 23 (τέλος) would suggest that he might be sympathetic; J. HÉRING, *First Epistle*, 165 denies strongly that all of humanity is implied in the second «all». Not all men live in Christ. There are two humanities, the old and the new, with their respective heads. One changes from the old to the new through faith in Christ. E.B. ALLO, *Première Épître*, 406, also denies the inclusive nature of the second «all».

[64] The question of sovereignty involves a change in lordship which lends support to the universalist view. The verb βασιλεύω is used 5 times in this chapter of Romans. Boring phrases the point of the passage as a question: Who is in charge? Who is in control of the world and humanity? He traces the movement of the answer to that question from sin and death at first, then to Jesus Christ, and finally to God who is all in all. M.E. Boring, «Universal Salvation», 283.

[65] Fitzmyer sees the argument of this chapter as being of an *a minori ad maius* type, stressing contrasts between Adam and Christ: the superabundance of Christ's

This is followed by v. 19, which Crockett believes to be the parallel to v. 22, which reads «For as through the one man's disobedience the many were made sinners, even so through the obedience of the one the many will be made righteous». Paul uses οἱ πολλοί (the many), as he does in v.15, which might seem to indicate a limited number. Crockett argues, however, that Paul uses this word in its «Hebraic inclusive sense»[66].

De Boer draws attention to an important term in this passage, ζῳοποιεῖν, and suggests that its use instead of ἐγείρειν signals a deeper soteriological and eschatological meaning implying the resurrection of all to eternal life and complete salvation. There is some support for this idea, for the term ζῳοποιεῖν in verse 22 seems to govern the entire passage since πάντες ζῳοποιηθήσονται appears to be directed wholly towards πάντα ἐν πᾶσιν. It is announced that all will be made alive (πάντες ζῳοποιηθήσονται), and this is in the future. This term πᾶς is repeated 10 more times, ending only in verse 28 when God will be πάντα ἐν πᾶσιν. All enemies must be destroyed, including death, and everything subjected to Christ before God can rule his universe in its entirety. In this case, vv. 23-24 specify the sequence and manner in which all are made alive. Each in his own rank or order: first Christ, then at the parousia those who belong to him. This is followed by τὸ τέλος, that problematic expression. There is no reason why it cannot mean «the end» and still include the remaining people to be made alive. The extensive, repetitive use of the inclusive and universalist «all», the emphasis on the conquest and neutralization of all powers opposed to God, and the idea that God's sovereignty will only be complete when the entire cosmos is restored to him, all at least lend support to the claim that salvation is intended for all[67].

---

effects, and the fact that while Adam is head of the old aeon, which is death, Christ is head of the new aeon, which is life (J. FITZMYER, *Romans*, 405-406). Boring also makes the point that each verse affirms that whatever humanity might have lost in Adam is more than compensated for in what it gains in Christ. M.E. BORING, «Universal Salvation», 285.

66 Throughout ch. 5 of Romans, «the many» and «all» seem to be almost synonymous. «Through Christ in verse 15b the gift (of life) comes to τοὺς πολλούς; the same life in verse 18 comes to πάντας» (W. CROCKETT, «Ultimate Restoration», 83). Barrett also points out that in the OT, «many» is often contrasted with one or some, rather than with all (C.K. BARRETT, *Romans*, 108-109).

67 Here and in Rom 4,17, allusion is made to a liturgical formula taken from the Second Benediction: «the God who makes alive the dead». The gift of eternal ζωή is given in the new age from the source of life itself. In each of the 11 times that the term is used in the NT, it is associated with the spirit and the action of God, and at times is contrasted with the flesh or the law. It is used in John 5,21; 6,63; Rom 4,17; 8,11; 1 Cor 15,22.36.45; 2 Cor 3,6; Gal 3,21; and 1 Pet 3,18. M.C. DE BOER,

4.3 *Conclusion*

In conclusion, it seems fairly clear that although Paul hoped that all would be saved, he in fact expected that some would not, for the language indicates that although salvation is *extended and offered* to all, it is only by *accepting* this in the form of faith in Christ that one is granted the pardon and grace promised by God. The passages which hint at universal salvation speak of possibilities: Christ, in reconciling the cosmos, makes possible the salvation of all. It is at the implications of Paul's cosmic christology that we must look in our analysis of 1 Cor 15, rather than in specific statements regarding personal salvation.

From the above passages, it is clear that the Pauline writings envisaged two classes of people, those who are being saved and those who are perishing, whatever is meant by that term. Verses 50-53 of 1 Cor 15 make it clear that «flesh and blood cannot inherit the kingdom of God». It is only the transformation of our bodies by God at the last trumpet that makes it possible for us to put on imperishability and immortality. Obviously, one must be in Christ to experience this glorification. Being in Christ in the form of faith is the deciding factor in assigning a person to one group or the other.

4.4 *Other Approaches to the Question*

In defining Paul's view of salvation in this passage, a look at the structure can be of some help. Aletti analyzes the unity of the themes of verses 20-28 and shows that the relationship between Christ and the believers draws its meaning from the universality that the resurrection gives to Christ. Verses 20-28 have an inclusive emphasis not found in other verses: all Christians, all men, all of creation, God. The point is made emphatically that Christ's resurrection has universal effects. Additionally, verses 20-28 are centered on Christ's total victory over death and his connection with the risen dead[68].

Defeat of Death, 113. Lindemann draws the close connection between v.22b and the rest of the passage, and holds that the passage is very much about the relationship between God and Christ and the reign of God. A. LINDEMANN, «Parusie», 104-105.

[68] J.-N. ALETTI, «L'argumentation», 74-75:

a = 12-19 living and dead Christians
b = 20-28 Christians, all men, all of creation, God
a[1] = 29-32 living and dead Christians
a = 12-19 Christ not risen: defeat and disaster
b = 20-28 Christ and dead raised: victory
a[1] = 29-32 no resurrection of dead: vanquished by death

The total nature of Christ's victory over death, the totality of its effects, and the link between Christ's resurrection and that of humanity, suggests that the logic leads in the direction of universalism.

E.P. Sanders writes of a «participation eschatology», in which one is saved by transferring from the old to the new reality by means of faith and commitment. Only those who do so will be saved; all others will be destroyed at the eschaton. Sanders is probably correct in saying that one must participate in the new reality to be saved. But are there different ways of participating? Is it a foregone conclusion that all those who do not will be lost[69]?

Boring resolves the problems of Paul's apparent contradictions by a theory of symbolic meaning. For example, when God as judge is the operant symbol, such as in 1 Thess, «two-group» language is used (us and them) which stresses the salvation of some and the perdition of others. On the other hand, in passages in which kingly conquest is used to describe God's actions, «one-group» thinking is stressed, in which God's complete rulership of the cosmos and his victory over all enemies is described[70].

The fact that passages implying limited salvation are numerically more numerous is not decisive. In fact, it is this latter type of imagery which enables Boring to state that

> Those who are pictured as the enemy subjugated by the assertion of God's eschatological kingly power are not one of the two groups into which humanity is ultimately divided, not a group of non elect or nonbelieving hu-

[69] This seems to square with the many passages which imply that it is by accepting the salvation that is offered through faith that one is saved. On the other hand, Sanders very rigorously consigns those without faith to destruction. He notes 1 Cor 6,9-11, which lists those who will not inherit the kingdom of God, and takes the exhortation to stand firm until the day of the Lord as a warning that the believer stands a chance of losing all. Although Paul uses similar words at many times, there is no clear proof that he meant all unbelievers or complete annihilation. Sanders describes a «soteriology of cleansing», in which believers await salvation in a pure state with the possession of the Spirit as a sign of future salvation. By participating in Christ, the believer shares in his death and thereby dies to the power of sin which characterizes the old aeon. He now belongs to God. E.P. SANDERS, *Paul and Palestinian Judaism*, 447-474.

[70] «the range of Paul's soteriological language - that is, how inclusive it is - is not determined by propositional systematic consistency, nor by the developments in his theology, nor by the tension between depth and surface structures, but by the demands of the central encompassing images within which his language functions, images that necessarily involve him in conflicting language games» (M.E. BORING, «Universal Salvation», 275).

man beings, but superhuman powers, every ἀρχή, ἐξουσία, and δύναμις that has kept God's creation from being what it was intended to be, such as θάνατος, the last enemy. They are defeated; their power is taken away. All creation becomes subject to the gracious kingly rule of God. Not only is there no room left for hell in this picture; there is no room for destroyed, annihilated creatures who have been defeated by sin and death[71].

This use of symbols and their functions to explain Paul's statements enables Boring to say that

A Pauline theology of evangelism will refuse to reduce human responsibility and will thus always contain an urgent call to decision; but it will also refuse to reduce the sovereignty of the gracious God who has already decided and acted for all human beings [...] Paul affirms *both* limited salvation *and* universal salvation [...] Paul affirms both human responsibility and the universal victory of God's grace. As propositions, they can only contradict each other. As pictures, they can both be held up, either alternatively or, occasionally, together, as pointers to the God whose grace and judgment both resist capture in a system, or in a single picture. And this is ultimately what Paul did[72].

Beker states that God's final apocalyptic triumph does not permit any pocket of evil or resistance to him. This line of argumentation probably is the most fruitful in discerning universalistic threads in Paul's theology. We have seen in the section on death that death was not God's plan or his doing, being the result of human sin and disobedience. Death created a scar or rift in the universe, a portion of creation alienated from God. God's reconquest of the cosmos involves the subjection of every enemy and adversary, the last being death itself. Then the Son, everything having been subjected to him, is himself subjected to the Father, so that God will be all in all. The issue here is God's total and undivided sovereignty over his creation.

These other approaches to the question are less than satisfying, for they depart from the text and leave one with the uncomfortable feeling that modern categories and sensibilities have triumphed over the intent of the original text. As we have seen, Paul's letters were occasional and ad hoc. We should not expect a fully developed theology in all areas. He was dealing with church discipline and the burning question of the relationship of Christianity to Judaism and the status of Jews and Gentiles before God. Using Boring's model, we see that he used various images at

---

[71] Boring points out that the πάντες in v.22 is not explicitly universalist, while the τὰ πάντα ἐν πᾶσιν in v. 28 is. This is not because Paul has changed his mind, but because another image, that of kingly conquest, has come into play, rather than a juridical image. M.E. BORING, «Universal Salvation», 281.

[72] M.E. BORING, «Universal Salvation», 291-292.

different times and for different purposes. As someone steeped in the Jewish apocalyptic tradition of the intertestamental period, he believed in some sort of retribution for sinners (cf. Rom 2,1-11 and 2 Cor 5,6-10), and yet, if his theology is carried out to its logical consequences, one might be forced to admit that the eternal loss of a large portion of humanity has no part in God's plan for humanity.

In chapter 3, it was shown that even in Jewish apocalyptic literature, the fate of the wicked and the nature of the resurrection was vague and at times contradictory. Most taught that the wicked would be punished; some were simply silent as to their fate. The focus is always on the life of the elect. Paul does not mention any specific punishment as such for the wicked; he states simply that many are perishing or will face destruction. «Glory» was seen as a manifestation of God's creative power; for the Christian, this is manifested by means of being in Christ which is tantamount to experiencing the resurrection. It was by being glorified with Christ that one received a glorified and therefore immortal body. Those who are not in Christ probably go through the process of death and destruction bereft of the regenerative power of Christ's glory; i.e., they «perish». If God is to punish the wicked in some direct way, it would appear that this would have to be either without a resurrected body or through some sort of body granted through means not discussed in the NT.

The salvation of unbelievers as distinct from the wicked was just not a major issue, therefore we do not find the sort of discussion that we would expect. The closest to it was the question of Israel's salvation. Even though he states in Rom 11:26 that all Israel will be saved, he does not elaborate as to the means or the time.

It is fairly clear that Paul believed that only those who were «of Christ» or «in Christ» would be raised up and glorified. But what does it mean to be «in Christ» or «of Christ»? For Paul, it was to be a member of the Christian community, i.e., live a life of faith in Christ. But perhaps one need not be explicitly so. This is the idea developed by Karl Rahner in his theology of the «anonymous Christian». Did Paul believe in universal salvation? We cannot know for sure. If he did, he failed to develop and explain this part of his theology. But his theology points in that direction and sows the seeds for its future development.

5. The Importance of the Apocalyptic Message

What is special about the apocalyptic message of this passage? Is it different from normal eschatology? Is the apocalyptic message relevant for today, and if so, in what way?

Beker sees a fourfold positive message in apocalyptic literature: 1) vindication: with the death and resurrection of Christ, God renews his covenant with Israel and the gentiles and inaugurates the righteousness of God, and his sovereignty at the beginning and end of time is equal; 2) universalism: God's wrath and judgment level all that is opposed to him, all human judgments, all elitism. It is a manifestation of the power and glory of God over all that is earthly or human, and institution of new values. Related to this is a cosmic anthropology that demands righteous action and a reconciliation of the world. The individual must take an active and selfless part in God's plan of cosmic redemption; 3) dualism: world to come – God's world – always set in contrast with this world that is still being controlled by evil forces. All of this will be transformed in the world to come. This calls for saying «No» to structures and being willing to endure suffering; 4) imminence: the sense of the impending actualization of the reign of God intensifies all else and hopes for the elimination of all dualistic structures. There are three aspects to this imminence: a) necessity: the expectation of the return of Christ is made necessary by the resurrection of Christ, since resurrection language *is* apocalyptic language; b) incalculability: the coming of the reign of God cannot be deduced from historical events, but its imminence can be deduced from God's promises. The so-called delay of the parousia is not a problem, nor was it so for Paul; what is called for is radical openness and faith in God's promises; c) patience/impatience: Beker holds that passion and sobriety, apocalyptic fervor and missionary strategy all go hand in hand, since God is the one who chooses the moment of fulfillment[73].

Beker warns us of the manifold and grave consequences of ignoring the apocalyptic message. Apocalypticism becomes Christology, and the focus of theology looks back to the Christ event as the fulfillment of God's promises rather than to the future. The message becomes privatized and spiritualized. During the patristic era, eschatology is replaced by mysticism and the indwelling of the Spirit, the soul becomes spiritual and progresses into the angelic order[74].

---

[73] J.C. BEKER, *Paul's Apocalyptic Gospel*, 30-53.

[74] This «collapse of apocalypticism into Christology» leads to individualism and spiritualization, as well as a misunderstanding of Paul's anthropology and ecclesiology resulting from the «spiritualization of the somatic worldly component of his thought». The church should be viewed, according to Beker, as the «avant-garde of the new creation in a hostile world, creating beachheads in this world of God's dawning new world and yearning for the day of God's visible lordship over his creation, the general resurrection of the dead». This is sacrificed when the apocalyptic nature is lost. Taking a swipe at both Protestant and Catholic ecclesiologies, he says that the church then becomes an «aggregate of justified sinners» or a «sacramental

What does this do to the resurrection? Beker foresees a process of closure to the future and to the coming of the kingdom of God, a loss of the
sense of being in the midst of the end time. Beker insists that Paul's
apocalyptic is a «necessary consequence of the truth of the gospel [...] he
does not celebrate apocalyptic *notwithstanding* Christ but *because* of
Christ [...] for the death and resurrection of Christ are future-oriented
events, not "closure" events». Additionally, there is a process of individualism that encourages a preoccupation with one's own personal salvation. There is also a tendency towards substituting the church for the
kingdom of God, although this criticism may reflect Beker's own confes-
sional stance[75].

Making apocalyptic relevant without compromising either its message
or its power is difficult. Beker theorizes that Paul's apocalyptic gospel
cannot be transferred directly into our time, culture and situation. He
sees its role as a catalytic one. This function will be able to distinguish
between the coherent permanent gospel and the time-conditioned or contingent interpretations. The rewards of taking seriously Paul's apocalyptic
gospel include an ethical fervor, a concern for the entire cosmos and an

---

institute». While his point about the change in focus of theology and spirituality is
well taken, perhaps he is overly critical and reductionist in his analysis of non-
apocalyptic theology. The statements concerning mysticism and the indwelling of the
Spirit reflect a prejudice on Beker's part; indeed, it is clear from a reading of the
Qumran documents that the indwelling Spirit of God and living in the company of
angels is certainly not incompatible with a fervent apocalyptic eschatology. J.C.
BEKER, *Paul the Apostle*, 154-155.

[75] 1) The resurrection interprets Jesus' life as a closure event, that is, as the final
confirmation of the divine status of Jesus in his incarnate life. And so the «life of Jesus» becomes a «foundation story» that occupies the position of the «center of history»
and loses its firm connection with the coming kingdom of God and the final resurrection of the dead. 2) It stresses in antidocetic fashion the reality of Jesus as the
Christ and thus centers more on the identity of Jesus as the eternal Son of God than
on the Jesus as the inaugurator of the final resurrection and the kingdom of God. 3) It
confirms the divine preexistence of Christ and his incarnation and so construes an
analogy between the incarnation and the resurrection: just as the post resurrection
Jesus is divinity in the flesh, so the incarnate Jesus is divinity in the flesh. 4) The
resurrection signifies the exaltation of Christ, whose grace is available through the
sacraments of the church, «the kingdom of Christ», and whose reign can now be lo-
cated in the hierarchical offices of the church. 5) The resurrection of the dead becomes an individualistic postmortem immortality and an individualistic «last» judgment. 6) The cosmic resurrection of the dead and the future kingdom of God become
a far-off proper «conclusion» to the created order. They function, as it were, as the
proper end for systematic doctrinal thought: just as our transient creation has a beginning, it has an end in the eternal being of God, so that both «beginning» and «end»
are embraced by the timelessness and eternity of God. J.C. BEKER, *Paul the Apostle*,
84.157.

elimination of sectarianism and elitism, an emphasis on humanity as a whole rather than individualism, and most of all, a change of emphasis regarding Christian ethical activity. This well-meaning ethical activity on the part of Christians often becomes, Beker believes, a «romantic and tragic exaggeration of human ethical capability», since the emphasis is always on the individual and his own efforts. Ethical activity rooted in an apocalyptic gospel, on the other hand, is always viewed «against the horizon of God's initiative». In other words, God's prerogatives, power and glory are safeguarded, and all humanity must justify itself to God instead of the other way around[76].

There is much that is attractive in Beker's views concerning Paul's apocalyptic gospel. It could provide an antidote to the individualism, complacency, and compromise with worldly powers and values that seems to have taken hold of Christianity. There is a captivating passion and fervor and a constant reference to the power and initiative of God rather than human beings, which is missing in much of our social teachings and liberation theology. There is a concern for the regeneration of the cosmos as a whole, which seems to be tailor-made for our concern with ecology. There is a leveling of structures, and a refusal to recognize external distinctions between people. And yet, there are reservations. First of all, although Beker realizes that a first-century world view cannot be transplanted intact into our time, he is not specific enough in his efforts to explain how it is to become a catalyst. How is this done, without compromising the apocalyptic nature of the gospel, which is something that Beker criticizes bitterly in modern theologians? Additionally, although apocalyptic is the great leveler, it is elitist in the sense that it is very quick to divide humanity into the sheep and the goats, and it seems to revel in the fact that the wicked will perish or be punished. There also does not seem to be an obvious way to keep this apocalypticism from degenerating into the neo-apocalypticism that Beker decries so much. He rightly accuses it of being deterministic, non-participatory, non-christological and self-centered, but how could any apocalyptic theology keep from falling into the same trap? Beker has highlighted admirably the beauty and power of apocalyptic theology, but has failed to show how it can speak to our own time without being seriously compromised.

---

[76] The impossibility of transferring Paul's first-century world directly into our own is obvious: the matter of cosmology, exclusivity, disintegration and renewal, etc. presents problems, although perhaps in recent times even these aspects are more credible than we might suppose. Paul's apocalyptic gospel must be *defended* rather than slavishly copied, and it is this that will act as a catalyst, enabling us to reflect on his language in a new way. J.C. BEKER, *Paul's Apocalyptic Gospel*, 84.86.105.

E. Schüssler-Fiorenza agrees with Beker's fundamental principle that one should not seek to explain away or dilute the apocalyptic message. She is also more clear as to the nature of its effect on modern readers.

Early Christian apocalyptic should therefore not be delineated by abstracting the theological eschatological essence or the existential eschatological stance towards life from its apocalyptic language and thought-world. Apocalyptic language is not simply the vehicle for theological-eschatological ideas or concepts but as mytho-poetic language evokes imaginative participation. The metaphoric and symbolic character of apocalyptic language resists any attempt at logical reduction and closed one-dimensional interpretation. Its aim is not explanation and information but the expression of literary wholeness. It elicits understandings, emotions and reactions that cannot fully be conceptualized and expressed in propositional language. Since apocalyptic language appeals to the imagination it has to be analyzed from a literary perspective.[77]

She warns against looking upon the NT writings merely as self-consciously created literary works, insisting that they are religious proclamations, and as such, should be the spark for audience participation and catharsis.

Paul expanded apocalyptic expectation by calling Christ the «firstfruits of those who have fallen asleep» (15,20) and combining the concept of the resurrection of Christ with the apocalyptic symbol of the general resurrection of the dead. Resurrection becomes an «apocalyptic tensive symbol» evoking a wide range of meanings as expressed in the symbolism of 1 Thess 1,10; Phil 1,23; and 1 Thess 4,15ff.[78]

Early Christian apocalyptic language formed the creative core of Christian theology. Christ is the Lord who continues to live in the community, and the apocalyptic literature reveals him as such, and that the end-times have been inaugurated in the Christ event. Between the Jesus who spoke in the past and who will come as eschatological judge in the future, there is his voice that continues to speak through the apostles and prophets of the community, making Christian apocalyptic literature prophetic in character.

Schüssler-Fiorenza is more specific in how this theology can continue to speak to us in her reliance on the impact of apocalyptic on the imagination, and she is correct in viewing it as prophetic in nature and as hav-

---

[77] E. SCHÜSSLER-FIORENZA, «Phenomenon of Early Christian Apocalyptic», 305.

[78] She also believes that the hellenistic concepts such as immortality, transformation of the perishable nature and the putting of of the imperishable nature as a garment are added to 1 Cor 15, but there is no real reason to insist that these are only hellenistic concepts. E. SCHÜSSLER-FIORENZA, «Phenomenon of Early Christian Apocalyptic», 305-307.

ing a life within the community. However, it is difficult to control or evaluate what issues from the imagination, and it is very easy to use the emotive power of apocalyptic for one's own ends or to service various ideologies. Passion for justice there must be, but it must be God's justice.

It must be emphasized that this thirst for a just world which is seen by Schüssler-Fiorenza and others as the abiding value of apocalyptic theology is already a distortion of the original message. It is difficult, for us to understand the intensity with which the people of the first century yearned and waited for the sudden, violent, all-encompassing irruption of the transcendent God into human history and the termination of that history. The basic message of apocalyptic was spiritual: the believer must decide whose side he is on and make sure his heart is right with God. Correct ethical living was the result. Apocalyptic theology must not become the fuel for ideologies, sects, and social crusading. If it is compromised with human agendas, then it is no longer truly apocalyptic.

CHAPTER V

The Exegesis of 1 Cor 15,12-28 During the Patristic Period

1. Introduction

The first five Christian centuries provided the fullest opportunity for a wide spectrum of interpretations of this passage. A diachronic survey of these exegeses and interpretations is important for understanding the role of this passage in the early proclamation of the gospel, the spread of the church, and the development of Christian doctrine. This will also enable us to discern whether the full import of the apocalyptic message has been understood and utilized, and whether there was a shift away from an apocalyptic to a christological interpretation. If there is a shift towards a christological interpretation, does it represent a legitimate theological development, or a misunderstanding of the basic message of the passage?

The history of the exegesis of this passage is intertwined with the history of the theological debates of early Christianity. The first real controversy in which this passage is enmeshed is that of the resurrection, which was the preoccupation of the Church during the first two centuries. The resurrection was indeed central to the New Testament faith; however, the symbolism and resurrection accounts of the NT are not unambiguous in what they mean for the human race and for the individual believer. Many questions were unanswered, especially those concerning the relationship between the soul, the body, and the material world[1].

2. The Phases of Interpretation

The first phase of exegesis of 1 Cor 15 was the soteriological phase, in which the fate of individual believers and humanity as a whole was debated and refined. Emphasis was also given to ethical perseverance and

---

[1] J.T. LIENHARD, «The Exegesis of 1 Cor 15, 24-28», 340-359; P. PERKINS, *Resurrection*, 331-332; E. SCHENDEL, *Herrschaft*, 2-5.

fidelity in anticipation of the parousia. The primary use of the passage in question was to defend the reality of and need for the resurrection. A verse from the passage under discussion was used primarily as a prooftext, with little speculation, to lend support to the argument of the author[2].

Sometimes the connection with the author's argument was rather thin. During this period, there was a preponderance of quotations from the first half of the passage, in particular, verses 12-24. Verse 22 was a favored passage, as it explains the need for a physical resurrection against opponents who denied the participation of the flesh in salvation[3].

Part of the exegetical background of this first phase was the eschatological expectation during the first two Christian centuries of the end of the world with its general resurrection and final judgment. A variation of the eschatological expectation was the amorphous movement called millenarianism, which was widely diffused throughout the very early centuries. This idea was based on the expectation of a first resurrection of only the just, followed by a thousand-year reign with Christ in the heavenly Jerusalem descended on the earth, with every sort of good and happiness. This would then be followed by a second general resurrection and the universal judgment. This idea had a twofold basis: the belief that the duration of the world was only 7,000 years, and a literal reading of Rev 20 and 21[4].

The next phase, christological and cosmological in nature, begins with Origen, reaches a peak during the Christological controversies of the fourth and fifth centuries, and finally passes from the scene in the late fifth century. This phase was fueled by the rise of the Alexandrian school of exegesis, whose most prominent spokesman was Origen. This approach favored the allegorical and symbolic interpretation of Scripture over the historical, with Christ as the hermeneutical key[5].

---

[2] Tertullian is one of the first to begin to actually interpret the text, but it is Origen who really opened it to speculation. E. SCHENDEL, *Herrschaft*, 30.

[3] The Church Fathers found themselves sometimes debating on two fronts. Against gnostics and others of similar views, they had to prove that flesh was not evil and that it was capable of participating in immortality, while they had to convince more conventional Christians that the soul was not naturally immortal. P. PERKINS, *Resurrection*, 332.

[4] Simonetti characterizes the more literal and materialistic intepretation of scripture as being part of an Asiatic cultural ambience filled with pagan, stoic, and Jewish ideas; while the Alexandrian culture and its exegesis, which supplanted the former, was more rigorous, scientific, and spiritual. Besides being rather stereotypical, this explanation also does not explain the obviously Eastern roots of Alexandrian culture. M. SIMONETTI, «Il millenarismo in Oriente», 37-58.

[5] The historical sense was not denied, but was subordinated to the allegorical, especially in passages that were deemed offensive, crude, incredible, or unworthy of

The allegorical and spiritual exegesis applied by Origen and his followers quickly brought to a virtual end the literal exegesis of eschatological passages such as Rev 20 and 21 and the resulting millenarianism[6].

The Alexandrian allegorical tradition, especially as represented by Origen, was bitterly attacked for centuries after his death. Most vehement in opposition were church fathers such as Augustine and the later Jerome, and the exegetical school of Antioch, which flourished in the latter fourth and early fifth centuries. These opponents protested the excesses of this exegetical tradition and held it responsible for many heresies. The school of Antioch interpreted Scripture in a strictly historical and literal manner, although at times some typology was accepted in the exegesis of the OT[7].

The coming of the Arians in all shades signalled the beginning of the Trinitarian controversy surrounding this passage, for many of them appealed to it as a prooftext for their doctrines. It is easy to find in this passage verses which suggest the Son's inferiority to the Father, and the Arians were quick to do so. This gave rise to an important exegetical problem from the standpoint of Christology, that of the subjection (ὑποταγή) of Christ. Exegetes struggled mightily to explain this passage while preserving the divinity of Christ and his equality with God the Father. Additionally, the phrase «God will be all in all» in verse 28 (ὁ θεὸς τὰ πάντα ἐν πᾶσιν) immediately provoked the question, What happens to Christ at this point? Does he still exist and maintain his identity and rule? Or is he absorbed into the Godhead?

The anti-Arian exegesis of verse 25 by Marcellus of Ancyra also incited much polemical activity, especially his interpretation of «until» (ἄχρι οὗ) and rule (βασιλεύειν) as implying that the kingdom of Christ was temporal in nature and would come to an end. This gave rise to a doctrine of two kingdoms, one of Christ and the other of God, with the former being temporal in nature[8].

God. The Alexandrian tradition had its roots in Philo, was first developed for Christians by Clement, and reached its peak with Origen. Others followed in Origen's tradition; for instance, Didymus the Blind, Cyril of Alexandria, Rufinus, and briefly, Jerome. R.M. GRANT, *Interpretation*, 52-62; K. FROEHLICH, *Biblical Interpretation*, 15-19; J. TRIGG, *Biblical Interpretation*, 23-31.

[6] M. SIMONETTI, «Il millenarismo in Oriente», 37.

[7] The Antiochenes also used the word *theoria*, but they meant it in the sense of a deeper meaning of a passage, but based firmly on the literal sense. Some of the better known Antiochene exegetes were Diodore of Tarsus, Theodore of Mopsuestia, John Chrysostom, and Theodoret of Cyrrhus. Ironically, while the Alexandrian school was accused of fostering Arianism, the Antiochene school gave birth, it is said, to Nestorianism. R.M. GRANT, *Interpretation*, 63-72; K. FROEHLICH, *Biblical Interpretation*, 19-22; J. TRIGG, *Biblical Interpretation*, 31-38.

[8] This doctrine of two kingdoms, one of Christ and the other of God, is handled by various authors, including Gregory of Nazianzus, Gregory of Nyssa, John Chry-

The doctrinal prominence and speculative force of this passage diminishes after the great christological debates of the fifth century, and fades away definitively after the anti-Origen condemnations of the Fifth Ecumenical Council of 553.

2.1 *Apostolic and Post-Apostolic Age*

a) Clement of Rome

One of the first uses of this passage outside the NT was in I Clement XXIV.1, written about the year 96 A.D. The purpose of this letter was to deal with authority problems in the Corinthian community, as it urged a group of dissidents to obey church order and the established authority structures. It is likely that the Corinthian community was still experiencing problems with an overly realized eschatology as in Paul's day, for a major portion of the letter (chapters 23-28) deals with defending the tradition concerning resurrection and judgment in spite of the delay experienced by the community.

Clement's argumentation concerning the reality of the resurrection begins with a reference to Christ as the firstfruits (1 Cor 15,20), although instead of following it up with the rest of Paul's argument, Clement employed a device that became standard; that is, the analogy between the resurrection and transformative events in the natural order, the prime examples being the seasons and grains of seed. Additionally, he utilizes prophecies from Scripture, stories from mythology, and arguments for God's omnipotence and providence, all designed to show that the resurrection is indeed possible and likely within God's created order[9].

He presents a traditional NT eschatology: the imminent coming of the Kingdom, the sudden return of Christ and the universal judgment[10].

The purpose is to illustrate that the resurrection is in keeping with creation and history, and that given its unfolding and evolutionary nature, it will arrive in its own good time, when all is ready. It remains for the believer to lead a holy life in expectation of God's judgment, especially concerning proper order in the community[11].

---

sostom, and Severian of Gabala. They deal with the problem in various ways, although all of them discuss a double kingdom, and a beginning or end of at least one and sometimes both of them. They do not, however, follow Marcellus by claiming that the temporary kingdom belongs to Christ and the eternal one to God, but hold that both kingdoms are Christ's and God's. A. GRILLMEIER, *Christ in Christian Tradition*, I, 290-292; J. LIENHARD, «The Exegesis of 1 Cor 15, 24-28», 354-355.

[9] The myth of the phoenix, found in Pliny the Elder's *Natural History* 10.2 and in some Jewish apocryphal writings, is his mythological analogy. P. PERKINS, *Resurrection*, 337.

[10] 42,3; 50,3; 23,3-5; 28.

[11] CLEMENT OF ROME, in *The Apostolic Fathers*, 51; B.E. DALEY, *Hope*, 10; 28.1-29.1.

b) Ignatius of Antioch

Ignatius of Antioch wrote his letters to the seven churches about 110 A.D. while being taken to Rome under military escort for eventual martyrdom. His eschatology reflects the belief that the last days are very near, and he is convinced that it is a time for ethical decision. His letters are filled with hope, the foundation of which is the resurrection, which he considers a stage of the passion. In his *Letter to the Trallians*, he warns believers not to listen to anyone who speaks to them «apart from Jesus Christ», i.e., who deny the fleshly reality of Jesus, his life, death and resurrection. As Christ was raised bodily from the dead, so will all those who believe in him, and apart from him we have no true life. A complete bodily resurrection is reserved for believers, while bodiless but painful punishment awaits sinners and deniers of the resurrection. Eschatological renewal is more than transformation of the material world, but is the gift of life which has already begun for believers in Christ, who is the prototype[12].

c) Conclusion

In this apostolic and immediate post-apostolic period, the emphasis in the interpretation of this text is given to patience concerning the return of Christ, the final judgment, ethical decision, and proper order within the community. The resurrection of Christ is looked upon as the guarantee of our own. Speculative exegesis is absent.

2.2 *The Challenge of Gnosticism*

Gnosticism was the Church's first major theological challenge. There were many varieties of Gnosticism with diverse characteristics. In general, however, they all shared a cosmological dualism of spirit and matter, a separation of God from creation, denigration of matter and the body, a rejection of the OT and its God, whom they believed to be the inferior creator or Demiurge, and a denial of salvation history[13].

---

[12] IGNATIUS OF ANTIOCH, *Letter to the Trallians*, IX.2.95; B.E. DALEY, *Hope*, 12-13; P. PERKINS, *Resurrection* 334-335.

[13] Gnosticism is comprised of many different philosophies and systems, but in general it may be characterized according to the Congress of Messina in 1966: «The Gnosticism of the second-century sects involves a coherent series of characteristics that can be summarized in the idea of a divine spark in man, deriving from the divine realm, fallen into this world of fate, birth and death, and needing to be awakened by the divine counterpart of the self in order to be finally reintegrated. Compared with other conceptions of a "devolution" of the divine, this idea is based ontologically on the conception of a downward movement of the divine whose periphery (often called

There were many forms of gnosticism; however, the Valentinian variety probably represented the greatest threat to the church. It was clearly and intellectually articulated and of all the diverse forms, it was probably that closest to orthodox Christian theology. The Valentinian anthropology consisted of the body, which is dust and destined to perish; a vivifying animate element or soul, which will be preserved; and the intellect or spiritual element, which is the true self and will be reunited with God. Since the body could not survive nor the other two elements die, words such as «arise» and «resurrection» were interpreted in an existential and cosmological sense: the soul escaped the fetters of material existence and «rose» or «ascended» through the spheres to another, superior form of existence[14].

A prime example of the Valentinian gnostic theology with which the Church struggled is the *Treatise on the Resurrection* from the Nag Hamaddi trove. The author held that the resurrection was a matter of faith, not subject to philosophical proofs. The resurrection is not as understood by orthodox Christians in that the spiritual body is not re-created at the parousia of Christ. When an elect believer dies, the inward «living members», which are intellectual in nature, separate from the outer perishable body. The resurrection body is clothed with a garment of light, and there is continuity of the person's identity[15].

The author also taught that rather than the fullness of the resurrection being held in abeyance until the parousia, the resurrection is present for the believer, since one has already proleptically participated in the passion and resurrection of Christ[16].

Christ «swallowed up» death by being able to put aside the perishable world and transforming himself into an imperishable aeon[17].

It is important to realize that both gnostic and orthodox writers appeal to the same texts as proof of their doctrines. Paul has traditionally been viewed as the zealous hammer of the gnostics, especially in regard to their denial of the resurrection[18].

Sophia or Ennoia) had to submit to the fate of entering into a crisis and producing, even if only indirectly, this world, upon which it cannot turn its back, since it is necessary for it to recover the pneuma, a dualistic conception on a monistic background, expressed in a double movement of devolution and reintegration» (G. FILORAMO, *Gnosticism*, 143).

[14] B. LAYTON, *The Gnostic Scriptures*, 316-317.

[15] *On the Resurrection*, NHLE, 52-53 paragraphs 45-47. This is the so-called *Epistle to Rheginos*; P. PERKINS, *Resurrection*, 357-60.

[16] *On the Resurrection*, NHLE 45,24-28. Cf. 2 Timothy 2,18.

[17] 45.14-18; *NHLE* 51. This image is found in several gnostic writings: The *Apocryphon of John*, NHLE 99; the *Apocalypse of Peter*, NHLE 344, and this may be an «exegesis» based partly on a reference to 1 Cor 15,54. P. PERKINS, *Resurrection*, 357

[18] E. PAGELS, «The Mystery of the Resurrection», 276-288. Schmithals, as Bultmann before him, painted Paul as an untiring and orthodox anti-gnostic polemicist,

E. Pagels insists, however, that the gnostics did in fact believe in the resurrection, but not in the way understood by the church[19].

Strangely enough, various gnostic groups, especially Valentinians, not only were not embarrassed by Paul's alleged polemics, but actually embraced his teachings on the resurrection in this chapter as proof of their own doctrines. Pagels shows that the Valentinians, through an extremely intricate and subtle symbolic exegesis of chapter 15, sought to prove that Paul was speaking on various levels: some statements were meant for those who were on the psychic (*psychikos*) level, while others referred to the initiates, those who were spiritual (*pneumatikoi*) and the perfect (*teleioi*)[20].

This is to be expected, for the gnostics used this form of exegesis on their own and all sacred writings, believing them to bear cryptic messages[21].

It is important to bear in mind, then, that as the Church Fathers use certain proof texts to refute the gnostics (and others) these same texts will be claimed by their adversaries[22].

---

and 1 Cor 15 as the very climax of his anti-gnostic polemic. See W. SCHMITHALS, *Gnosticism in Corinth*, 156-285.

[19] This is based on statements by Origen and others to the effect that the gnostics do not believe in the resurrection *in this flesh (in hac carne)*, and that they consider belief in the *bodily* resurrection the «faith of fools». E. PAGELS, «Mystery», 278.

[20] «Valentinian exegetes resolve what we have come to call the "Pauline sense of paradox" rather simply: they insist that Paul's contradictory statements apply to different persons, to psychics and pneumatics respectively. For example, when Paul speaks of the Christian as one already "raised with Christ" in baptism, already "alive in Christ", he is speaking of the pneumatic, whose "resurrection", like Christ's, has already occurred; pneumatics live the "new life" now. On the other hand, when Paul describes the resurrection as a future event, which is to occur at the end of the age, he is speaking of the raising of psychics who await the eschatological transformation as their future hope» (E. PAGELS, «Mystery», 287).

[21] The gnostics believed that they alone possessed the keys to intepret correctly sacred texts, so the use of this method on a text that is supposedly anti-gnostic is not surprising. G. FILORAMO, *Gnosticism*, 17-18.

[22] The angels, who have never descended to this physical sphere of existence, were baptized when the dove descended on Jesus at his baptism in the Jordan. They are the counterparts of the gnostics on earth, enabling them to rise through the spheres to the Pleroma (22,4-5). The gnostics interpreted our text in a completely different way, as we see from the polemics in *excerpta ex scripti Theodoti*. The gnostics claim that Paul was the apostle of the resurrection, but as the type of the Savior or Paraclete. Rather curiously, the gnostics interpret verse 29 to mean that angels are baptized on the behalf of those who are spiritually dead and who live «down here», i.e., the human race. *excerpta ex scripta Theodoti*, 23,2; 22,1-3; P. PERKINS, *Resurrection*, 356.

2.3 *The Church's Response To Gnosticism*

a) Irenaeus of Lyon: The Goodness of Creation

The gnostic vision of God and reality prompted the vision of millennial hope that is found in Irenaeus of Lyon. Irenaeus is the first anti-gnostic author that we have, and he as well as Tertullian rely heavily on Paul's letters for their anti-gnostic writings[23].

Utilizing unity as a guiding principle, Irenaeus labored to counteract the dualism and existential pessimism of the gnostics, for whom separation and division were guiding principles. The gnostics separated God the Father from the Creator; spirit from matter; salvation from history and human life; and material, natural man from pneumatic or spiritual man. Irenaeus, then, asserted the unity of God with his creation and the importance of the created order, the continuity of the Old Testament with the New, and the solidarity of God and Christ with the flesh of humanity. His economical and soteriological conception of salvation history enable him to speak of the temporal nature of Christ's reign without prejudice to his divinity[24].

Whereas the gnostics had distinguished between the Demiurge and the Father and the *hylic* or natural man and the pneumatic or spiritual man, Irenaeus hoped to prove that they were no divisions in the Godhead or in humanity. Both body and soul are necessary for salvation (V 6.1). There is only one God who both creates and saves; likewise, man is at the same time carnal and spiritual. His anthropology and view of salvation were evolutionary: in the beginning man was created through the breath of God, which was temporal, while at the end, after the eschatological event of the incarnation, man is perfected and given the gift of eternal life through the Spirit of God. Irenaeus uses verse 22 to show that the body does not possess incorruption, but has the capacity to receive it, which man was unable to do until the coming of Christ. Christ came in a way which we were able to see and accept, and recapitulates in himself the history of the old Adam[25].

By far the most important aspect of his theology of hope is the resurrection of the body, which will take place when Christ returns. The material reality of the resurrection of the body is something which he must

---

[23] Justin Martyr wrote a *Compendium Against All Heresies*, but it is not extant. Irenaeus, bishop of Lyon, wrote *Adversus haereses* in Greek, comprising 5 books, but in complete form only a Latin translation survives. G. FILORAMO, *Gnosticism*, 3.

[24] B.E. DALEY, *Hope*, 28; M. O'ROURKE BOYLE, «Irenaeus' Millenial Hope», 5-16; E. SCHENDEL, *Herrschaft*, 201.

[25] For Irenaeus' anthropology see especially *A.H.* V 1,3; V 6,1; V 14,2; V 12,2.; V 16,1-2; IV 38,1-4; and III 22,1. J. DANIÉLOU, *Gospel Message and Hellenistic Culture*, 398-406.

establish in opposition to the gnostic vision, which believed only in the immortality of the spiritual soul[26].

Irenaeus must counter the gnostics' frequent appeal to 1 Cor 15,50: «Flesh and blood cannot inherit the Kingdom of God» by responding with the principles set forth in vv. 53 and 54: Christ's humanity was real and of flesh, and he saves the whole human person, body and soul, by raising and transforming our bodies with the gift of his Spirit. The transformation begins now, and is completed at the coming of Christ and the general resurrection. The flesh and blood of v.50 is taken to mean those who do not have the Spirit, and the corruption and death swallowed up by victory is taken differently from the gnostics, meaning the body that has been vivified by the Spirit[27].

His most frequent scriptural quotations from 1 Cor 15 are vv. 22 and 23, which describe the image of the old and new Adam[28].

There is also appeal to the image of Christ as firstfruits of the resurrection of man, for the assumption of human nature by Christ who is the head of the body makes possible the resurrection of every human found to be part of this body[29].

The symbol of the New Adam is used to show the material reality of the resurrection, its necessity and results. Christ is the New Adam who regenerates humanity through his assumption of human nature, counteracting the devastating effects of the first Adam's disobedience. Irenaeus insists that it was necessary and in accordance with divine mercy for the first Adam to taste salvation first in order for the human race to be revivified. Showing that separation from God and death both are the result of Adam's disobedience, he portrays death, the last enemy, as being destroyed once the old Adam has received new life[30].

The image of the old and new Adam (1 Cor 15,22) is used at the beginning to show the continuity between the fallen and redeemed humanity, as well as the means by which God breathes life back into fallen humanity in his act of recreation[31].

---

[26] In 3.12.3, the resurrection of the dead is designated as the content or essence of apostolic preaching. It is this that Irenaeus seeks to protect in his argumentation, cf. *A.H.* 1.10.1; 1.22.1; 3.16.6.

[27] *A.H.* V 8,1; III 19,1.

[28] His first use of the passage under study is in *A.H.* 3.18.3, where he appeals to the primitive profession of faith in I Cor 15,3-4 to show that the Jesus who suffered and died is not distinct from the Christ who is risen, despite the claims of the gnostics. This is followed by his insistence that Christ is preached as having risen from the dead, and that this is the reason for the incarnation, for since death came into the world by one man, so also the resurrection of the dead (I Cor 25,23).

[29] *A.H.* III 19,3; III 22,4; III 23,7; III 23,8.

[30] I Cor 15,26.54.55.

[31] *A.H.* V 1,3.

A clear distinction is made between man's animal nature, called a living soul, and his spiritual nature which is given by the new Adam[32].

This argument is establishing continuity between the flesh and the resurrected body, thereby countering the gnostic attempts to make a radical distinction between the two. A chain of verses 12-19, 22 and 32 provides the means by which Irenaeus proves that Paul was referring to the body of flesh as that which undergoes both death and resurrection[33].

The same Adamic image is used to show that the Word would never have taken on flesh unless flesh were destined to be saved[34].

The concept of ἀνακεφαλαιώσασθαι or recapitulation, best explains the salvific work of Christ. All of humanity is restored in the Son, who reverses the warped history of the human race by making the correct decisions when undergoing similar experiences and choices as the first Adam. In this way, sin and death lose their power and man is revivified[35].

Irenaeus' vision of millennial hope presented human salvation as taking place within salvation history and as being in accordance with God's plan from the beginning. Our immortal and incorruptible life is a gift of God, not something we enjoy by nature. There is only one God, and he has made himself known through the Scriptures and the Prophets as well as through the events of salvation history. Even creation itself becomes the means by which God is revealed. In a loose allusion to 1 Cor 15,24-28, he portrays the Son as the revelation of the Father, and the Son becomes the standard by which all will be judged, and all creation, men, angels, demons, even death itself, must give testimony to Christ in either a positive or negative manner, since all is subjected to Christ[36].

Irenaeus describes the end of human history in vivid terms: the appearance of the Antichrist with the persecutions and tribulations that he will bring, the coming of Christ and the defeat of the Antichrist, Christ's judgment with the punishment of the wicked and reward of the just[37].

Borrowing heavily from Jewish apocalyptic symbolism, he describes a millennial kingdom of earthly peace and plenty which is the locus of man's encounter with God through Christ, as well as being the beginning of incorruptibility and a final preparation.

---

[32] *A.H.* V 12,2.3.

[33] *A.H.* V 13,4.

[34] *A.H.* V 14,1. Verse 22.

[35] M. O'ROURKE BOYLE, «Irenaeus' Millennial Hope», 13-14; *A.H.* III 18,7.

[36] *A.H.* IV 6,7.

[37] *A.H.* V 25; V 28-30; IV 31,1; V 30,4; IV 4,1; IV 33,1; V 27,1; V 28,4; V 29,1. Quoted in B.E. DALEY, *Hope* 30; E. NORELLI, «Il duplice rinnovamento», 89-106; G. JOSSA, «Storia della salvezza ed escatologia», 107-125; E. SCHENDEL, *Herrschaft*, 26. Irenaeus in reality expresses two eschatological doctrines, that of the Antichrist and that of the *recapitulatio* (V 25-36).

It appears that Irenaeus taught the existence of two resurrections: one of the just, over whom Christ would rule, and the other at the end of time for the universal judgment. The period in between the two resurrections is the reign of the Son, and is temporal in nature[38].

Irenaeus' rather inconsistent presentation of the double parousia presents some problems[39].

In the final chapter of his work, Irenaeus insists that all will be raised and the world shall not be annihilated, but the new heaven and earth will be graded with various levels, with each person being allotted a place according to spiritual rank. Everything will be subject to God, eventually even the Son himself, so that God may be all in all (1 Cor 15,25-28)[40].

Likewise, in the *Demonstratio*, Irenaeus argues for the necessity of the incarnation. Christ is the first born of the dead and the head and source of the life oriented to God. He appeals to verses 12-17 to paint a grim picture of the consequences of there being no incarnation or resurrection: if Christ was not born, then he did not die; if he did not die, he was not raised from the dead; if he was not raised, death is not conquered and its reign has not been abolished; in light of all this, we cannot «mount on high into life»[41].

The Word had to become visible and perceptive in order to take us into full communication and incorruptibility. The death that we gained due to Adam's sin is reversed by the new Adam's obedience[42].

b) Tertullian: The Latin Church's Answer to Heresy

The life of the Christian church in the first few years of the third century was characterized by a sectarian, rigorist, and anti-intellectual attitude. Much Christian polemical writing at this time contained bitter attacks against pagan culture and Jewish ideas. A fervent expectation of a

---

[38] Irenaeus bases his doctrine of the two resurrections and the reign of the Son on Rev 20,1-21,4. Because he spoke of the economies of God, his dealings with the world for the sake of salvation, Irenaeus was able to speak of the temporal nature of the reign of the Son without jeopardizing his divinity, since the Trinity was eternal before creation and is without beginning or end. E. SCHENDEL, *Herrschaft*, 27-29. *A.H.* V 35,2; 36,3.

[39] According to V 32,1, Christ will come at the beginning of the Kingdom to rule over the just, while I.10.1 and III.16.6 give the impression that Christ will come first for the completion and the judgment, and then begins the Kingdom. Some reach the conclusion that he always spoke of only one parousia, basing this on I 10,1; III 4,2; V 20,1 while others hold for two, one at the Incarnation, the other at the end of time, based on a reading of IV 33,1 and IV 22,2. E. SCHENDEL, *Herrschaft*, 29.

[40] *A.H.* V 36,2. M. O'ROURKE BOYLE, «Irenaeus' Millennial Hope», 15-6; E. NORELLI, «Il duplice rinnovamento del mondo», 89-106; E. SCHENDEL, *Herrschaft*, 26.

[41] IRENAEUS, *Demonstratio*, 39.

[42] *Demonstratio* 31.

violent and imminent universal end encouraged the use of biblical eschatology for polemical and moralistic purposes[43].

Tertullian (160-220 A.D.) was the epitome of this tendency. His polemical works were passionate, uncompromising attacks on pagan culture
and skepticism, Gnosticism, and after his adherence to the Montanist
sect, the Church itself. Tertullian vigorously asserts the reality of the resurrection of the fleshly body as well as the millennial tradition. According to Tertullian's eschatology, the universal end would be a settling of
accounts between God and man, and should be anticipated with fear and
dread[44].

The soul is in a way corporeal, but without the solid substance necessary to suffer fully; therefore, the resurrection is necessary so that all can
undergo complete judgment and retribution[45].

Together with Irenaeus, Tertullian taught a double resurrection, tying
the resurrection of the just with the establishment of the 1,000 years reign
as foretold in Rev 20-21, after which would occur the general resurrection and the final judgment[46].

Tertullian was the first to offer a short interpretation of the verses beyond a mere citation[47].

His analysis of verses 24-28 play an important role in his theology as
expressed in *Adversus Praxean*. In this work, written around 212 after
his break with the Great Church, Tertullian defends the distinction of
persons in the Godhead against the claims of Praxeas and the so-called
patripassionists, who held that the Father himself was born of the Virgin
Mary and suffered on the cross[48].

---

[43] B.E. DALEY, *Hope*, 34; J. DANIÉLOU, *The Origins of Latin Christianity*, 251-258; P. SINISCALCO, *Ricerche sul "de resurrectione" di Tertulliano*.

[44] B.E. DALEY, *Hope*, 34; «the fulness and perfection of the judgment consists simply in representing the interests of the entire human being. Now, since the entire man consists of the union of two natures, he must therefore appear in both; as it is right that he should be judged in his entirety...as therefore he lived, so also must he be judged, because he has to be judged concerning the way in which he lived» (*De resurrectione*, XIV).

[45] «the soul is corporeal, possessing a peculiar kind of solidity in its nature, such as enables it both to perceive and suffer [...] souls are even now susceptible of tor-ment and of blessing in Hades, though they are disembodied [...] it will still need the flesh; not as being unable to feel anything without the help of the flesh, but because it is necessary that it should possess such a faculty along with the flesh [...] it also re-quires the conjoining of the flesh to endure suffering, in order that by its aid it may be as fully able to suffer, as without its assistance it was not fully able to act» (*De resurrectione*, XVII).

[46] Irenaeus' description of the double resurrection is found in *A.H.* V 32,1. E. SCHENDEL, *Herrschaft*, 67-68.

[47] E. SCHENDEL, *Herrschaft*, 30-31.

[48] This work is notable for its contributions to Trinitarian theology, being the first time that the terms *persona* and the concept of «one substance, three persons» appears

In 4.2 and 4.4 of this work, he utilizes verses 24,25,27 and 28 of 1 Cor 15 to illustrate that the rulership of the Son is not an obstacle to the monarchy or supremacy of God the Father, as the Son's power is derivative, all things are subjected to the Son by the Father, and this power will be restored to the Father when all enemies have been overcome. This also shows that there are two distinct persons, Father and Son, and yet the monarchy remains unimpaired[49].

In *On Prescription Against Heretics*, Tertullian seeks to reassure believers who are shaken by the abundance of heresies present in the world. Heresies are necessary, and are a form of testing. Heresies are caused by philosophical speculations and appeal to Scripture by heretics. Once the faith has been received, speculation and searching should cease. Heretics have no right to argue from Scripture, as it is the property of the church. The apostolic tradition is sound, all knowledge was revealed, there being no secret tradition communicated to an elite. Anything not stemming from apostolic tradition is false. Tertullian rummages through the letters of Paul to find ammunition to use against the heretics, especially the gnostics Marcion, Valentinus, and Apelles. He finds various theological statements of Paul that he uses as a parallel to those of contemporary heretics, claiming that they have their roots in NT times and have already been condemned by Scripture. He aims 1 Cor 15,12, concerning those who deny the resurrection, squarely at Marcion and Valentinus[50].

Very brief references, in the form of assertions of the truth of the resurrection, are found in two other works: *De patientia* and *Ad nationes*. In the first, the resurrection renders grief for the dead futile, patience being the only acceptable response. In the second work, it is stated that the Christians take for granted the resurrection: it is a given[51].

His work *De resurrectione* vigorously defends the dignity of the flesh, and the necessity of both the soul and the body, since both come from the Logos. He blasts the gnostics for holding the flesh in contempt, states that those who deny the resurrection of the flesh hate the Creator and pervert the Scriptures. Many conventional second-century arguments for the resurrection of the flesh are used[52].

(*EncECh*, 819). Tertullian's main concern in this work is to prove the difference of the Father and the Son, preserving both their common substance and distinct persons. E. SCHENDEL, *Herrschaft*, 201.

[49] IV 2; IV 4, LNPF vol. III, 600; CCL 2 (1159-1205).

[50] *De praescriptione haereticorum* 33.3. LNPF vol. III, 259.

[51] *De patientia* 9.2, page 713 LNPF. This was written about 202. *Ad nationes* I.19.2 page 127 LNPF, written about 217.

[52] In addition to stock arguments such as the seasons, the Phoenix myth, the creative power of God, etc., Tertullian insists on the authority of Scripture, holding that doctrines must be read from it, and admitting that many doctrines are not philosophi-

He also adds a christological argument: the unity of the flesh and the spirit is assured by the union of God and humanity in Jesus. The soul should love the flesh like a brother, almost as much as the Lord, and pray for it[53].

Verses 12-18 are used to sharpen what is at stake: the consequences of there being no resurrection are appalling, namely, a complete lack of any hope. Verse 22 also shows us the need for the revivification of the flesh in Christ, for Tertullian is also dealing with the favorite proof text of the gnostics: verse 50, in which it is stated in no uncertain terms that flesh and blood cannot inherit the kingdom of God. But a revivified flesh can. The references in verses 29-32 to battling the beasts at Ephesus and to vicarious baptism are for Tertullian further proof of the resurrection of the body. Christ sitting at the right hand of the Father is a guarantee of the resurrection of the flesh, for death is the last enemy. Christ's session at the right hand means that it has been defeated and that corruption will not inherit incorruption[54].

Perhaps some of his most sustained polemics are to be found in *Adversus Marcionem*, in which he defends the unity of God, the goodness of matter, the reality of Christ's incarnation, and the reality of the bodily resurrection against Marcion and others who attempted to sunder God from creation and spirit from matter. He must also defend the continuity between the OT and the NT, and he pays special attention to the teachings of Paul, showing that Paul used Jewish phrases and symbols in describing Christ, and that the claims of the heretics are in fact refuted by his teachings. In defending the reality of Christ's incarnation, verses 13-18 show the consequences if he had not been incarnated. All that he did while on earth is nullified. His resurrection – and ours – are false, we are still in our sins, and our hope is vain[55].

In defending the doctrine of the resurrection in 5.9, verses 25 through 27 explain that the Christ of the New Testament and the God of the Old

---

cally defensible. Also, he insists on a literal reading of Scripture, looking upon allegorizing as perversion of the sense of Scripture. P. PERKINS, *Resurrection*, 367-371.

[53] «Both natures has He clearly united in His own self; He has fitted them together as bride and bridegroom in the reciprocal bond of wedded life. Now, if any should insist on making the soul the bride, then the flesh will follow the soul as her dowry [...] Why, then, O soul, should you envy the flesh? There is none, after the Lord, whom you should love so dearly; none more like a brother to you, which is even born along with yourself in God. You ought rather to have been by your prayers obtaining resurrection for her; her sins, whatever they were, were owing to you» (*De resurrectione*, LXIII).

[54] *De resurrectione* 48,3; 48,8; 48,9; 48,10; 48,11; 48,12; 51,7.

[55] *Adversus Marcionem* 3.8.5; 3.8.7.

Testament are the same God, since God places the enemies under Christ's feet, and Christ then hands the kingdom over to God. This undercuts Marcion's claim of a radical discontinuity between the two. Verse 22 also explains the need for a bodily resurrection; since it was the fleshly body that sinned and died, that same body must rise and be revivified by the new Adam[56].

c) Conclusion

Irenaeus and Tertullian both have roughly the same goals, but use different approaches and models in their theologizing. Although too early to be identified with any «school», the thought of Irenaeus resonates more with the Greek traditions, while Tertullian is uncompromisingly Latin, literal, and polemical. Irenaeus seeks to join God, creation, the OT, and the resurrection in an evolutionary and transformative approach to redemption and salvation, while Tertullian uses the requirements of justice, Christian hope, and the dignity of the flesh due to the union of the divine and human in Christ as the basis for his approach to the resurrection. The ideas introduced by Irenaeus will have a longer life than those of Tertullian, since they satisified to a greater degree very important anthropological and theological questions. As we have seen in the preceding chapters, this anti-gnostic response was still within the general framework of the apocalyptic message of 1 Cor 15: the relationship between spririt and flesh.

2.4 *The Alexandrian Tradition*

a) Clement of Alexandria: Beginnings of the Alexandrian Approach

Clement of Alexandria (150-215 A.D.) also views man in rather evolutionary terms, and in his writings, we have the beginnings of the Alexandrian allegorical exegesis of Scripture. The true and complete man is the spiritual man (II 8,49.1), and justification is similar to likeness to God, perfection, and possession of the Holy Spirit. Adam was perfected only when he became an adult. The spirit does not belong to man by nature, because human freedom plays a part. Because of the sin of Adam, Christ had to introduce a historical element. Not a great emphasis was given to guilt or transmission of original sin; in fact, it was an «extension consequent upon sin of an original state of imperfection»[57].

---

[56] *Adversus Marcionem*, 5.9.2; 5.9.5; 5.9.6; 5.9.13; 5.10.1.

[57] *Stromata* II 8,49.1; IV 23,150.4; VI 12,96.1-2. Clement refers to verse 32 and 33 because of its reference to Greek philosophy.«Let us eat and drink, for tomorrow

b) Origen: Master of Speculative Exegesis

The explosion of speculative exegesis of 1 Cor 15 and other passages relating to the resurrection begins with Origen. It is difficult to paint a completely clear picture of Origen's thought, as he was speculative and not what we would call systematic. Many of his writings were in fact written ad hoc against various theological challenges, or were homilies and commentaries. Throughout the corpus of his material, he appears in many places to contradict himself, a good example being his views on the matter of eternal punishment. Much of his writing lacks precision of definition, failing to resolve the tension inherent in antitheses. He had a tendency to hold one position for «ordinary» Christians, and to break loose in his speculative mode for those whom he considered the spiritually advanced. Additionally, many of his surviving works are in fragments preserved either in less than reliable translations, such as that of Rufinus, or are quoted, often inaccurately or without understanding, in the works of his enemies[58].

Although sharing many of the eschatological beliefs of late Judaism, Origen broke with the tradition concerning millenarianism[59].

Having nothing but scorn for the concept of the millennium, Origen tended to be more rational and philosophical in his exegesis and speculation. The Son and his incarnation were always his interpretative keys for exegesis[60].

Engaging in a sort of demythologizing of eschatological passages, Origen allegorizes the passage and applies it to the present ethical and spiritual life of the believer and its orientation towards the end or τέλος. The

---

we die. Be not deceived; evil communications corrupt good manners». *Stromata* I,14; LNPF, II, 314; J. DANIÉLOU, *Gospel Message*, 412-413.

[58] Crouzel criticizes Trigg for trying to over systematize Origen's theology and for failing to understand Origen the spiritual and allegorical exegete («The Literature on Origen», 505). Crouzel insists that Origen lacks the type of precision and systematization that modern people would expect. One must resist the temptation to superimpose a modern scheme on material from another age and mentality. H. CROUZEL, *Origen*, 167-179; ID., «The Literature on Origen 1970-1988», 499-516; J.W. TRIGG, *Origen*, 244-248.

[59] Late Jewish apocalyptic included a belief in the millenium in some form, marked by the end of the world, a cosmic duel between God and his adversaries, and a destruction or upheaval of human institutions and the foundations of the world, with a new order coming to birth out of the destruction. The millennial tradition was shared by Justin Martyr, Hippolytus and Irenaeus and others, who expended a great deal of energy trying to fix dates for the end and establish warning signs. A. MONACI, «Apocalisse ed escatologia», 139-152.

[60] A. MONACI, «Apocalisse ed escatologia», 149; M. SIMONETTI, «Il millenarismo in Oriente», 37.

«end of the world» becomes so in the one who reaches spiritual maturity[61].

The *apokatastasis*, or universal restoration of all things, is at the very heart of Origen's theology. It is based on 1 Cor 15,24-28, especially 28, and is one of Origen's most controversial teachings[62].

This restoration is a return of all things to a perfect state which existed previously, and implies a cyclical view of history. Cosmic and universal in its vision, it looks to the time when all souls will regain their intelligible qualities after having undergone progressive purification and instruction. Origen also held that although the *apokatastasis* is comprehensive and takes place for all of creation at the same time, it also can be used to describe the state of the individual soul, since each individual soul is a reflection of the cosmos. Each soul proceeds towards God at its own pace; therefore, some may reach the state of perfection long before others, and there will be a point where all have reached that state and God will be «all in all» in the entire universe. In *De principiis* III.6, Origen says that

> I am of the opinion that in saying God is all in all it means that He is all in each individual person. He will be all in each individual in this way that all that a rational nature can feel, understand, think, all that will be God and it will do nothing except feel God, think God, see God, God will be all its movement and thus God will be all for it[63].

It is unclear whether he ever in fact taught that doctrine as it is often presented, and we have his own denials in a letter in which he accuses others of adulterating his teachings. Careful research absolves him for the most part from charges of pantheism, teaching the salvation of the devil and the demons, and a denial of the bodily resurrection. Most of these charges are based on misinterpretations of his teachings that have been perpetuated over the centuries, or on a lack of familiarity with the entire corpus of his teachings[64].

---

[61] The eschatological passage Matt 24,3-34 undergoes special allegorizing treatment. Origen had a disdain for the «Jewish sense» of apocalyptic (Prin. II.11.2; Comm. in Matt 17,35); B.E. DALEY, *Hope*, 47-48.

[62] The word itself was a medical, juridical, military and astronomical term; in the latter sense, it was used to describe the completion of a revolution of a heavenly body to its starting point. In the LXX, the verb form of the term is used to describe conversion (שׁוּב) as in Jer 15,18. Origen was probably the first to link the use of the term to the return to a primitive state. A. MÉHAT, «Apocatastase», 96-214.

[63] Excerpt from *De principiis* III 6 quoted on page 323 of C. RABINOWITZ, «Personal and Cosmic Salvation in Origen», 319-329. This doctrine of the restoration of all things at the end of time is usually attributed to Origen and Gregory of Nyssa. In the *Commentary on John* (II 8,61), Origen refers to *apokatastasis* as if it is a known concept, implying that it was not something original with him. H. CROUZEL, *Origen*, 257-258.

[64] Both Jerome and Rufinus, in their heated exchange of letters, refer to a letter by Origen (*Letter to Friends in Alexandria*) in which he indignantly denies teaching the

In *De principiis* (περὶ ἀρχῶν), Origen develops a soteriology that is much more integrated with the destiny of the cosmos. By far his favorite verses are 24-28, emphasizing the defeat of inimical powers and God being all in all respectively[65].

The work explains how the world and its diversity came into being, and how it shall return to the divine unity at the time of the consummation, when God will be «all in all».

For Origen, the question of the duration of Christ's reign and the manner of his subjection are soteriological rather than relational[66].

Subjection is synonymous with salvation, and the subjection of all powers is very closely linked to the final consummation which is perfection. At the final consummation, each soul will pay for its sins; however, the goodness of God will restore all of creation to unity with even his enemies being conquered and subdued[67].

A key concept in his cosmology is the belief that the beginning is like the end. From the one beginning proceeded all differences and variations as creatures fell away from their unity with God, being pulled in different directions according to their motions and impulses. Their conditions were thereby changed, and they were distributed throughout creation in various ranks according to merit, not having goodness in them essentially, as with the Trinity, but only accidentally. Through subjection to Christ, the entire creation and all rational creatures will be restored to primal unity[68].

Origen believes in a succession of different worlds, called «ages». The continual falling away from God of rational creatures is the cause of these worlds, along with the variety and diversity of this world. Creatures advance or decline in their relative positions in these successive worlds according to their spiritual development and conduct, hoping to

---

salvation of the devil, accusing others of having misrepresented his teachings. H. CROUZEL, *Origen*, 257-266.

[65] *De principiis*, I 2.10; I 6.1,2,4; II 3.1,3,5,7; III 5,6,7,9; III 6.1,2,3,5,6,8,9; IV 3.12. All of the references from 1 Cor 15 are from verses 24-28; Origen probably wrote this work to counter the anti-intellectual criticism that he received because of his philosophical and allegorical interpretation of the Bible. It was probably composed in 229 A.D., and was a mature work. Only fragments of the Greek remain; the rest, in a Latin translation by Rufinus, must be used with caution because of the latter's alterations designed to render Origen more safe and orthodox. It is a philosophical genre of literature, discussing first principles, and for that reason, it is not systematic. At times, Origen presents more than one solution to a problem and leaves it to the reader to decide which one is best. J. TRIGG, *Origen*, 91-93; H. CROUZEL, *Origen*, 45-46; ID., «L'Anthropologie d'Origène», 36-49.

[66] Origen's trinitarian theology was subordinationist in nature. E. SCHENDEL, *Herrschaft*, 202.

[67] *De principiis*, VI 1. Quoting verse 25, 27, and 28, Origen then explains what it means for all to be subjection to Christ.

[68] *De principiis*, I 6.2.

rise from what is seen and temporal to what is unseen and eternal. The end of the world means the beginning of the world to come[69].

This succession of different worlds will continue until the perfection or culmination of the universe – the *apokatastasis* – which is greater than the ages. In this period, things will no longer belong to an age, but will all be in God[70].

Although this appears to be a rather mechanistic process, the intervention of God in the form of His Son was necessary, since the world and the human race were rushing headlong towards doom and destruction. This was due to a fundamental corruption and perversion of the ruling principle of the universe, the sense of structure and hierarchy: both the ruling and the ruled had been corrupted. Christ's intervention was needed to teach obedience and to restore in himself these corrupted laws of «ruling and reigning», This is what is meant by the «subjection of enemies» and the ruling of Christ «until all his enemies are subdued». Christ's action restores the capacity for ruling, reigning and obeying, since he fulfills in himself what he wishes to be fulfilled in others, including in himself all those whom he had subjected to the Father. Then, as the head of all things, and with them and the subjected enemies subsisting in him, he shall subject himself to the Father[71].

Replying to objections to the term subjection when used with regard to the Son, Origen insists that subjection is a good and positive thing, the crowning glory of His work. Through the subjection, Christ offers to the Father all the corrected and renewed laws of the obedience and subjection due from the human race[72].

«All in all» (verse 28) takes on a variety of meanings within Origen's theology. The first creation was incorporeal; we will be delivered from bondage of corruption and recover incorruption and freedom when we have received the glory of the Son of God and when God shall be all in all[73].

«All in all» does not include evil or irrational animals nor lifeless things. At the end, God will not only be in all things, but be all things. For although God is present in all things, we must be careful in saying

---

[69] Origen argues that if bodily nature ceases, it will have to be created again when the new world or age is created, since rational creatures continually tend to fall away from God. *De principiis*, III 1,3.5.7.

[70] *De principiis*, I 7; II 3.1; II 3.3; II 3.7.

[71] Verses 27 and 28 form the structure for this argument. *De principiis*, III 5.6.

[72] Verse 28 forms the core of this argument. *De principiis*, III 5.7.

[73] Man received the image of God in the first creation; the perfection of God's likeness is reserved for the time of the consummation after having striven to acquire it through the imitation of God. *De principiis* III 6.1.

that God is in all things, since we would not want to say of him that he resides in an unworthy vessel[74].

God is also «all in all» when he is all things in each person. When a rational mind is completely purified of all vice and wickedness, then God becomes its total reality; it is no longer conscious of anything else save God. There is no longer any contrast between good and evil, since it no longer exists for a mind that perceives only God[75].

When death, the last enemy, is destroyed, it will not mean that the substance of death will be destroyed, but that its hostile purpose and will, which derived from itself rather than from God, will come to an end. It will not cease to exist, but will no longer be an enemy. This «destruction» will occur so that there will no longer be the sadness that comes from death or diversity. In arguing for the bodily nature of the resurrection, Origen states that the body that has returned to dust will be raised again and will advance to the glory of a spiritual body as the merits of the indwelling soul dictate[76].

In explaining further the end of death portrayed in verse 26, he draws attention again to the glory of the spiritual body at that time when all things are restored and «God shall be all in all». It will not happen suddenly, but gradually and in stages, during the «lapse of infinite and immeasurable ages, seeing that the improvement and correction will be realized slowly and separately in each individual person». Some will advance quickly, others at a medium pace, some others will lag far behind. Each soul will proceed at its own speed, making progress and eventually being reconciled to God. In the end, even death will be reconciled, no longer being an enemy[77].

God has created two universal natures, one of which is visible and bodily, the other invisible or incorporeal. The invisible, of which the rational nature is comprised, is only changed by action of the mind and will, since it is endowed with free will. The visible nature can undergo a change in substance, since God is the creator and can do anything. The question is asked, then, when God shall be all in all, of which species will the whole bodily nature consist? Returning to Gen 1:1 in which God made the heavens and the earth, Origen believes that at the end and consummation of all things, there will be a return to the beginning. People will dwell on earth, but since creation is a shadow of heavenly things, they will be instructed in the precepts of the true and eternal law[78].

---

[74] *De principiis*, III 6.2.

[75] This is developed in some of his other works, such as *On Prayer* and *Commentary on John*. *De principiis*, III 6.3.

[76] *De principiis*, III 6.5. Verse 26.

[77] *De principiis*, III 6.6.

[78] *De principiis* III 6.9.

The souls that are advancing first inhabit this other earth and through instruction are prepared for «better precepts to which nothing can ever be added». Christ himself will take over the kingdom, and will instruct those who are capable of receiving it in his wisdom after they have had preparatory instruction in the virtues. He will reign until he subjects all of them to the Father who subjected all things to him, which according to Origen, is another way of saying until they are capable of receiving God. Then God will be to them «all in all»[79].

Origen believed in two resurrections: the first is the change in the believer brought about by baptism and following the Christian life. This is the imperfect resurrection. The «living» are those who have not sinned mortally after baptism and are able to pass to the second resurrection, while the «dead» are those who have sinned after baptism and have not repented. The second resurrection is face to face and total, and will involve different orders and classes, according to merit. Between death and resurrection, souls are clothed with a corporeal envelope or vehicle and sent to a school for souls in the heavens to be instructed in various spiritual truths, so that they might advance in spiritual and moral progress[80].

The body, according to Origen, was constantly in a state of flux and change. The individual remains the same in the soul ($\psi\upsilon\chi\acute{\eta}$) and the underlying principle of continuity called the $\epsilon\tilde{\iota}\delta o\varsigma$. At the resurrection, the soul produces the $\epsilon\tilde{\iota}\delta o\varsigma$, which constructs a new body, which will be different in appearance, being suited to its new environment[81].

Punishment, however, is one of Origen's most controversial topics. In many homiletic works, he writes of the need for sinners to be punished, and even speaks of everlasting punishment. In his more careful and reflective works, however, he speaks of each sinner lighting his own fire with his conscience, and implies that it is not eternal, and that its purpose is medicinal and purgative, purifying the individual to receive the vision of God[82].

---

[79] De principiis, III 6.9.

[80] De principiis, III 6.9; II 11.6-7; H. CROUZEL, Origen, 240-244, 248-249; ID., «La "première" et la "seconde" résurrection», 3-19.

[81] This is taken from a lost fragment of the Commentary on Psalm 1.5 which is quoted by Methodius in his De resurrectione. H. CROUZEL, Origen, 255-256; B.E. DALEY, Hope, 53-54.

[82] The eschatological fire of purification is equated with God, and is for all those who are headed for heaven, saint and sinner alike. If there is an eternal punishment, it is reserved for «hardened» sinners. Sinners are the only ones who will really feel the pain of the eschatological fire. Personal and general judgment are basically the same. Origen uses this passage on which to base his conception of purgative punishment. He holds that Christ is the only true foundation; all other foundations, be they of gold, silver, precious stones, wood, hay or straw, will become manifest as each man's work is laid bare on the Day. On the Day, it is fire that will do the revealing,

The *Dialogue with Heraclides*, in defending the resurrection, argues for Christ as the firstfruits, and the consequent importance of the bodily nature of Christ and the bodily nature of his death, so that those who are Christ's will be raised[83].

In his treatise *On Prayer*, Origen personalizes and spiritualizes the message of chapter 15 in his exegesis of the Our Father. The Kingdom of God is immanent and eschatological. In answering the question: «Why do we pray for the coming of the Kingdom, which is already present, as if it were not?», Origen replies that just as with knowledge and wisdom, we will keep growing in our inward capacity to receive it, and after the inimical powers within us have been subjected, we will have reached a state of perfection, when the mind will be without sense perception, but will be in immediate contact with spiritual realities. Christ subjects the enemies within us, reigns over us inwardly, and after all other rule, authority and power has been abolished, delivers up the Kingdom to the Father so that God is all in all. Our corruptible nature puts on sanctification in holiness, purity and incorruption; the mortal clothes itself with the Father's immortality, and death is conquered within us. Even now we can share in the good things of regeneration and resurrection[84].

In the prologue of the *Commentary on the Song of Songs*, Solomon is the type of Christ. As the putative author of Proverbs, Ecclesiastes and the Song of Songs, he shows three aspects of Christ: becoming a servant, drawing all to himself, and uniting all rational creation within him and defeating inimical powers. When perfection has been reached – in other words, when all the powers have been subjected to the Father and God is all in all – then Christ will be called Solomon (peaceable) and nothing else[85].

Origen did in fact produce a commentary on Corinthians. Of the extant fragments in *Fragmenta e catenis in epistulam primam ad Corinthios*, very little is useful for our purposes[86].

The *Commentary on Romans* dwells at length on chapter 5, the chapter that discusses the entry of death into the world and its subsequent reign[87].

---

and if anyone's work survives this cleansing fire, he will receive a reward. H. CROUZEL, «L'Exégèse origénienne de I Cor 3.11-15», 273-283; L.R. HENNESSEY, «The Place of Saints and Sinners», 295-312.

[83] ORIGEN, *Dialogue with Heraclides*, 5 and 6 (verses 12-20; 23).

[84] ORIGEN, *On Prayer* 290-291 (vv. 23-25.28).

[85] ORIGEN, *Commentary on the Song of Songs*, 53-54.

[86] This *catena* consists of the verse in question followed by a brief statement of the importance of the passage or how the heretics interpret it. The section on vv. 20-23 uses the analogy from nature to discuss the resurrection. Unfortunately, verses 24-28 are not present. C. JENKINS, «Origen on 1 Corinthians», 43-48.

Following the exegetical method of the patristic period, the citation of one passage of Scripture is used to explain another, in this case 1 Cor 15,22 explains Romans 5:12, then verses 21-27 elaborate on death's entry into the world, its transmission throughout the human race, its dominion, and its eventual overthrow. Of interest is Origen's description of three different kinds of death; the common or physical death which we all suffer, which is neither good nor bad, the spiritual death in which the soul is separated from God, and the death to sin, which conforms to the death and resurrection of Christ. The spiritual death is the result of sin, and it is personified in the tyrant to whom the Son was temporarily subjected[88].

There was a definite link between sin and physical death, although at times it is unclear whether physical or spiritual death is the result. In several of his works, Origen insists that Christ's redemptive death makes our death to sin possible. Christ will reign throughout a long process, until each soul is perfected in virtue, death destroyed, and God is all in all[89].

Various references in his *Commentary on Matthew* to the verses dealing with death explain why Jesus had to go to Jerusalem, be delivered up, and taste death; the purpose, of course, was to defeat death[90].

His discussion of John 2,19, in which Jesus states that if the temple is destroyed, he will raise it up in three days, is related to the process of the resurrection and the defeat of death, which will occur in proper order rather than all at once. It represents the corporate nature of the resurrection: all Israel, that is, the Church, will be wakened[91].

There is again reference to the two types of death: one is indifferent and is the lot of all humans; the other, the result of sin, is that referred to in verse 22, and this imposed the temporary reign of a murderer on the human race. This is the enemy which Christ will defeat[92].

God will be all in all when we can see God without a mediator, as Christ does. This comes about when we are purified and all sin has been

---

[87] ORIGENE, *Commento alla Lettera ai Romani*. Libri I-VII. III 1; III 8; V 1; V 2; V 3; V 6; V 7; V 10; VI 5; VI 6; VII 4; VII 5; VII 12; VIII 13; IX 41.

[88] *Commentary on Romans*, VI 6. Cf. also *Dialogue with Heraclides* 24-27. The second type of death is the «wages of sin». Often cited to explain this concept in Romans 6:14 is 1 Cor 15:26. ORIGENE, *Commento alla Lettera ai Romani*, 306, n. 7; H. CROUZEL, *Origen*, 235-237; «Mort et immortalité chez Origène», 19-38.81-96.181-196; E. SCHENDEL, *Herrschaft*, 83.

[89] *Romans*, VI 5; V 3. Love is the greatest of these virtues, which in its perfected state leaves no room for sin. V 10; H. CROUZEL, *Origen*, 237.

[90] *Commentary on Matthew*, 12,5; 12,20; 12,33; 13,8.9; 14,20; 15,23; 16,3; 17,29.

[91] The third day begins in the new heaven and the new earth, when all Israel is awakened and death is conquered. This passage is used in conjunction with his commentary Ezek 37,1-14. *Commentary on John*, X 21; X 23; XIII 8.

[92] *Commentary on John* XX 224; XX 39.

taken from the world, so that we are ready and able to accept God the Father[93].

John 13,3, in which Jesus knows that the Father has given everything into his hands, refers to the events in verses 22-27: the defeat of powers, death, and the revivifying of the human race[94].

Origen's use of 1 Cor 15's verses in his commentaries on the OT is varied and diverse. His allegorical exegesis finds many prophecies of the resurrection in OT texts[95].

The *Homily on Leviticus* discusses priestly regulations, in particular the prohibition against the priests drinking wine. This prohibition is taken as a reflection of the human condition: the presence of sin and death. Wine will be drunk again when death has been destroyed. The sword mentioned in Lev 26,8 is the Word of God, which will destroy death[96].

A mention of Judah in Jeremiah 11,1-10 alludes to Christ, since it was during his stay in Judah that he despoiled death (v. 24). The treasures mentioned in 10,13 refer to the rank and order in the hereafter in proportion to merits, while verses 25-26 help us to understand in Jer 17,11 how God destroys the foolishness of this world by contraries[97].

The prophecy in Isa 4,1 in which the seven women of Jerusalem take hold of one man and beg to be called by his name to take away their reproach is understood by Origen as referring to Christ, who carries many names, such as wisdom, understanding, good counsel, fortitude, knowledge, piety and fear of God[98].

He expresses his conviction that the resurrection is something ordered and graded with a reference to verse 23[99].

Origen makes much of the fact that Joshua and Jesus are essentially the same name. In his *Homily on Joshua*, he allegorizes the taking of the city of Ai as the defeat of death, and the hanging on a tree of the king of Ai

---

[93] *Commentary on John*, I 16; I 37; XX.48; Origen believes that this unmediated knowledge of God is the highest goal. E. SCHENDEL, *Herrschaft*, 100.

[94] *Commentary on John*, XXXII 27,28,29,30,31,32,34,39.

[95] He opposed millenarians in his exegesis, especially in interpreting passages such as Ezek 37,1-14. They insisted that the body would be exactly as it was on earth, with the very same flesh. He had to defend himself against two of their favorite prooftexts: Isa 40,5 «all flesh will see the salvation of God»; and Job 19,25-26 (a corrupt text, translated in various ways) «then from my flesh I shall see God». H. CROUZEL, «Les prophéties de la Resurrection», 980-992.

[96] ORIGEN, *Homilies on Leviticus*, VII 2; IX 3; IX 11; XVI 7. Reference is also made to Christ's statement that he would not drink wine until he could do so in the Kingdom of God, which is taken to mean the defeat of death described in 1 Cor 15,24-28.

[97] *Homiliae in Ieremiam*, VIII 6; VII 3; IX 1; VII 3.

[98] *Homily on Isaiah*, III 3.

[99] PG 17, 28.

in 8,29 is seen as a type of Christ. In reference to the subjection of all to
the Christ, it is pointed out that at present only those who believe are
subjected to Christ, though at the second coming all will be. The Leviti-
cal towns in 25,4 reflect the celestial hierarchy and rank, something dear
to Origen's heart[100].

He finds the Book of Numbers filled with prophecies of the resurrection. Of particular fascination for him is the ordering of the tribes and the
Hebrew camp, for they symbolize the ordered and ranked nature of the
resurrection[101].

Christ's victory over death and various aspects of his reign form the
bulk of the other references[102].

In the three centuries following Origen's death, his teachings were
distorted, misunderstood and misrepresented. Many of his works were
interpreted by others according to the controversies and heresies of their
own day, rather than those of the time in which the work was written.
Additionally, Origen wrote in the early third century, a period in which a
philosophical background was taken for granted. Later interpreters in an
age concerned more with authority and organization failed to appreciate
the subtleties of his works. His teachings on the pre-existence and the fall
of souls, limited versus eternal punishment, the nature of the body at the
resurrection, and the *apokatastasis* all aroused particular controversy. By
the 6th century, Origenism, as distinguished from the teachings of Origen
himself, was a strong current in the church, causing many sharp disputes,
especially among the monks of Palestine. Origenism was finally condemned in 553 at the Fifth Ecumenical Council[103].

c) Conclusion

Origen is one of the first to depart radically from an apocalyptic interpretation of this passage. The apocalyptic categories are then spiritualized
and individualized, so that they become statements about the individual
soul rather than the body of believers. Eschatology is removed from the
realm of history or the world and its structures. The «all in all» of v. 28

---

[100] *Homily on Joshua* VIII 4; XVI 3; XXV 4 refer to verses 22-26.

[101] *Homily on Numbers*, I 3; XVII 2,4,5. H. CROUZEL, «Les Prophéties», 984.

[102] *Homily on Numbers*, X 1; XII 3; XI 4; XI 6; XII 3; XVI 6; XVII 2; XVII 4;
XVII 5; XIX 2; XXVII 13; XXVIII 4. For the ordering of the resurrection according
to spiritual merit see I 3 (v. 23) and XVII 2,4,5 (v. 23). Victory over death is cov-
ered in XII 3 (Num 21,16) XVI 6 (Num 23,21) and XVII 5 (Num 24,7-8). The Sons
of Adam were dispersed at the beginning of the world; at the end of the world, they
will be brought together, and God will be all in all (XXVIII 4, verse 28).

[103] H. CROUZEL, *Origen*, 167-179.235.249; B.E. DALEY, *Hope*, 168.188-190; J.
TRIGG, *Origen*, 244-258.

becomes a statement about God's relationship to the individual and the removal of his spiritual and intellectual limitations. This individualized and spiritualized interpretation is one that was followed by many after him, in varying degrees.

2.5 *Some Enemies of Origen*

a) Methodius of Olympus

Methodius of Olympus cannot be dated with complete certainty; however, this avowed anti-Origenist is thought to have lived in the last quarter of the third or first quarter of the fourth century[104].

His chief concern was to emphasize the participation of the body in future salvation – a risen body that will be just as it is now, not another spiritual body. It will differ only in quality. He placed great emphasis on chastity, virginity, and asceticism, suggesting that the first two are most important for the Kingdom of God, representing as they do the life of purity and fidelity of the eschatological church[105].

In the *Symposium*, verse 22, the Adam image, serves to explain why Christ, who was in the beginning with God, assumed human nature. Man had been created incorruptible, but suffered death because of Adam's transgression. Man had caused the curse, so man had to undo it[106].

An elaboration is given in *De resurrectione*: in I 13, verse 22 (in conjunction with vv. 50 and 54), the purpose for the incarnation and the feasibility of flesh and blood achieving salvation is discussed, and it is stated that the body does not possess life, but life possesses the body. Similarly, verse 20 underlines the priority of Christ as the firstfruits and firstborn of the dead[107].

b) Peter Alexandrinus

Peter Alexandrinus (d.303 A.D.) was an anti-Origenist whose works, at least according to the few extant fragments, emphasized the identity of every feature of the risen body with the present earthly one[108].

His use of verse 20 stresses the corporeal reality of the resurrected Christ, who is firstborn from the dead; and also insists that all the dead will be resurrected just as Christ was[109].

---

[104] Methodius retained some of Origen's ideas and methods of exegesis. B.E. DALEY, *Hope*, 61-64; A. GRILLMEIER, *Christ in Christian Tradition*, 165-166.

[105] B.E. DALEY, *Hope*, 62.

[106] *Symposium*, 3.6.102.31.

[107] *De resurrectione*, I 26.1.253.6.

[108] B.E. DALEY, *Hope*, 61; *EncECh* 677-678; A. GRILLMEIER, *Christ in Christian Tradition*, 165-166.

[109] *De resurrectione*, 426-429.

c) Victorinus of Pettau

Victorinus of Pettau lived in the second half of the third century and was martyred under Diocletian, probably in 304. He is considered the forerunner of Latin biblical exegesis; unfortunately, his work on the apocalypse is the only extant work[110].

Victorinus was a millennialist, although his adherence to it was neither total nor unconditional. His exegesis, usually literal, was tempered with some light allegorizing that betrays some of the influence of Origen, especially in his exegesis of chapters 20 and 21 of the Apocalypse, the heavenly Jerusalem[111].

In explaining allegorical method, he points out that when a will is written, it remains sealed until the death of the testator, when it is opened and published. In like manner, Christian doctrines can now be disclosed following the death of Jesus, who liberates and represents man.

In his exegesis of Rev 5,5, he equates the Lion of Judah with Christ, who is the conqueror of death. He points out that Moses spoke in a veiled language in the Pentateuch which would only be clarified with the coming of Christ. Verse 21 again illustrates the saving power of one man's death, since death came through one man. In his commentary on chapter 21, the heavenly Jerusalem, verse 25 is given an eschatological meaning and association: Christ will reign until all enemies are conquered. It is an association with his comment on Rev 21,25, the reign of Christ[112].

2.6 The Christological Controversies: Third Century

a) Novatian

Although Novatian (mid-3rd century) does not actually cite chapter 15 of 1 Cor, he does refer to verses 24-28 indirectly in De trinitate, in which he defends the eternity and divinity of the Son, who does nothing of his own will and determination, but everything in total obedience to the Father. Although divine by nature, it cannot be said that there is any dissonance or that there are two gods, for all is subjected to the Son by the Father, to whom the Son remits all of subjected creation in a communion rather than a union of substance (per substantiae communionem ad Patrem revolvitur), thereby preserving his identity[113].

---

[110] EncECh, 867. In Apocalypsim comes to us through three different recensions.

[111] Victorinus believed in a first resurrection, when the just will rise and Christ will rule for 1,000 years, after which all the dead will rise to be judged and rewarded or punished accordingly. The second death will be reserved for condemned sinners. B.E. DALEY, Hope, 64-65; C. CURTI, «Il Regno Millenario», 419-433.

[112] In Apocalypsim16-154. 64,15; 65,13; 152,5.

[113] De trinitate, XXXI; A. GRILLMEIER, Christ in Christian Tradition, 130-133; E. SCHENDEL, Herrschaft, 73-79.

b) Hippolytus

Hippolytus is problematic: we are not sure of his dates, and he is assigned to the first half of the third century. Many of his works are in
pseudonymous fragments, while others are attributed to him without sufficient proof[114].

Contra Noetum is a polemic against the so-called *patripassionists*,
those who denied the distinctions between the persons of the Trinity, insisting that God the Father was born as Jesus and suffered and died on
the cross. Hippolytus argues that God the Father and Jesus are distinct
persons, and he utilizes verses 23 through 28 in support of this argument.
Since God is excepted in being subjected to Christ, and since Christ
hands over the kingdom to God the Father, they must be distinct persons[115].

A fleeting reference to verse 20 in *De resurrectione ad Mammaeam*
designates Christ as the firstfruits and explains the importance of the incarnation and resurrection: Christ took the same flesh, raised it from the
dead, and made it the firstfruits for the righteous so that all who believe
in the Risen One may also have the resurrection[116].

In his commentary *in Danielem*, Hippolytus argues that the Ancient of
Days in Dan 7 is God the Father, and he draws parallels between the
eternal power in this chapter and that in 1 Cor 15,27, Eph 1,22, Heb 2,8,
Rev 5,13 and Col 1,15. Verse 23 serves to show that the Word was
united with the Protoplast in order to become the first of our resurrection[117].

There is one vague reference to verse 20 and 23 in *demonstratio de
Christo et Antichristo*: the Savior is the beginning of the resurrection for
all men; from his place at the right hand of the Father, he will judge humanity at the end of the world[118].

2.7 *The Arian Controversy and Its Aftermath: Fourth Century*

a) Marcellus of Ancyra

Much of the exegesis of this passage during the latter portion of the
fourth century and after is strongly influenced in one direction or another
by the theological views of Marcellus of Ancyra (d.374?), a strong defender of Nicene orthodoxy who himself fell afoul of official orthodoxy
in another direction. His anti-Arian polemic *Contra Asterium*, composed

---

[114] *EncECh*, I, 383-384.
[115] *Contra Noetum*, V 226.6.245.20.
[116] *De resurrectione ad Mammaeam*. GCS 1,2 (1897) 251-253; LNPF V, p. 240.
[117] *In Danielem*, 4.11.5.284.
[118] *Demonstratio de Christo et Antichristo*, 46.29.8.

between 325 and his deposition in 334, sparked a fierce fourth century controversy concerning the end of Christ's reign and his subjection to the Father[119].

Marcellus proposed a view of history and a Trinitarian theology that were eschatologically determined, based for the most part on his exegesis of 1 Cor 15,24-28, especially vv. 24-25[120].

The relation of the Logos and the Spirit to God the Father was expressed in terms of historical or «economical» development. Although completely one, God has interacted with human history in different ways at different times, according to an unfolding plan. The first economy or stage was from the creation of the world to the Incarnation; the second, an economy according to the flesh which is the age of Christ; and a third economy of the Holy Spirit, which is the age of the Church[121].

Marcellus held that there are two kingdoms: an eternal kingship of the Logos which is without beginning or end, and a temporary kingdom of the incarnate Christ. The latter kingdom began 400 years previously as Christ began to reign in his humanity. The eternal Logos assumed this temporary reign by virtue of the economy of salvation, in order to take on our flesh and reveal it to the whole Godhead bodily[122].

An important element of Marcellus' theology is that since it was humanity that was deceived by the devil and fell, so it was humanity that became king through the Word. This was the purpose of the temporary

---

[119] His works are reconstructed from the extant fragments found in the works of his chief opponent, Eusebius of Caesaria. Schendel says of him, «*Markell von Ankyra* is für das 4. Jahrundert mit seiner Deutung des Paulustextes der grosse Provokateur» (F. SCHENDEL, *Herrschaft*, 204); A. GRILLMEIER, *Christ in Christian Tradition*, 274-296; J. LIENHARD, «Exegesis of 1 Cor 15,24-28», 310-343.

[120] Marcellus uses a slightly different text of 1 Cor 15. Verses 24,25,27a and 28b are the verses quoted in the extant fragments of his work, with the following changes: verse 24b (cited once) τοῦ διαβόλου is inserted after πᾶσαν ἀρχήν; verse 25b (cited three times), πάντας is omitted; verse 28 (cited three times) ὁ υἱός is omitted. The change in 25b is apparently without any real significance, while that in 24b is in line with his view of salvation history. The omission of ὁ υἱός is of greater importance, as Marcellus liked to reserve the title «Son» for the incarnate Christ, for it is as the Logos that he will be subjected. J. LIENHARD, «Exegesis of 1 Cor 15,24-28», 341.

[121] *Eusebius Werke IV. Gegen Marcell*, GCS 14. In particular see fragments 4,9,17,19,43,70,100,117. The third economy is represented by fragments 111-2. The Logos is reunited with God the Father and God is all in all. E. SCHENDEL, *Herrschaft*, 119-121.

[122] Some of the favorite texts of Marcellus and others of like thought were: Pss 96,1; 110,1; Acts 3,21 and 1 Cor 15,24-28. Marcellus' exegesis of these psalms, especially the parts which speak of Christ's assumption as man of the economic kingdom, had a lasting effect on even such orthodox writers as Gregory of Nazianzus (Or. 30). G.W.H. LAMPE, «Notes on the Significance», 58-73; ID., «The Exegesis of Some Biblical Texts», 169-175.

kingdom of Christ: to join fallen man to the Word and establish him as king, and to remain joined until the effects of the devil's deception had been counteracted. He did not make a clear distinction between the humanity of the Word and humanity in general[123].

This kingdom is also partial, and will endure only until every rule of the devil, authority and power has been destroyed by Christ. Just as the second economy had a temporal beginning, so it will have an ending. The enfleshed Logos will leave aside the flesh and the temporal kingdom which have accomplished their purpose and be reunited with the Father, to be king of all and reign with the Father[124].

When the partial kingdom comes to an end, the Logos will be what it was before, and God will be all in all[125].

A pseudo-Athanasian work, *De incarnatione et contra Arianos*, has recently been reevaluated and attributed to Marcellus. Although dealing with verses 24-28, it concentrates on the meaning of «subjection». Subjection means subjection of the world to the flesh of Christ, and takes place in two stages. In the first, humans are subjected to the Son, recognized as his members, and become Sons of God in him. In the second stage, the Son is subjected to the Father in our place, meaning that the subjection is really that of his members; namely, believers, to God. This part of his theology, if by Marcellus, is not far from orthodoxy[126].

b) Eusebius of Caesarea

One of his most determined opponents was Eusebius of Caesarea, a follower of Origen who joined battle with Marcellus in two works composed between 334 and 339. In these two works, *De ecclesiastica theologia* and *Contra Marcellum*, he refutes Marcellus' exegesis of 1 Cor 15, 24-28 and establishes his own[127].

---

[123] Fragment 117 refers in depth to this relationship between man and the devil: «For the Word itself, in its own right, did not have a beginning of its reign. But man, who was deceived by the devil, became king through the power of the Word in order that, when he had become king, he might conquer the devil who had earlier deceived» (J. LIENHARD, «The Exegesis of 1 Cor 15, 24-28», 342-343).

[124] Marcellus later made a profession of faith at a Roman synod in 340, in which he attempted to mollify his critics by claiming that while the kingdom of Christ will not end, the separation of man from God and the conflict between the Church and its enemies will come to an end. E. SCHENDEL, *Herrschaft*, 122-123; B.E. DALEY, *Hope*, 78-79.

[125] «Marcellus was best known as the heretic who proposed that Christ's kingdom would end; and he is probably the reason why the phrase "of whose kingdom there will be no end" appears in the creed of Constantinople» (J. LIENHARD, «Exegesis of 1 Cor 15, 24-28», 340-341); G.W.H. LAMPE, «The Exegesis of Some Biblical Texts», 170.

[126] J. LIENHARD, «Exegesis of 1 Cor 15, 24-28», 346.

[127] Eusebius was Origenist in his theology and exegesis. In other works, he gave special attention to salvation within the political and historical order, and wrote ex-

In his exegesis, he first of all attacks Marcellus' understanding of «until» (ἄχρι οὖ or ἕως ἄν) in verse 25, the verse which was an important *crux interpretum*. He uses a stock argument in his denial that these prepositions imply a cessation: in other places in Scripture, e.g., Matt 28,20, these prepositions do not mean a cessation («I will be with you to the end of time» – and thereafter!). There are also the words of the archangel Gabriel to Mary in Luke 1,33, namely, «his kingdom will have no end»[128].

It is the subjection of the Son in verse 28 that becomes the focal point of most of Eusebius' argumentation. The problem lies with the understanding that Marcellus (and many others) had of the double subjection of 1 Cor 15: first all things are subjected to the Son, then the Son to God the Father. Eusebius accuses Marcellus of holding that this second subjection is an absorption into the Godhead, with subsequent loss of identity[129].

In his counter-argument, Eusebius points out that by analogy, this latter understanding of the subjection of Christ would mean the extinction of all those things which had been subjected to Christ, since there would be coalescing and mixing (συναλοιφὴν δέ τινα καὶ σύγχυσιν) and a loss of identity[130].

He proposes that the subjection be understood as glory, honor and obedience given in complete freedom[131].

Those who have been subjected to Christ participate in him through many of his attributes: life, wisdom, reason (λόγος), light, justice, holiness, and anointing[132].

Turning to 2 Cor 6,16 and John 10,38, he interprets verse 28 (ὁ θεὸς τὰ πάντα ἐν πᾶσιν) as referring to the indwelling presence of God[133].

---

tensively on the Emperor Constantine as the agent of Divine Providence. Despite his acceptance of the historical order and the fact that he was in no way a millenarian, Eusebius looked forward to the Second Coming as Christ's complete vindication after his historical humiliation and vindication, and as the time when the wicked would be punished and the virtuous rewarded. J. LIENHARD, «Exegesis of 1 Cor 15, 24-28», 343; B.E. DALEY, *Hope*, 77-78; E. SCHENDEL, *Herrschaft*, 143-153); F.S. THIELMAN, «Eschatology of Eusebius of Caesarea», 236-237.

[128] *De ecclesiastica theologica* III 14. There are references to our passage in the following places: 2,9; 3,13; 3,14; 3,15; 3,16; 3,17; 3,18; 3,19; 3,20. The references deal exclusively with verse 24 and 27-28. E. SCHENDEL, *Herrschaft*, 144-145.

[129] *De ecclesiastica theologica*, III 14.

[130] *De ecclesiastica theologica*, III 15.

[131] *De ecclesiastica theologica*, III 15.

[132] *De ecclesiastica theologica*, III 15.

[133] The passage from 2 Cor 6,16 refers to Ezek 37,27, «My dwelling place shall be with them; and I will be their God, and they shall be my people». *De ecclesiastica theologica*, III.16; J. LIENHARD, «Exegesis of 1 Cor 15, 24-28», 344.

There are passing references in other works, chiefly those of Scripture commentary and exegesis. A messianic interpretation of psalms 72 and 75 views all references to worship, submission, incorruption and conquest as foreshadowing the coming of Christ and the subjection of God's enemies, especially death, as expressed in verses 24-26. A similar messianic interpretation is given to Isaiah, and the commentary on chapters 24,26 and 63 refer to verses 24-26 as reflecting the action of the prophesied Messiah[134].

c) Cyril of Jerusalem

The *Cathechetical Lectures* of Cyril of Jerusalem (d. 386), also an opponent of Marcellus, reflect his traditional hope in resurrection and eternal life. They provide the usual apology for the resurrection, namely, the creative power of God, analogies in nature, and the requirements of justice. But these lectures go further, for they strive to inculcate a hope in resurrection with Christ and to meet any possible objections. He deals first with the Manichees who deny the reality of the resurrection by the use of Scriptural quotations[135].

Turning to the opinions of Marcellus, he bases his objections on three points: the eternity of the kingdom, the meaning of «subjection», and the meaning of «until». He answers the first and third points by appealing to Scripture[136].

Most of his explanation, however, is reserved for clarifying what is meant by «subjection». He denies that the Son is absorbed into the Father. The Son is not an obedient servant by necessity, but by choice and affection; he is Lord of all things, but as an obedient Son he does not seize the Lordship but receives it by nature[137].

The fragmentary pseudo-Athanasian *Epistula ad Antiochenos (Sermo maior de fide)* also deals with this passage. The work is concerned with subjection, and asks who the one not subjected to God before everything

---

[134] *Commentarii in Esaiam*, 1,54; 1,85; 1,89; 2,53; 2,58. *Commentarii in Psalmos*, 876,B,1; 809,A,16; 868,A,9; 656,A,4; 868,B,1; *Demonstratio evangelica* 10,6; 8,1.

[135] He quotes verses 14, 15, and 17 in *Cathechetical Lectures* 13,37 and 14,21. He appeals to the consequences of there being no resurrection: Christ is not risen, and we are still in our sins 13,37; 14,21; 18,16.17. B.E. DALEY, *Hope*, 80; J. QUASTEN, *Patrologia*, 365-369; E. SCHENDEL, *Herrschaft*, 153-157.

[136] If Christ was king before, he must be king after; «until» does not mean cessation or end of kingdom and dominion. Marcellus misunderstands v. 25 about Christ's reign (15,27.29.30.31). If creatures endure when God is all in all, so must the Son through whom all things were made (15,32; 10,9).

[137] In the latter example, he cites ps 110 as proof that Christ is not a servant, but rather a Son: both the Father and the Son are referred to as Lord (15,32; 10,9).

is subjected to him is. He distinguishes between, ὁ ἐκ πατρὸς λόγος and ὁ ἀναλημφθεὶς ἄνθρωπος, the former being Christ and the latter Jesus, who is the one to whom all things are not yet subjected. Subjection in verses 23-4 means conversion to Christianity[138].

He does, however, definitely hold two kingdoms, the human and the divine. The human kingdom has a beginning and an end, and the reign of Christ proceeds in two stages, human and divine, «So that God might be all in all, reigning through him as through God the Word, after reigning through him as through a man, the Savior»[139].

d) Hilary of Poitiers

Hilary of Poitiers (315-367) sought to refute the arguments of the Arians about the inferiority of the Son. Book XI of *De trinitate* deals extensively with this problem. Steering a course between Arianism and Sabellianism, he makes a distinction between the impassible divinity and the assumed humanity, holding that this latter dispensation was strictly for the promotion of the assumed humanity[140].

He denies that Jesus ceases to possess authority by handing over the kingdom to the Father or that Jesus undergoes any diminution of his divinity by the subjection[141].

Jesus will abolish every power, sweeping aside all prerogatives of power; in fact, he will so subject these powers to himself that God will subject them[142].

The victory over death is the resurrection, and those raised will be given a new form and promoted to something higher[143].

---

[138] The authorship has been vigorously contested. Its most recent attribution is to Marcellus of Ancyra. Lienhard points out, however, that the exegesis of the passage in this letter is very different from that of Marcellus and so the letter is probably not from his hand. J. LIENHARD, «Exegesis of 1 Cor 15, 24-28», 345-346.

[139] The work is dated about 360, at a later stage of Marcellus' thelogical «development». The very strong emphasis on a beginning and end of the human kingdom would tend to favor the authorship of Marcellus, but as Lienhard points out, a form of this teaching is also held by later authors. J. LIENHARD, «Exegesis of 1 Cor 15, 24-28», 147.

[140] Hilary was moderately allegorical in his approach to Scripture, and was under the theological influences of Cyprian and Tertullian. His eschatological outlook was classical apocalyptic in nature: the coming of the Antichrist, the resurrection of both the saved and sinners for reward and punishment, Christ's triumphal return to Jerusalem, and so on. B.E. DALEY, *Hope*, 94-96; J. QUASTEN, *Patrology*, IV, 36-42; E. SCHENDEL, *Herrschaft*, 156-159.

[141] Hilary of Poitiers, *De trinitate*, XI 27-30. It is impossible for the Father to have lost any of his rule when he gave it to the Son, or for the Son to lose it when he restores it to the Father. E. SCHENDEL, *Herrschaft*, 163-164.

[142] Hilary of Poitiers, *De trinitate*, XI 32-33.

[143] Hilary of Poitiers, *De trinitate*, 35.

The time when God will be all in all is treated as a mystery in which those subjected to Christ will be conformed to his body in the kingdom of the Father and will share in the splendor with which he reigns in the body. In fact, we who are conformed to his body shall form the Kingdom of God[144].

Christ reigns in his glorious body until authorities are abolished, death conquered and his enemies subdued. His subjection is like a process of the divinization of humanity, after which God will be all in all,

the nature of the Father's divinity imposing itself upon the nature of our body which was assumed. It is thus that God shall be all in all: according to the Dispensation He becomes by His Godhead and His manhood the Mediator between men and God, and so by the Dispensation He acquires the nature of flesh, and by the subjection shall obtain the nature of God in all things, so as to be God not in part, but wholly and entirely[145].

This has important consequences for the human person, for this process leads to the completion of the entire reason for the Dispensation of the flesh, the «promotion» of humanity to a higher state:

The end of subjection is then simply that God may be all in all, that no trace of the nature of His earthly body may remain in Him. Although before this time the two were combined within Him, He must now become God only; not, however, by casting off the body, but by translating it through subjection; not by losing it through dissolution, but by transfiguring it in glory: adding humanity to His divinity, not divesting Himself of divinity by His humanity[146].

e) Jerome

Jerome answers several questions from his friend Amandus in *Ep. 55*, one of which concerns vv. 25-28, especially the subjection[147].

Referring to Hilary's treatment of the passage in admiring terms, he realizes that the chief stumbling block is the subjection. But what is the

---

[144] Hilary of Poitiers, *De trinitate*, 36.38.

[145] Hilary of Poitiers, *De trinitate*, 38.40. E. SCHENDEL, *Herrschaft*, 163-164. Against the Arians who claimed that the temporal subjection of the Son was a diminution, Hilary distinguishes between the divinity and humanity; it is the latter that is subjected. God's action in the Son does not mean inferiority of either; God's essence remains in the Son throughout the Son's birth.

[146] Christ does not cease to be; His humanity is eternal, although he is no longer man. His subjection is one of piety, a demonstration of the divine order of unity and reciprocal honor. HILARY OF POITIERS, *De trinitate*, 40.

[147] Jerome stresses the unity of honor, power, being, and indivisibility of the Father and the Son, denying that there can be any gain or diminution in either. E. SCHENDEL, *Herrschaft*, 171-177.

subjection to the Father, he asks, in comparison to the shameful and humiliating death which Christ endured for our sakes[148]?

In an intriguing interpretation which seems to imply universal salvation, he states that all believers, and even the entire human race, are members of Christ's body. But in unbelievers (Jews, pagans, heretics) Christ is not subject, for those members of the body are not subject to the faith. At the end of the world, however, when all the members of His body will actually see Christ reigning in their bodies, then they will be subject too, so that all of Christ's body can be subject to God the Father, making God all in all. «God» not «Father» is used, Jerome notes, because it is the Trinity itself which is implied, meaning that humanity itself will be subject to the Godhead[149].

f) Zeno of Verona

Zeno of Verona (d.372) writes in a manner reminiscent of both Hilary and Tertullian. His opponents were the followers of Arius, Marcellus, and Photinus[150].

For Zeno, the problem of the subjection is a trinitarian problem which is dealt with by viewing it through the economy of salvation. In his polemics, he is careful to preserve the divinity of the Son as well as his coeternal nature. Passages from Scripture that suggest inferiority on the part of the Son are ascribed to his humanity. Christ must be viewed as the joining of the divine and human; with only the divinity, the incarnation is meaningless, while humanity alone would leave us without eschatological hope. In the mystery of the divine economy, the world would not be able to exist without the divine rulership; therefore, it is not lost when it is given by the Father to the Son or vice versa[151].

Christ is certainly subject to the Father, but not in any sense that implies inferiority or loss. In a way, he is always subject to the Father, but through love, rather than necessity or slavery[152].

---

[148] Jerome insists that Christ's subjection was accomplished with a totally free will. Christ's complete obedience is grounded on his obedience even to the cross, and this obedience is transferred to the faithful in Christ, rather than being an example to imitate. E. SCHENDEL, *Herrschaft*, 175.

[149] He does not actually say that all will be saved, but that all will be subject. Verse 28 is also mentioned without detailed exegesis in *Against the Pelagians*, Book I.18. Both he and Ambrose modify Origen's doctrine of the *apokatastasis*, reserving complete destruction only to those who are completely godless. Jerome, *Ep. 55.5*; E. SCHENDEL, *Herrschaft*, 174, referring to Jerome's *Dialogus contra Pelagianos*, I 28.

[150] E. SCHENDEL, *Herrschaft*, 167-171.

[151] *Tractatus* 6,1-4.

[152] Zeno holds rather conventional views of the resurrection, and defends them with the usual sort of arguments: from nature, from OT examples, and from pagan

g) Epiphanius of Salamis

Epiphanius of Salamis (315-403), was a zealous defender of orthodoxy and a vehement anti-Origenist, holding Origen's speculation and allegorical method responsible for most other heresies, Arianism in particular[153].

His chief accusation against Origen is that he denied that the present flesh will rise again and that he interpreted the resurrection in an overly spiritual manner.

In his book the *Ancoratus*, Epiphanius develops his own eschatology and doctrine of the resurrection, which is close to that of Methodius; in other words, very literal[154].

The resurrection is an event which encompasses the total man, recomposed according to the image of the Triune God. All dualism and metaphysical speculation, especially Platonism, is rejected. Jesus was a complete man: comprised in a tripartite manner of body, mind and spirit. Our salvation is our hope in the resurrection, assured to us through the divine promises. We will rise again in the same flesh[155].

In the text of the *Ancoratus* itself, there is little reference to our passage: verse 20 is a support for his insistence that the body of Christ is perfectly similar to ours, that he is the firstborn of those who have fallen asleep, and will not die again, and his suffering, which took place only in his humanity, was solely for us. Verse 13 proves that the Holy Spirit did in fact speak through the apostle Paul, and is one of a long list of citations bolstering this claim[156].

Epiphanius shows his heresy hunting skills at their peak in his chief work, the *Panarion*, or *Medicine Chest Against All Heresies*, an encyclopedic polemical refutation of all the known heresies of his day, the early days of the Church, and even the time before Christ. His first use of 1 Cor 15 is in the section dealing with Cerinthus, in which he focuses on Cerinthus' claim that Christ suffered, was crucified and buried, but did not rise and will not do so until the general resurrection, as well as with others who deny the resurrection altogether. He utilizes the usual prooftexts to show that Christ has been raised and the dire consequences for humans if he has not been raised[157].

---

ideas concerning immortality. Bodies will be restored to their angelic state with some continuity with earthly bodies. There will be appropriate rewards and punishments. B.E. DALEY, *Hope*, 96-97.

[153] E. SCHENDEL, *Herrschaft*, 179-182; J. QUASTEN, *Patrologia*, 387.

[154] B.E. DALEY, *Hope*, 89-90.

[155] C. RIGGI, «Catechesi escatologica dell'*Ancoratus*», 163-171.

[156] *Ancoratus* 92,2; 92,5; 68,13. EPIFANIO, *L'ancora della fede*, 144.184.

[157] Verses 14-16,20,29 in *Panarion* 28,6.3.

In his polemic against Marcion, he attempts to refute Marcion's positions by appealing to those works of the NT which Marcion acknowledged as divinely inspired. His goal is first of all to show that Christ is definitely in continuity with and to be found in the OT, and the truth of the resurrection. In *Scholia* 16 and 24, he appeals to verse 17 and to other verses in Corinthians, Galatians etc., in order to prove that the resurrection is real and that Marcion is a heretical innovator[158].

It is Origen and Arius who are the villains in the *Panarion*. Epiphanius is countering what he perceives to be Origen's over-spiritualization of the resurrection, and therefore the prooftexts that he chooses are those stressing the factual and physical nature of Christ's resurrection and its consequences for humanity: verse 12-15,17, and 20[159].

Sections 69,74-77 are devoted to refuting the errors of Arius, and they center on the misinterpretation of verse 25 – for apparently the heretics interpreted this to mean that the one who was ruling (Christ) will be overthrown and cast down when the kingdom is handed over to the Father – and verses 27 and 28, which were seen as meaning the inferiority and possible extinction of the Son after his subjection to the Father. The reign of Christ was seen as limited and fixed, with all of his status and power coming to an end[160].

Epiphanius takes great pains to deny that handing over the kingdom means an end of Christ's reign. His favorite prooftext is Luke 1,33, in which the angel says to Mary concerning Jesus «and his kingdom will have no end». This text has added value because it was revealed by an angel. He explains that verse 24 means that the dominion of Christ's fleshly reign in time comes to an end, but that his divine nature was always with God and is without beginning or time[161].

Verse 27a is rather vague, causing him to ask who the subject is where it says ὅταν δὲ εἴπῃ ὅτι πάντα ὑποτέτακται. He shows the logical absurdities that ensue if it is held that either the Father or the Son is the subject, and decides that the subject is the Holy Spirit[162].

He must also struggle against the claim that the Son himself is inferior to the Father since he is subjected to him. But he insists that the Son is not subjected as a slave or as one having no power, but as one begotten of the Father of the same nature and divinity. It is not according to force, necessity, want or lot (λῆξις) that he is subjected, but as lawful, only-begotten Son ruling with the Father forever, with one unity and privilege

---

158 *Panarion*, 327.
159 *Panarion* 64,18.2; 64,63.9; 64,64.10; 64,65.1; 64,68.2.
160 *Panarion* 69,74.5.
161 *Panarion* 69,75.
162 *Panarion* 69,76.

of honor ruling all creation and teaching his Church. This is what is meant by «God will be all in all», one divinity, lordship, doxology of the Father, Son and Holy Spirit[163].

h) Conclusion

The controversies generated by the Arian interpretation of this passage and the writings of Marcellus seem to be based on the assumption that this is primarily a christological passage. To be sure, there are christological elements contained within it, but the emphasis is on the function of Christ rather than his nature. By concentrating on one element of the passage apart from the whole, and by superimposing controversial concerns on it, sight is lost of the fact that the resurrection and the defeat of death are the real focus of 1 Cor 15.

2.8 *Speculative and Pastoral Interpretations: Fourth and Fifth Centuries*

a) Ambrose of Milan

Ambrose, Bishop of Milan (337-97) is credited with making Neoplatonic philosophy and Origen's method of exegesis acceptable in the Western Christian Church's theology. His views on punishment, redemption, and death are all rather diffuse and inexact. It appears that he believed in a gradual progression of the soul homeward to God[164].

Ambrose's defense of the resurrection in *De excessu fratris* utilizes verses 13 and 19-23 as proof texts for the primacy of the resurrection. The incarnation was necessary because the flesh was assumed in order for it to be raised up and given life. Man rose because man died; Christ is the firstfruits, and the rest of humanity comprises the «remaining fruits», thus reassuring us of our resurrection, but in different degrees, as in v. 21. Christ did not need the resurrection for his own sake, but for us. Heaven, earth, and the universe rose again in him; therefore, if he did not rise, all is lost[165].

Book V of *De fide ad Gratianum* deals extensively with the troublesome subjection. The subjection of Christ cannot be understood in any disparaging way. Here we are in Christ's kingdom; after the subjection, we will be in the kingdom of God, when the Trinity will reign together. Christ received the kingdom as the Son of Man and delivers it up as such;

---

[163] *Panarion* 69,77.

[164] Ambrose rejected millenarianism, although he did hold that the world had grown old and lost its vital energy, the end being near. In some instances, he wrote of eternal punishment, while in others, he indicated that it is a medicinal process (*In Ps* 1,47). B.E. DALEY, *Hope*, 97-100; E. SCHENDEL, *Herrschaft*, 171-178.

[165] AMBROSE, *De excessu fratris*, II 91-3; 102.

his subjection is under the conditions of the flesh, not the majesty of his divinity. The Father and the Son exercise a unity of honor; the Father puts all things under the Son, who restores all things to the Father; all the giving and receiving by the Father and the Son is without loss to either[166].

The subjection is always to be understood as referring to the humanity rather than the divinity of Christ, as the Godhead cannot be subjected. If understood in the Sabellian or Marcionite sense, the subjection would mean the reabsorption of the Son into the Father and the loss of his identity, and as a consequence, the same fate would befall everything which had been subjected to the Son. It should be understood as an expression of the perfect unity of the wills of the Father and the Son which has existed since before time, and which rules out any weakness or temporal subjection[167].

Obedience is what accomplishes the subjection, and the prime example of this obedience and subjection of the assumed humanity is the obedience of Christ unto death on the cross. He was subject in his flesh in order to overcome the weakness and unruliness of our flesh and to make us partakers in the divine nature[168].

This obedience and subjection is soteriological in its scope: «When therefore, all things have become subject to Christ, through Christ's obedience, so that all bend their knees to His name, then He Himself will be all in all. For now, since all do not believe, all do not seem to be in subjection. But when all have believed and done the will of God, then Christ will be all in all. And when Christ is all in all, then will God be all in all; for the Father abides ever in the Son»[169].

b) Augustine of Hippo

A sampling of Augustine's works discloses that he concentrated his exegesis on two particular portions of this passage: vv. 21-22 and v. 28. Verses 21-22 were essential to his doctrine of original sin and grace, stressing the fact that all have sinned and are liable to death and it is only through Christ that one can have life. Augustine does not seem to be

---

[166] AMBROSE, *De fide*, V 12, 147-9.

[167] AMBROSE, *De fide*, V XIII 161-164.

[168] Many minor examples of Christ's human subjection are given, such as his obedience to his parents. AMBROSE, *De fide*, V, XIV 171,174,178.

[169] AMBROSE, *De fide*, V, XV 182. «In general, Ambrose seems to sympathize with the Origenist doctrine of universal salvation, although he never makes it entirely clear how strictly universal he expects it to be» (B.E. DALEY, *Hope*, 99). *De excessu fratris*, 116; *In Ps* 39,17; *In Ps* 118,20.29 all provide examples of Ambrose's view that there is the possibility that all (with the exception of demons) may be saved.

overly interested in christological interpretations of this text beyond the role of Christ as mediator[170].

Verse 28 is spiritualized and interpreted in an epistemological and psychological manner which reflects the ability of the individual to know beyond himself and to know and experience God. God's sovereignty is also expressed, but mostly as it will be perceived by the individual[171].

c) Gregory of Nazianzus

Gregory of Nazianzus (329-390) devoted much of his theological work to a vigorous defense of the Trinitarian theology of Nicea against the later Arians, or Eunomians as they were called. Since he was a skilled rhetor, many of his works, especially those on eschatology, were more poetic and vivid than precise and systematic. Gregory was a moderate Origenist, and this is reflected in his cautious acceptance of the purgative nature of punishment and the hope for universal salvation[172].

Gregory's *Oratio 30* is directed against Eunomius and concentrates on the texts which the Eunomians use in defense of their views, one of which is 1 Cor 15,25[173].

Verse 25 is disposed of quickly: a measurement of time does not exclude what follows afterwards; the «until» in verse 25 does not mean a cessation. Coming dangerously close to Marcellus' notion of the two kingdoms, Gregory teaches that Christ's kingdom or rule can be understood in two senses. In the first sense, he is king over all, whether people want it or not, and in this sense, the kingdom is permanent and without end. In the second, we are subjected to the Son and placed under his dominion, albeit willingly. Once this subjection has taken place, there is no

---

[170] In discussions ranging from the fate of unbaptized infants to whether those alive at the time of the parousia will experience death, Augustine is consistent: since all die in Adam, all must be given life through him. *De moribus ecclesiae catholicae et de moribus manichaeorum*, I 19,35; *Ep.* 92, 147, 148, 166.

[171] «God will be the source of every satisfaction, more than any heart can rightly crave, more than life and health, food and wealth, glory and honor, peace and every good - so that God, as St. Paul said, may be all in all» (*Civ. Dei* XIX 15; XXII 29,30).

[172] In many orations, such as his *Carmina Moralia*, he opts for a traditional Christian eschatology with scenes of judgment, punishment, reward, heavenly joys, etc. Examples of his acceptance of the purgative and hopeful nature of punishment are found in *Oration* 3,7; 39,19; 40,36. B.E. DALEY, *Hope*, 83-84; J. MOSSAY, *La Mort et l'au-delà*, 102-108.

[173] He also attacks those whom he calls Sabellians, in reality followers of Marcellus. This work was written about 380. J. LIENHARD, «Exegesis of 1 Cor 15, 24-28», 347.

further need to bring about subjection. Therefore, this kingdom is temporary and has an end[174].

The submission of Christ to the Father is for a salvific purpose. Christ, having taken on sin and suffered for us, has refashioned our nature by means of the passion. Now he subjects himself to the *Father* in accordance with the Father's will. He does so as head of his body, the Church. He cannot be subjected to *God*, since he is himself God[175].

In his exegesis of verse 28, he points out that it is God – not the Father alone – who will be all in all. The Son is not reabsorbed into the Godhead. The phrase «all in all» means this: there will not be any more multiplicity caused by motions and passions, and we shall be in the divine form, receiving and carrying within us God alone. This for Gregory is the meaning of perfection[176].

There are some scattered references in his poetry and orations[177].

d) Gregory of Nyssa

Gregory of Nyssa (335-94) was able to both affirm and refine many of Origen's eschatological ideas, thereby having a lasting influence on Greek patristic and Byzantine theology. He believed firmly in a restoration of intellectual creation to an original unitive state with God, and the resurrection was the first stage in this process[178].

This original state was not a disembodied preexistence, and our physical existence was not the result of a fall. At the resurrection, the perfection or fullness of the rational creature's possible reality as it exists in the mind of God is restored. When God created humans, this included the σκόπος or goal, the final reality of each creature. This is a process realized through time; in the end, all will reach the end or fullness[179].

---

[174] *Oratio 30.4*. Matt 28,20, which became a standard prooftext in refuting this argument, is used here.

[175] The ecclesial understanding of the submission of Christ is based upon Col 1,18. J. LIENHARD, «Exegesis of 1 Cor 15, 24-28», 348; *Oratio* 30,5.

[176] *Oratio* 30,6; J. LIENHARD, «Exegesis of 1 Cor 15, 24-28», 348.

[177] GREGORY OF NAZIANZUS, *Carmina historica*, (Carmen de se ipso 11) 136,96 (vv. 20,22); *Carmina theologica*, PG 37,2.34 (vv.22-23); *Orationes*, 37,6; 38,4; 30,4.5.6, SC 250, 318, 358; and *Christus patiens*, SC 149 298,99; 334,40. This latter work is of questionable authorship.

[178] *De hom opif* 17,2; *De an et res*, PG 46, 148 A1; *De orat dom* 4; *Or catechet* 26; *In beat* 8; B.E. DALEY, *Hope* 85-87.

[179] *De hom opif* 16, 28.4; *De an et res*, PG 46, 152A1-11, 113B1-D2, 125A1-C2. Gregory mentions exclusion from heaven for sinners in a couple of places, such as *In inscr psal* 2.16, but for the most part he is unambiguous: every creature will achieve the fullness and completion ordained by God.

Gregory concentrated much of his speculative work on the *apokatasta-sis* or hope for universal salvation, devoting, in fact, a whole treatise to 1 Cor 15,28. *In illud: tunc et ipse filius* grapples with the whole problem of the subjection of Christ[180].

In the first part of the treatise, Gregory examines the different mean-ings and nuances of the term ὑποτάσσειν, and finds that none of these meanings really applies to the subjection of Christ. The subjection, how-ever, lies in the future, since ὑποταγήσεται is a future tense.

Salvation consists of both sin and death passing completely into non-being. The subjection takes place through us, for it is through the imita-tion of Christ the firstfruits that fallen human nature becomes separated from evil and purified by the divinity in him. Every evil force and power in us will be destroyed; submission to God is complete separation from evil. All that will be left is that which has its origin in God as in the be-ginning, before the admixture of vice. We come under the hegemony of the perfect good in Christ, and perfect subjection to God occurs when this process is complete and the soul is no longer subjected to evil[181].

The complete abolition or non-being of evil defines the time when God will be all in all; if there is anything opposed to God, he cannot be all in all, since God cannot be in evil. The fact that God will be all things to all beings shows the simple and unitary nature of the life to come in which we hope. We will no longer search for many and varied things in life, since God will be all that we need, having assumed everything and hav-ing become every reality for us. To obtain God and all that is in him is impossible without being united with him, which in turn requires that we be incorporated into him, which we accomplish by becoming one with the body of Christ. When the good pervades everything, then our entire body is subjected to the vivifying force, and it can be said that through the subjection of this body, the subjection of the Son takes place, as he is united to his body which is the church[182].

Gregory alludes to the strange and unusual ways in which Paul uses terms, pointing out that at times, words are used in other than the com-mon sense. For example, «subjection» means «salvation»; what is called «subjection» in the letter to the Corinthians is «reconciliation» in the letter to the Romans, and so on[183].

---

[180] GREGORY OF NYSSA, *In illud: tunc et ipse filius*, 1-28; GREGORIO DI NISSA *Commento al Nuovo Testamento*, 141-165.

[181] *In illud: tunc et ipse filius*, 1313-1316; J. LIENHARD, «Exegesis of 1 Cor 15, 24-28», 348-349.

[182] *In illud: tunc et ipse filius*, 1317.

[183] *In illud: tunc et ipse filius*, 1324-1325.

Perhaps this freedom with terms is preparation for Gregory's interpretation of βασιλεύειν, which he interprets to mean ἀριστεύειν, «to excel or be the best». This perhaps is taken to mean that Christ will definitely be in command until all enemies, including death, have been conquered or destroyed. When no one dies any longer, and there are no more enemies, Christ will have led all men to God and can then hand over the kingdom to God the Father. Christ will be subjected to God in our subjection, understood not as «servile humility, but as a kingdom and incorruptibility and blessedness»[184].

This is fundamentally the exegesis found in his other works. Verse 28 receives special attention in *De anima et resurrectione*, in which Gregory explains the meaning of «all in all». Everything free will be united with virtue; the Divine Being is the fount of all virtue; those who have parted with evil will be united with Him, so that God will be all in all. God distributes himself proportionally to every mode of existence, so that we need nothing, as he becomes the fulfillment of every need and longing. Evil will be completely annihilated, since God, who is all in all, cannot be in what does not exist[185].

Verses 19-21 help Gregory in his polemical work *Contra Eunomium* to defend orthodox views of the incarnation and resurrection[186].

Gregory defends the resurrection in *De opif hom*: if Christ, with all of his wounds and brokenness, is risen from the dead, then how can anyone say that there is no resurrection[187]?

Employing the usual patristic method, Gregory exegetes two passages from the Song of Songs by relating them to the NT and shows that when all powers are destroyed and evil passes into non-being, then God will be all in all. God is the end of our desire, and if we view only that, then no evil remains. We are joined to God by our communion with the good, which is Christ[188].

Scattered throughout his many treatises, orations, homilies etc., are many other references to 1 Cor 15; it is of interest, however, that verse 25 is rarely mentioned in his works. This is surprising when one considers the strenuous exegetical activity sparked by this verse from the time of Marcellus of Ancyra and onwards[189].

---

[184] *In illud: tunc et ipse filius*, 1325; J. LIENHARD, «Exegesis of 1 Cor 15, 24-28», 349-350.

[185] *De anima et resurrectione*, LNPF vol. V, 452.

[186] *Contra Eunomium*, II (v. 20); V v. 21); and X (v. 19).

[187] *De opif hom*, 25.

[188] GREGORIO DI NISSA, *In Canticum Canticorum*, 14 and 15. Gregory is dealing with Song of Songs, 5,15 and 6,9.

[189] The sole reference is found in *In illud: tunc et ipse filius*. Most of Gregory's attention is focused on verse 28. His other references to verses from 1 Cor 15 are

e) Didymus of Alexandria

Some interesting and original interpretations are preserved in two *catenae* fragments on 1 Cor 15, 24-28 attributed to Didymus of Alexandria (d.398). He proposes two meanings for βασιλεία: the common meaning, that is, «those ruled over», and as a second meaning, «the Son's own flesh». This is because Didymus views Christ's flesh as being involved in a progress or process, from being ruled over in the form of a slave (Phil 2,7) to the point where it is the flesh of the Logos. The Son hands over his own flesh to the Father for improvement. On the question of subjection, Didymus claims that the purpose of the subjection of the Son to the Father is to refute Greek mythology and its parricides. The subjection is twofold: that of the Church, as the Son takes to himself its persecutions and sufferings, followed by that of the Son[190].

2.9 *Antiochean Exegesis in the Fourth-Century Church*

f) John Chrysostom

During the fourth century, eschatology diminished in importance and became more focussed on the individual. Eschatology became the concern of spiritual writers and preachers, with the aim of inciting the believers to live a Christian life[191].

This is evident in the works of John Chrysostom (344/54-407), the bishop of Constantinople. His sermons dwelt often on eschatological themes: especially strong was his insistence on the importance of judgment and retribution, lest justice be rendered meaningless and people be encouraged to sin. He held that judgment, retribution and punishment actually enhanced human dignity, making us choose and be responsible for our actions. He was an anti-Origenist in that he denied the medicinal nature of punishment, insisting that it was fearsome and everlasting, and that reward and punishment began immediately after death without any intermediate state[192].

In his *Homily 39 on 1 Corinthians*, he deals with the problems of chapter 15 in various ways. In commenting on verses 12-22, he merely

---

found in: *Oratio in diem natalem Christi* (v. 21); *In inscriptiones psalmorum* 2,8 (vv. 21-2); *De oratione dominica* 5 (v.22); *De mortuis non esse dolendum* (v. 26); *In ascensionem Christi* (v. 26); *De tridui inter mortem et resurrectionem Domini nostri Iesu Christi spatio* (vv. 24,28); *De infantibus praemature abreptis* (v. 28); *Adversus Arium et Sabellium de Patre et Filio*; *Antirrheticus adversus Apolinarium* (vv. 14, 20-1); *De beatitudinibus* 7 (v. 19); *In sanctum pascha* (v. 19); *De perfectione christiana ad Olympium monachum* (vv. 20, 23); *Refutatio confessionis Eunomii* (vv. 20, 23).

[190] J. LIENHARD, «Exegesis of 1 Cor 15, 24-28», 350-351.

[191] B.E. DALEY, *Hope*, 105.

[192] His homilies on Matthew and on the letter to the Hebrews are especially vivid and uncompromising. B.E. DALEY, *Hope*, 106-109.

restates, explains and praises Paul's arguments. It is not until verse 23 that he begins to provide anything original. In verse 23, «each in his own order» is taken to mean that reward as well as punishment will not be alike, but apportioned according to what each deserves. Then, referring to enemies, meaning Marcellus and his followers, he deals with the issues raised by verses 24-28. Verse 24 must be understood in a way that is worthy of God (θεωπρεπῶς) in order to avoid the implication that the Father was not king before Christ handed over the kingdom, or the Son after the handing over. He bolsters his argument with John 5,17 and Dan 7,14. The only rule that is «put down» is that of the devils. Likewise, he denies any interpretation of «until» in verse 25 that would be unworthy of God. John claims that Paul made no mention of the Father in vv. 24-26, making the Son the subject. To prevent anyone from thinking that the Son was greater than the Father, however, the Son subjects all things to the Father in v. 27, thereby showing «His great concord with the Father, and that He is the principle of all other good things and the first Cause, who hath begotten One so great in power and in achievements»[193].

He differentiates two ways in which Paul speaks of God: when speaking of the Godhead itself, he uses exalted language; while speaking of the economy of the flesh, however, he uses language and images that are human and limited. Knowledge of this resolves apparent contradictions. He solves the problem of the duration of the kingdom by positing two kingdoms: one is by creation, the other by appropriation (οἰκείωσις). In the first, God is king of all, including Greeks, Jews, demons and enemies; while in the second, which alone has a beginning, he rules believers, the willing and the subjected. Verse 28 means this: when God is all in all, all things must be dependent on him, for there cannot be two powers without beginning, nor a separate kingdom, nor anything independent. When all enemies have been subjected, and when the Son is in complete concord with the Father in total perfection, then God may be said to be «all in all»[194].

g) Severian of Gabala

Among the spurious works attributed to John Chrysostom and recently reevaluated as belonging to Severian of Gabala (408-431) is a homily titled *In psalmum 96*. When this psalm states «the Lord is king», the royal accession cannot be predicated of the kingdom of God, since it is eternal.

---

[193] *Homilies on First Corinthians 39*, LNPF XII, 239; J. LIENHARD, «Exegesis of 1 Cor 15, 24-28», 351.

[194] *Homilies on First Corinthians*, LNPF XII, 239-240; J. LIENHARD, «Exegesis of 1 Cor 15, 24-28», 351-352.

In an exegesis reminiscent of Marcellus, the author holds that the kingdom of the Savior is twofold in nature: one kingdom exists before the world and is timeless, ruled by the Savior who is king by nature. The other kingdom, the economy of salvation, begins at the incarnation. In this «economy» Christ is king according to human form. Before the incarnation, the world was tyrannized by demons, death and sin. The temporal reign of Christ has a beginning and an end, but the eternal reign does not. He distinguishes between two meanings of the word βασιλέια: the one meaning refers to the dignity of rulers, the other to the nations who are ruled, and it is the latter that is of importance in explaining the passage. It is the kingdom of sin and death that will end, and humanity, formerly ruled by sin and death, will be freed from captivity, created anew, and handed over to God the Father[195].

There is further elaboration on the nature of the kingdom in a fragment attributed to Severian: the kingdom was seized by the Evil One when he overthrew Adam and his descendants; in other words, the devil is a usurper and a tyrant. After the kingdom is handed over, the Son and the Father rule together[196].

h) Theodoret of Cyrrhus

Theodoret of Cyrrhus (c.393-466) is seen as more or less the last to be involved in the controversy surrounding 1 Cor 15,24-28[197].

The expression of his eschatological hope was the expectation that after the resurrection, the body and soul would both share in the immortality, incorruptibility, stability, and changelessness which are the characteristics of God[198].

All sin and sorrow will disappear, and life will be happy and filled with divine, intelligible light. Resurrection and salvation are not identical, since sinners will also rise if only to be judged and punished. The full

---

[195] *In psalmum 96*, PG 55, 604-5; Luke 1,31-33 is used as a prooftext to show that Christ's kingdom will have no end. There are two meanings to the word kingdom, «the dignity of the rulers» (τὸ αξίωμα τῶν βασιλευόντων), and «the nations who are ruled» (τὰ ἔθνη τὰ βασιλευόμενα); G.W.H. LAMPE, «Exegesis of Some Biblical Texts, 171-172; Lienhard, «Exegesis of 1 Cor 15, 24-28», 352.

[196] In explaining that «until» does not mean a cessation, he quotes Isa 46,4, which is used for the same purpose by John Chrysostom and Theodoret of Cyrrus. J. LIENHARD, «Exegesis of 1 Cor 15, 24-28», 352.

[197] Theodoret was an Antiochene who was involved in refuting many heresies and opposing views, among them the Monophysites. He defended Nestorius after the latter's condemnation in 431. J. LIENHARD, «Exegesis on 1 Cor 15, 24-28», 353.

[198] B.E. DALEY, *Hope*, 115.

transformation we have already begun to experience through the Holy Spirit; the rest begins immediately after death, when believers will be united in the glorified humanity of Christ[199].

He engages in commonplace exegesis in his *Interpretatio epistulae I ad Corinthios* until he reaches verse 24, and he is aware that Arius, Eunomius and others have used verses 24-28 for their own purposes. He denies that the word «until» means any cessation, and he insists that Christ's handing over of the kingdom to the Father is not taking away power from himself, but only the devil and his minions, for only when they have been scattered into outer darkness will creation be wholly subject. Additionally, there is only one kingdom, which is eternal as is God, and the Son who is coeternal. He does not, however, explain exactly what he means by that[200].

He avoids the implication of subordinationism by pointing out that in Phil 3,21 the Son is the one who acts, while in 1 Cor 15,27, it is the Father. He spends the most time on the most delicate question, that of Christ's subjection: references to the subjection of the Son do not refer to the divine nature of the Only-begotten, but to his human nature; handing the kingdom over to the Father does not mean that he does not possess it already; and subjection also means that Christ makes his own what is ours, both our present disobedience and future subjection, and he is said to be subjected after we have been subjected, which occurs after having been freed from sin and corruption[201].

Finally, a unique distinction explains verse 28. God has two modes of being omnipresent: the first, by nature (κατὰ τὴν οὐσίαν), is invariable, since he cannot be circumscribed. The second, however, is according to favor or good pleasure (κατὰ μέντοι τὴν εὐδοκίαν, οὐκ ἐν ἅπασίν ἐστιν), is not yet complete, and in this sense, God is not yet «all in all». Those who fear him, hope in his mercy, and are just, are those to whom God is present in the second way. God will be all in all when all have been freed from sin and converted to him[202].

3. Summary and Conclusion

There are several reasons for terminating the survey of the exegetical tradition of this passage with Theodoret. First of all, the Arian and anti-

---

199 B.E. DALEY, *Hope*, 115.
200 PG 82, 355-357; J. LIENHARD, «Exegesis of 1 Cor 15, 24-29», 353.
201 PG 82, 357-358.
202 PG 82, 359-60; J. LIENHARD, «Exegesis of 1 Cor 15, 24-28», 353.

Arian polemics had fairly well run their course by the end of the fifth century. Although some christological controversies remained, this passage did not play a major role in them. Gnosticism and Manicheaism had ceased to be any threat by this time. No longer did the passage play a prominent role in the development of doctrine.

During the fifth and sixth centuries in the west, the theological tradition declined considerably. Political and social upheavals, the «fall» of the western empire, the barbarian invasions and the Gothic wars, all took their toll. Most of the eschatological tradition was focussed on moral exhortation and preparation for the end, which was thought to be near, with special emphasis on judgment and punishment. This absence of fertile theological reflection on this passage does not invite further research in the west into the exegetical tradition of this passage.

For the first hundred years or so following the writing of this passage, the exegesis was still rooted in a Jewish milieu. Although a deep understanding of the apocalyptic approach may have been lacking, a *basic* comprehension of the apocalyptic message of the passage prevailed. Scripture, especially of the prophetic variety, was rooted in history and described in cryptic form what God was going to do in this history in the near future and the consequences of this intervention for every human being. It was practical, immediate, and urgent in its appeal. There was very little speculation on the deeper meanings of this passage. Instead, individual verses were chosen for appropriate prooftexts for the resurrection, since the resurrection was understood as the «firstfruits», the inaugural event of the new age. There seems to have been a firm understanding of the fact that Christ's resurrection was linked to the resurrection of the believer, and that the parousia would signal the beginning of that resurrection. The emphasis was given to the immediate effect on the salvation of the believer. In this sense, as we shall see, the passage was interpreted according to the intention of the author, and with an appreciation of the apocalyptic meaning.

The next phase involved defending the value of the created order, the body, the Scriptures and salvation history. The *reality* of the resurrection of the body was the point of contention, and there are many verses in this passage that deal admirably with this problem: those stressing the dire consequenses for believers if there is no resurrection, and those stressing the continuity, if not complete identity, of the earthly body with that of the resurrected state (mostly in vv. 35-58). During this period, the end of time and the final judgment were thought to be imminent, and the purpose of theological use of this passage was pastoral, in that it prepared people to live with this in view. In defending and explaining God's creative power, his mastery over human history, the importance of the created order, the body, and appropriate ethical behavior, a fundamental grasp of the apocalyptic message was evident.

As fuel for the apocalyptic interpretation of this and similar passages, millenarianism was of great importance. Drawing on the images in Rev 20 and 21, believers expected not only God's intervention in history, but a new heaven and new earth. They believed that they were living in the end times, that time period initiated by the resurrection of Christ. Ethical choice and correct living as well as faith were crucial for the Christian community.

As Christianity spread throughout the Roman and Greek world, the interpretation of Scripture underwent a change. Alexandrian exegesis, especially as exemplified in the writings of Origen, dealt the death blow to apocalyptic exegesis, although it continued in a secondary and subordinate current within the Church. With the allegorical approach, the Jewish roots were effectively cut. Scripture was no longer primarily about God's imminent action in history, but was seen more as a repository of eternal divine truths. Apocalyptic literature is primarily sectarian in nature. As Christianity became less of a sect and finally a state religion, the very conditions which give rise to apocalyptic – persecution and alienation – began to disappear. Finally, the enemy of apocalyptic – time – took its toll. As time passes and the expected imminent intervention of God begins to recede, apocalyptic tends to lose its force and its appeal.

Origen was the first to begin to struggle with the cosmic implications of this passage by focusing his attention on verse 28, «so that God may be all in all», thereby building a teleological theology. His particular gift was to be able to see the cosmological and anthropological implications as well as the soteriological. He recognized that the resurrection and defeat of death had made a qualitative change in our existence, and that humanity was being swept along to greater spiritual heights.

This was done at the expense, however, of the historical application of the passage. It was removed from history to the realm of the intellect and spirit, with the apocalyptic characteristics of God's intervention in history, the judgment of sinners and vindication of the righteous, and the transformation of the created order being deemphasized. Opposition to Origen and the Alexandrian method continued with writers such as Methodius of Olympus, Peter Alexandrinus, and Victorinus of Pettau.

In the christological controversies which followed, the New Testament was seen through polemical lenses, and there was one burning question: What is the *nature* of Christ? Function was given an important but subordinate place in the theological reflection of this period. Marcellus of Ancyra was instrumental in igniting the controversy over this passage. Ironically, his notion of different economies within salvation history did in fact focus on Christ's function, and his eschatologically determined theology treated the kingdom of Christ as a messianic function in much the same way as did Jewish apocalyptic literature. However, within the theological ambience of the fourth century, the passage was seen as a christological statement instead of one pointing towards the total victory of God. By interpreting symbols such as the limited reign of Christ or his subjection to the Father in christological rather than function terms, exegetes started unwinding a ball of theological yarn that perdured for two hundred years. The view of Scripture during this period was one of revelation of theological truth rather than the hidden plan of God and his imminent intervention and victory. Many of the exegetes who followed spent much time in trying to answer the questions created by the writings of Marcellus. In the face of such problems as were generated during this time, the only solution seemed to be a spiritualization of the entire passage.

Authors such as Epiphanius of Salamis and Cyril of Jerusalem, and Hilary of Poitiers continued to focus on the traditional hope for the resurrection and eternal life and the importance of the flesh in this plan. They represent a more traditional and literal approach. Of particular interest is the continuation of a basically apocalyptic attitude in the representatives of Antiochean exegesis, primarily John Chrysostom, Severian of Gabala, and Theodoret of Cyrrhus. Antiochean exegesis is much closer to the original Jewish roots of the apocalyptic writings. Chrysostom in particular speaks in uncompromising terms of reward and punishment, God's justice, and the restoration of sovereignty to God.

It is not to say that any particular theological move in this period of evolution was in error, only that many were not apocalyptic in their understanding. A failure to appreciate what apocalyptic literature is trying to communicate, and the fact that a plethora of symbols is enlisted for this purpose without to much concern for theological coherence in the modern sense, can lead one on theological detours that obscure the majesty, power and urgency of the original message.

CHAPTER VI

Summary and Conclusion

The study of this passage focussed first on the rhetorical structure and
purpose of the passage, and determined that the resurrection and the defeat of death were its key elements. Surveying the Jewish apocalyptic literature of the period uncovered the operative theologies and symbols
pertaining to death, afterlife, judgment and resurrection, as well as the
role of the Messiah. After having arrived at a working definition of
apocalyptic, a comparison was made to determine if indeed 1 Cor 15 belongs to this genre. Finally, a survey was made of its history of interpretation during the first five centuries of this era, paying special attention to
the permutations that this interpretation underwent through time. We can
now add some other questions: What is the apocalyptic message of 1 Cor
15? Why is it important, and how does it differ from ordinary eschatology? What are the consequences of refusing to give credence to the
apocalyptic message of this passage? A summary of the itinerary already
followed in the analysis of this passage will respond to some of these
questions. This will be followed by a review of the observations of J.
Beker and E. Schüssler-Fiorenza, two prominent proponents of the value
and importance of Christian apocalyptic theology.

Contrary to the opinion of many commentators, Paul is not defending
his status as an apostle, but his reliability as a witness to the resurrected
Christ. At first, Paul emphasizes in the *narratio* the received tradition
and the common agreement with the Corinthians, especially in 15,3b-5.
The center of this tradition is the Risen Christ; Paul takes great pains to
emphasize that he is a reliable witness and to suggest the 500 others as
corroborating testimony. His very life and all that he has accomplished in
spite of what he was before is also offered as further proof. The resurrection of Christ is firmly reestablished as the foundation upon which
Paul will build the rest of his argument against the deniers of the resur-

rection of the dead. In the *propositio*, the problem is stated: there are some who say that there is no resurrection. Having already appealed to the received tradition, especially with regard to the resurrection of Christ, Paul will now begin his argumentation in the *probatio*. The consequences of there being no resurrection of the dead are first unfolded logically: the Christian life is empty and meaningless, and those who have already died will be without hope at the coming of Christ, since according to much Jewish apocalyptic theology, only those alive at the time of the coming of the Messiah will be saved. This is the consequence if the resurrection of Christ is treated as an isolated and unique event.

Beginning in v. 20, Paul's apocalyptic strategy becomes clear. The resurrection of Christ is to be portrayed as the beginning, rather than the end, of the apocalyptic process. It derives its meaning from the general resurrection at the end of time, not vice versa. Many commentators say that the general resurrection is shoved into the distant future; the opposite is true. The resurrection of Christ is a proleptic event, the firstfruits of what is to come[1].

The parousia of Christ is that event which brings history to an end and signals the general resurrection of those in Christ. This is accomplished after – and only after – certain conditions have been met. The inimical powers must be overcome and destroyed. These are almost always understood as otherworldly powers, although some have argued that they signify the rulers of this world, i.e., secular political powers. It is impossible to prove absolutely one way or another, but in a sense it does not matter. Jewish theology taught that evil supernatural powers were the driving force behind heathen nations and wicked rulers. Paul and his contemporaries would not have made such a clear distinction between them[2].

Verse 20 is completed by verse 28; what begins in Christ ends with God the Father being all in all. The terms ἀπαρχή and πάντα ἐν πᾶσιν become the two poles of the apocalyptic process: one begins, the other

---

[1] It is striking how seldom Paul elaborates his theology of the resurrection of believers. The received tradition, as seen in 1 Cor 15,3-5, speaks of the resurrection of Christ and his appearances but says nothing of that of the believer. Paul goes on to stress Jesus as both savior and judge (1Thess 1,10; 1 Cor 1,7-8; Phil 3,20; 2 Cor 5,10; Rom 2,16), the universal significance of his resurrection, and its connection with the resurrection of the faithful dead, thereby combining the received tradition with the apocalyptic concept of the resurrection of the dead at the end of the age.

[2] G.H.C. MACGREGOR, «Principalities and Powers», 22-23. This is contested by Carr, who claims that the «rulers of this age» in 1 Cor 2,6-8 refers only to the earthly rulers directly responsible for the death of Jesus, i.e., Pilate, Herod and Caiaphas. Given the cosmological orientation of much of Paul's theology and his apparent lack of interest in affixing blame for the crucifixion to anyone in particular, the thesis of Carr is unlikely. W. CARR, «The Rulers of this Age», 20-35.

ends; the entire apocalyptic process flows towards that final point. The last event before the parousia and handing over of the kingdom is the defeat of death, the last enemy, but it is unclear from the passage what death is and what this overcoming entails.

It is in the Jewish apocalyptic literature of roughly 200 B.C. to 100 A.D. that clues can be found as to the image that Paul had in mind when he called death the last enemy, as well as comparisons for the apocalyptic symbolism and language of 1 Cor 15. A survey of the literature in question discloses first of all that there was no one consistent image or theology of death, afterlife, resurrection and judgment. There were many symbols, images, and theologies, often side by side in the same document, and often they seemed to contradict each other. But this did not seem to disturb the authors; and in fact, some modern observers have suggested that this be seen as a theological richness rather than a weakness. In the descriptions of the post-mortem life, the language concerning resurrection of the body is inconsistent, at times seeming to favor a physical resurrection, while at other times describing what appears to be either exaltation and transformation or immortality of the soul. But rather than impose a modern desire for order and consistency on the data, perhaps it is better to ask the function of these symbols: they were not meant to be a treatise on the afterlife, but a clear and forceful statement of the vindication of the righteous and the justice of God. For the most part, they were parenetic in nature, reassuring the reader that the just will be rewarded and the wicked punished.

Death plays a key role in the apocalyptic agenda. Death, especially the unjust death of the just, seems to be the driving force behind the apocalyptic message. If the just cannot live a blessed and happy life on earth, where is the justice of God? A personified death is often seen as the force that is opposed to God, a symbol of a world alienated from God and controlled by evil and unjust forces. To defeat death is to vindicate God's sovereignty over the cosmos as well as his justice. The defeat of death means that the just, the faithful, will experience God's mercy and live a blessed life with Him, despite the outward appearances of circumstances.

It is evident that there was no clear cut, unequivocal role for the Messiah, and that there were many messianic theologies in existence. At times, active, at others, passive in his role, he was never more than an agent of God, rather than a mediator. His function was what defined him, rather than his origin or identity.

Before beginning that survey of the Jewish apocalyptic literature it is important to fashion a working definition and description of apocalyptic. Distinction is made between the genre apocalypse and apocalyptic eschatology. The first, according to the SBL paradigm, is a «genre of revelatory literature with a narrative framework, in which a revelation is mediated by an otherworldly being to a human recipient, disclosing a transcendent reality which is both temporal, insofar as it envisages eschatological salvation, and spatial, insofar as it involves another, supernatural world»[3].

A number of characteristics of apocalyptic eschatology have been noted: ethical dualism, the two ages, universalism, cosmic destruction and regeneration, heavenly mysteries, and so on. Many of these are not in themselves apocalyptic; however, when placed in relation to one another in the same document, such eschatological expressions as an approaching cosmic catastrophe, battles with angelic powers, a new aeon in discontinuity with the past, and parenetic discourse can be considered expressions of an apocalyptic eschatology. Many times apocalyptic eschatology is generated in an atmosphere of alienation and/or persecution. Its message is one of counseling patience, fidelity, perseverance and ethical fervor.

Utilizing the SBL paradigm for the genre apocalypse and the characteristics of apocalyptic eschatology, several conclusions can be reached: 1) apocalyptic imagery and clusters are sprinkled throughout the Pauline and deutero-Pauline corpus, playing an essential part in Paul's theology; 2) although this passage is not a representative of the apocalypse *genre*, it definitely reflects an apocalyptic eschatology and provides in a skeletal form the outline of an apocalypse; 3) Paul's theology of the resurrection in this passage is an integral part of its apocalyptic message.

A *crux interpretum* in this passage is whether the «all» of vv. 22-23 indicates that everyone will be raised up or saved. Again, an examination of all of the Pauline texts relating to salvation is inconclusive: some seem to favor universal salvation, others particular. It must be kept in mind that each letter was written within a particular context and in response to a particular problem; it is this contingency that determines the nature of the response. However, in answering the question whether Paul believed in universal salvation the following observations must be brought to bear: 1) it is clear that in Jewish apocalyptic literature, salvation was meant for the just, for those on «God's side». The nature of Jewish apocalyptic is sectarian and particular with regard to salvation, but universal with regard to the effects of the apocalyptic event; 2) although in many instances, the fate of the wicked or unbelieving is not mentioned or elaborated on, it is clear that most of the literature taught that the wicked would be punished or would perish; 3) Paul's letters are written to the Christian community to deal with specific questions and problems, there-

---

[3] J.J. COLLINS, «Morphology», 9.

fore universal salvation, except in the case of Israel, is simply not an issue. Paul's apocalyptic theology, however, is based on the idea of God's
reconquest of the cosmos, the elimination of every opposing force. It
could be said that the seeds for a doctrine of universal salvation are present within his theology, but that it was never developed. The «all» in 1
Cor 15, especially vv. 22-23, refers to the universal effects of Christ's
resurrection.

An examination of the history of the interpretation of this passage
during the first five Christian centuries is revealing. Beker claims that
when the apocalyptic message of a particular passage is lost, it collapses
into christology, and it appears that this was indeed the case with this
passage. The interpretation during the apostolic and sub-apostolic periods
focussed rightly on Christ as firstfruits (ἀπαρχή) and encouraged the believer to stand fast, live with ethical fervor and righteousness, and look to
his own resurrection as being the fulfillment of that promised by the resurrection of Christ. During the gnostic debates, writers such as Irenaeus
and Tertullian stressed the goodness of creation, especially the flesh, and
its resurrection as being a consequence and fulfillment of Christ's own.
They even maintained the literal millenarianism and transformation of
creation that was so much an integral part of the apocalyptic world view.
The radical turn began with Origen. With his allegorizing and spiritualizing approach to Scripture he first of all put to death millenarianism. His
rejection of the literal interpretation of Scripture also spiritualized the
turn of the ages and the renewal of creation. Secondly, the entire passage
was given a cosmological and spiritual interpretation that distanced it
from the realm of history and situated it within the spirit of the individual
believer. In the grand sweep of the return of creation to God, history
does not play an important part, nor does the world of human societies.
The locus of God's being «all in all» is shifted to the mind and spirit of
the individual believer.

The christological controversies completed the disintegration of the
apocalyptic interpretation of the passage. The debates of the patristic period over the meaning of various elements of this passage were the result
of taking words or phrases in isolation. Individual words and phrases are
merely constituents of the apocalyptic whole and it is this whole which
must be analyzed for a complete and clear understanding of its message.
The continual atomization and fragmentation of elements of the passage
finally led to either prooftexts for the christological controversies or to a
complete spiritualization and individualization of the message. The elements of the passage that caused the most difficulty were those implying
that Christ was less than the Father and that his kingdom was of limited
duration. This results if the passage is thought to be primarily christologi-

cal in its intention. But if the apocalyptic nature of the passage is used in its interpretation, and the focus is on the Father, his reconquest of the cosmos, and the place of the resurrection in this process, then problems are minimized. The passage does not focus on the *nature* of Christ, but his *function* within the apocalyptic event of God's reconquest of the cosmos. Christ's rule is his function within the apocalyptic process, and this function makes several inferences concerning his nature. The handing over of the kingdom to God the Father is not a diminishment of Christ, but his fulfillment as the Son when he can present to the Father a cosmos cleansed and healed of division and alienation.

Barth has stated that chapter 15 is not only the key to interpreting the whole letter, but all of Paul's letters as well. In what sense is this true? Chapters 1-2 certainly emphasize the death of Christ, with no mention whatsoever of the resurrection. Chapter 15, on the other hand, discusses the resurrection with almost no mention of the crucifixion. The intervening chapters are filled with seemingly mundane disciplinary and ethical matters, as well as ecclesial governance. How do they go together? Apocalyptic literature always aims to instill hope to stand fast in the face of adversity and persecution and to make the right ethical choices, to live correctly. Verses 29-34 and v. 58 echo this ethical imperative. The believer is urged to live correctly, to stop sinning, to be steadfast and faithful, so that his labor will not be in vain. This is not a theology of works, but one of being in Christ. The principal sign of the presence of the Spirit is love, and it is this that has been lacking among some of the Corinthians. The believer must live in hope of the resurrection, and that determines his behavior and mode of living in the world. Verses 29-34 show that without a fervent hope in the resurrection, ethical activity is difficult to sustain[4].

The apocalyptic message of 1 Cor 15 has not been fully realized, and it is seldom that one hears a sermon or homily based upon it other than as a bag of prooftexts for the resurrection of the dead. It does indeed teach that, but woven through this passage is a statement of what that means for us *now*. Living in Christ, filled with the Spirit, is a foretaste of that time when we shall be with the Lord and share in his glory.

Christian apocalyptic theology is of prime importance. It is something that is intensely personal, and yet communal in its outlook. It provides a

---

[4] The Holy Spirit is given in anticipation of the resurrection, and it is displaying the fruits of the presence of the Spirit that ensures that one is in Christ, and the principal sign is love. Bultmann insisted that chapter 13 rather than 15 was the climax of the letter. H.W. BOERS, «Apocalyptic», 50-65. Byrne highlights the strong link between belief in the resurrection and ethical fervor. B. BYRNE, «Eschatologies of Resurrection and Destruction», 288-298.

passionate, participatory spirituality and theology that engages the individual in ethical fervor and ardent hope in God's future. Properly understood, it does not compromise with the world or with earthly human structures, but levels all before the majesty, glory, and prerogatives of God. It can be something that fires the imagination, inspiring members of the Christian community to speak prophetically the message of Christ.

Problems do remain: how to avoid the tendency to sectarianism and exclusivity; how to deal with the problem of continuing history; how to make a literary/religious genre from a distant age potent and meaningful for our age without compromising its message and power.

ABBREVIATIONS

AB	Anchor Bible
ABD	Anchor Bible Dictionary
ACW	Ancient Christian Writers, ed., J. Quasten – D. Plumpe, Westminster 1946-
AH	Adversus haereses (Irenaeus)
AMWNE	*Apocalypticism in the Mediterranean World and the Near East.* Proceedings of the International Colloquium on Apocalypticism, Uppsala, August 12-17 1979, ed. D. Hellholm, Tübingen 1983.
ANF	*Ante-Nicene Fathers*, ed. A. Roberts – J. Donaldson, 1867-1872; reprinted Grand Rapids 1950.
ANL	Ante-Nicene Library, ed. E. Pusey, Edinburgh 1866-1872, 1897.
ANRW	*Aufstieg und Niedergang der römischen Welt*
ANT	Antiquities of Josephus
ApE	Apocalypse of Elijah
ApMos	Apocalypse of Moses
ApocBar	Apocalypse of Baruch
AsMos	Assumption of Moses
Aug	*Augustinianum*
BAGD	W. BAUER – W.F. ARNDT – F.W. GINGRICH – F.W. DANKER, *A Greek-English Lexicon of the New Testament*, Chicago 1979.
Bib	*Biblica*
BJ	Jewish Wars of Josephus
BJRL	*Bulletin of the John Rylands University Library of Manchester*
BLE	*Bulletin de Littérature Ecclésiastique*
BZ	*Biblische Zeitschrift*
CalTR	*Calvin Theological Review*
CBQ	*Catholic Biblical Quarterly*
CD	Damascus Document
CSCO	Corpus scriptorum christianorum orientalium
CSEL	Corpus scriptorum ecclesiasticorum latinorum
DRev	*Downside Review*
EncECh	*Encyclopedia of the Early Church*
EvQ	*Evangelical Quarterly*
EvTh	*Evangelische Theologie*
FC	Fathers of the Church, ed. R.J. Deferrari, New York 1947-
GCS	Griechische Christliche Schriftsteller, Leipzig, Berlin 1897-
Gr	*Gregorianum*
HRel	*History of Religions*

HTR	*Harvard Theological Review*
ICC	International Critical Commentary
Int	*Interpretation*
JBL	*Journal of Biblical Literature*
JETS	*Journal of the Evangelical Theological Society*
JR	*Journal of Religion*
JSNT	*Journal for the Study of the New Testament*
JSNTSS	Journal for the Study of the New Testament Supplement Series
Jub	Jubilees
LAB	*Liber Antiquitatum Biblicarum*
LCL	Loeb Classical Library
NEB	New English Bible
LNPF	A Select Library of Nicene and Post-Nicene Fathers of the Christian Church, ed. P. Schaff – H. Wace. Buffalo and New York, 1886-1900; reprinted Grand Rapids, 1952ff.
Neot	*Neotestamentica*
NJB	New Jerusalem Bible
NT	*Novum Testamentum*
NTA	*New Testament Abstracts*
NTApoc	*New Testament Apocrypha*, ed. W. Schneemelcher, trans. R. McL.Wilson, rev. ed., Louisville 1992.
NTS	*New Testament Studies*
OTP	*Old Testament Pseudepigrapha*, ed. J. Charlesworth, New York 1983.
PG	Patrologiae cursus completus, ed. Jacques-Paul Migne, Series Graeca, Paris 1857-1866.
PL	Patrologiae cursus completus, ed. Jacques-Paul Migne, Series Latina, Paris 1841-2864.
Ps-Philo	Pseudo-Philo
PssSol	Psalms of Solomon
RSV	Revised Standard Version
RTAM	*Recherches de Théologie Ancienne et Médiévale*
SC	Sources chrétiennes, Paris 1941-
Sibyl	Sybylline Oracles
SJT	*Scottish Journal of Theology*
SNTMS	Society for New Testament Studies Monograph Series
TAb	Testament of Abraham
TAsh	Testament of Asher
TBen	Testament of Benjamin
TDan	Testament of Dan
TDNT	G. KITTEL – G. FRIEDRICH, ed., *Theological Dictionary of the New Testament,* Grand Rapids 1993.
Test12P	Testament of the Twelve Patriarchs
TGad	Testament of Gad
TIss	Testament of Issachar
FpTJob	Testament of Job
TJud	Testament of Judah
TLev	Testament of Levi

TNaph	Testament of Naphtali
TReu	Testament of Reuben
TS	*Theological Studies*
TSim	Testament of Simeon
TSol	Testament of Solomon
TZeb	Testament of Zebulon
VChr	*Vigiliae Christianae*
WisSol	Wisdom of Solomon
ZNW	*Zeitschrift für die neutestamentliche Wissenschaft*
ZThK	*Zeitschrift für Theologie und Kirche*
2 Bar	II Baruch
4 Bar	IV Baruch
1 En	I Enoch
2 En	II Enoch
2 Ez	II Ezra
4 Ez	IV Ezra
2 Macc	II Maccabees
4 Macc	IV Maccabees

BIBLIOGRAPHY

1. Primary Texts and Reference Works

AMBROSE, *De fide*, PL 16; trans. H. de Romestin, LNPF 10, Buffalo – New York 1896 (reprint, Grand Rapids 1969).

————, *De excessu fratris*, trans. J.J. McGuire, FC 22, New York 1968².

AUGUSTINE, *De moribus ecclesiae catholicae et de moribus manichaeorum*, PL 32; trans. R. Stothert, LNPF 4, Buffalo – New York 1887 (reprint, Grand Rapids 1956).

————, *Civitas Dei*, trans. D. Zema – G. Walsh, FC 6, New York 1950.

Anchor Bible Dictionary, ed. D.N. Freedman, I-VI, New York 1992.

The Apostolic Fathers, ed. and trans. K. Lake, LCL 24-25, I-II, Cambridge 1977.

BERNARDINI, A.P., *Gregorio di Nissa*, Roma 1992.

Biblia Patristica. Index des citations et allusions bibliques dans la littérature patristique, ed. J. Allenback – A. Benoit, 5 vols., Paris 1975-91.

CLEMENT OF ALEXANDRIA, *Stromata*, ed. J. Ferguson, FC 85, New York 1991.

CLEMENT OF ROME, *Letter to the Corinthians*, trans. K. Lake, in *The Apostolic Fathers*, I, Cambridge 1977.

CHARLESWORTH, J.H., ed., *The Old Testament Pseudepigrapha*, I–II, New York 1983-1985.

DANBY, H., ed., *The Mishnah*, London 1938.

DOWNING, J.K., – al., ed. and trans., *Gregorii Nysseni Opera Dogmatica Minora*, Pars II, Leiden 1987.

EPIPHANIUS of SALAMIS, *Ancoratus*, ed. K. Holl, GCS 25, Leipzig 1915.

EPIPHANIUS of SALAMIS, *Panarion*, trans. F. Williams, in *The Panarion of Epiphanius of Salamis*, Book I Section 1-46, Nag Hammadi Studies 35, Leiden 1987; K. HOLL – J. DUMMER, ed., *Epiphanius II. Panarion Haer.*, *34-64*, Berlin 1980.

EUSEBIUS OF CAESAREA, *De ecclesiastica theologia*, ed. K. Lake, LCL 153, I, (1926, reprint 1980); ed. J.E.L. Oulton, LCL 265, II, Cambridge 1932 (reprint 1980).

——, *Commentarii in Esaiam*, ed. J. Ziegler, GCS, Berlin 1975.

——, *Commentarii in Psalmos*, PG 23, Paris 1857.

——, *Demonstratio Evangelica*, ed. I.A. Heikel, GCS 23, Leipzig 1913.

GREGORY OF NAZIANZUS, *Carmina historica*, PG 37, Paris 1857.

——, *Carmina theologica*, PG 37, Paris 1857.

——, *Orationes*, PG 46, Paris 1858; trans. C. Moreschini, *I Cinque Discorsi Teologici*, Roma 1986.

GREGORY OF NYSSA, trans. C. Moreschini, *In Canticum Canticorum*, Roma 1988

——, *De opificio hominis*, PG 44, Paris 1858; trans. H.A. Wilson, LNPF 5, Buffalo – New York 1893.

——, *De anima et resurrectione,* PG 46, Paris 1858; LNPF 5, Buffalo – New York 1893.

——, *De oratione dominica*, PG 44, Paris 1858; ed. H. Graef, ACW 18, Westminster 1954.

——, *In illud: tunc et ipse filius*, PG 46, Paris 1858; J.K. DOWNING, ed., *The Treatise of Gregory of Nyssa. In Illud: tunc et ipse filius. A Critical Text with Prolegomena*, in *Gregory of Nyssa, opera dogmatica minora*, Leyden 1966.

——, *Contra Eunomium*, PG 45, Paris 1858; LNPF 5, Buffalo – New York 1893.

HIPPOLYTUS, *Contra Noetum*, trans. S.D.F. Salmond, ANF 9, Grand Rapids 1869.

——, *In Danielem*, trans. G. Bardy – M. Lefevre, SC 14, Paris 1947.

——, *De resurrectione ad Mammaeam*, ANF 9, Grand Rapids 1869.

——, *Demonstratio de Christo et Antichristo*, ANF 9, , Grand Rapids 1869.

HILARY OF POITIERS, *De trinitate*, trans. S. McKenna, FC 25, New York 1954.

JEROME, *Ep. 55*, trans. W.H. Fremantle, LNPF ser.2, VI, Buffalo – New York 1892.

IRENAEUS OF LYON, *Adversus haereses*, trans. J. Dillon, ACW 55, Westminster 1992.

————, *Demonstratio*, trans. J. Smith, ACW 16, Westminster 1952.

JOHN CHRYSOSTOM, *Homilies on First Corinthians*, trans. T.W. Chambers, LNPF ser. 1, XII, Buffalo – New York 1889.

KLOSTERMAN, E., ed., *Eusebius Werke IV. Gegen Marcell. Über die Kirchliche Theologie. Die Fragmente Marcells*, GCS 14, Leipzig 1906.

LAYTON, B., trans. and ed., *The Gnostic Scriptures*, New York 1987.

METHODIUS OF OLYMPUS, *The Symposium*, trans. H. Mursillo, ACW 63, Westminster 1958.

ORIGEN, *Contra Celsum*, ed. and trans. H. Chadwick, Cambridge 1953.

————, *Commentary on the Song of Songs*, trans. R.P. Lawson, ACW 26, Westminster 1956.

————, *Commentary on Matthew*, ed. E. Klostermann, GCS 40, Leipzig 1935; trans. A. Menzies, ANF 10, Grand Rapids 1974.

————, *Commentary on John*, trans. R. Heine, FC 80, 89, New York 1986, 1993.

————, *Commentary on the Letter to the Romans*, PG 14; trans. F. Cocchini, *Commento alla Lettera ai Romani*, Casale Monferrato 1985.

————, *Homilies on Leviticus*, ed. W.A. Baehrens, GCS 29, Leipzig 1920.

————, *Homilies on Joshua*, ed. A. Jaubert, SC 71, Paris 1960.

————, *Homilies on Isaiah*, ed. W.A. Baehrens, GCS 33, Leipzig 1925.

————, *Homilies on Jeremiah*, ed. P. Husson – P. Nautin, SC 232 (1976).

————, *Homilies on numbers*, trans. M. Danieli, *Origène. Omelie sui numeri*. Roma 1988.

————, *On Prayer*, in *Alexandrian Christianity*, ed. and trans. H. Chadwick, Philadelphia 1954.

————, *Dialogue with Heraclides*, in *Alexandrian Christianity*, ed. and trans. H. Chadwick, Philadelphia 1954.

————, *De principiis*, trans. G.W. Butterworth, Gloucester 1973.

PITRA, J.B., ed., *Analecta Sacra*, Paris 1883.

Encyclopedia of the Early Church, ed. A. Walford, trans. A. Di Berardino, Institutum Patristicum Augustinianum, Cambridge 1992.

ROBINSON, J.M., ed., *The Nag Hammadi Library in English*, trans. Claremont Members of the Coptic Gnostic Library Project of the Institute for Antiquity and Christianity, Leiden 1988[3].

SAGNARD, F., ed. and trans., *Excerpta ex Scripta Theodoti*, SC 23, Paris 1948.

TERTULLIAN, *De resurrectione,* trans. P. Holmes, ANL 15, Edinburgh 1848.

————, *Prescription against heretics*, ANL 15, Edinburgh 1848.

————, *De patientia*, trans. R. Roberts, FC 40, New York 1959.

————, *Ad nationes*, ANL 15, Edinburgh 1848.

————, *Adversus Marcionem*, ANL 15, Edinburgh 1848.

THEODORET OF CYRRHUS, *Interpretatio epistulae I ad Corinthios*, PG 82, Paris 1959.

VERMES, G., *The Dead Sea Scrolls in English*, Sheffield 1987[3].

2. Books and Articles

ACHTEMEIER, P.J., «An Apocalyptic Shift in Early Christian Tradition: Reflections on Some Canonical Evidence», *CBQ* 45 (1983) 231-248.

ALETTI, J-N., «L'argumentation de Paul et la position des Corinthiens: 1Co 15,12-34», in *Résurrection du Christ et des Chrétiens 1 Cor 15*, ed. L. de Lorenzi, Série Monographique de "Benedictina", Rome 1985.

————, *Saint Paul Épitre aux Colossiens*, Paris 1993.

ALLO, E.B., *Saint Paul Première Épitre aux Corinthiens*, Paris 1934.

BARR, J., «Jewish Apocalyptic in Recent Scholarly Study», *BJRL* 58 (1975) 9-35.

————, *The Garden of Eden and the Hope of Immortality*, London 1992.

BARRETT, C.K., *The First Epistle to the Corinthians*, London 1971[2].

BARTH, G., «Erwägungen zu 1. Korinther 15, 20-28», *EvTh* 30 (1970) 515-527.

BARTH, K., *The Resurrection of the Dead*, trans. H.J. Stenning, New York 1933.

BARTH, M., *Ephesians 1-3*, AB 34, New York 1974.

BARTHES, R., *La retorica antica*, Milano 1972.

BEKER, J.C., *Paul's Apocalyptic Gospel. The Coming Triumph of God*, Philadelphia 1982.

————, *Paul the Apostle. The Triumph of God in Life and Thought*, Edinburgh 1980.

BEKER, J.C., *The Triumph of God. The Essence of Paul's Thought*, Minneapolis 1990.

BEST, E., *The First and Second Epistles to the Thessalonians*, London 1986.

BETZ, H.D., «On the Problem of the Religio-Historical Understanding of Apocalypticism», *JThCh* 6 (1969) 134-156.

———, «The Problem of Rhetoric and Theology According to the Apostle Paul», in *L'Apôtre Paul: Personalitè, Style et Concêption du Ministère*, ed. A. Vanhoye, BETL 73, Leuven 1986, 16-48.

BETZ, H.D., *Galatians*, Hermeneia, Philadelphia 1979.

BIANCHI, U., ed., *Arché e Telos. L'antropologia di Origene e di Gregorio di Nissa*, Milano 1981.

BLACK, M., «Πᾶσαι ἐξουσίαι αὐτῷ ὑποταγήσονται», in *Paul and Paulinism*, London 1982, 74-82.

BOERS, H.W., «Apocalyptic Eschatology in I Corinthians 15», *Int* 21 (1967) 50-65.

BOOMERSHINE, T.E., «Epistemology at the Turn of the Ages in Paul, Jesus, and Mark: Rhetoric and Dialectic in Apocalyptic and the New Testament», in *Apocalyptic and the New Testament*, Fs. J.L. Martyn, JSNTS 24, Sheffield 1989, 147-68.

BORING, M.E., «The Language of Universal Salvation in Paul», *JBL* 105 (1986) 269-292.

BRANICK, V., «Apocalyptic Paul?», *CBQ* 47 (1985) 664-675.

BROWN, R.E., «The Pro Christian Concept of Mystery», *CBQ* 20 (1958) 417-443.

———, «The Semitic Background of the New Testament *mysterion*», *Bib* 39 (1958) 426-448.

———, «The Semitic Background of the New Testament *mysterion*», *Bib* 40 (1959) 70-87.

BULTMANN, R., *Primitive Christianity*, Philadelphia 1949.

———, «ζῳοποιέω», *TDNT*, II, 874.

BÜNKER, M., *Briefformular und Rhetorische Disposition im 1. Korintherbrief*, Göttingen 1984.

BYRNE, B., «Eschatologies of Resurrection and Destruction: The Ethical Significance of Paul's Dispute with the Corinthians», *DRev* 104 (1986) 288-298.

CAIRD, G., «Everything to Everyone: The Theology of the Corinthian Epistles», *Int* 13 (1959) 387-399.

CALLAN, T., «Psalm 110.1 and the Origin of the Expectation That Jesus Will Come Again», *CBQ* 44 (1982) 622-636.

CANOBBIO, G., ed. and trans., *Apocalittica ed escatologia*, Brescia 1992.

CARR, W., *Angels and Principalities*, SNTSMS 42, Cambridge 1981.

———, «The Rulers of This Age – 1 Corinthians II, 6-8», *NTS* (1976-77) 20-35.

CAVALLIN, H., *Life After Death. Paul's Argument for the Resurrection of the Dead. Part I: An Enquiry Into the Jewish Background*, Lund 1974.

CHARLESWORTH, J.H., *The Messiah. Developments in Earliest Judaism and Christianity*, The First Princeton Symposium on Judaism and Christian Origins, Minneapolis 1992.

COHN-SHERBOK, D., «Paul and Rabbinic Exegesis», *SJT* 35 (1982) 117-132.

COLLINS, J.J., «Apocalyptic Eschatology and the Transcendence of Death», *CBQ* 36 (1974) 21-43.

———, «Cosmos and Salvation. Jewish Wisdom and Apocalyptic in the Hellenistic Age», *HRel* 17 (1977) 121-142.

———, *Daniel. A Commentary on the Book of Daniel*, Hermeneia, Minneapolis 1993.

———, «Apocalypse: Morphology of a Genre», *Semeia* 14 (1979) 21-59.

———, *The Apocalyptic Imagination. An Introduction to the Jewish Matrix of Christianity*, New York 1984.

———, «The Genre Apocalypse in Hellenistic Judaism», in *AMWNE*, 531-548.

———, *The Scepter and the Star. The Messiahs of the Dead Sea Scrolls and Other Ancient Literature*, New York 1995.

COLLINS, R.F., «New», in *ABD*, IV, 1086-1088.

CONZELMANN, H., *1 Corinthians. A Commentary on the First Epistle to the Corinthians*, Philadelphia 1975.

COPPENS, J., «"Mystery" in the Theology of Saint Paul and its parallels at Qumran», in *Paul and the Dead Sea Scrolls*, ed. J. Murphy-O'Connor – J.H. Charlesworth, New York 1990, 132-158.

CROCKETT, W., «The Ultimate Restoration of All Mankind: 1 Corinthians 15.22», *Studia Biblica 1978, III*. (1980) 83-87.

CROUZEL, H., «L'exégèse Origénienne de I Cor 3.11-15, et la purification eschatologique», in *Epektasis,* Fs. J. Daniélou, Paris 1972, 273-283.

CROUZEL, H., «The Literature on Origen 1970-1988», *TS* 49 (1988) 499-516.

——, «Mort et immortalité chez Origène», *BLE* 79 (1978) 19-38; 81-96.

——, *Origen*, Edinburgh 1989.

——, «La "première" et la "seconde" résurrection des hommes d'après Origène», *Didaskalia* 3 (1973) 3-19.

——, «Les prophéties de la résurrection chez Origène», in *Forma Futuri*, Fs. Cardinale M. Pellegrino, Torino 1975, 980-992.

CURTI, C., «Il regno millenario in Vittorino Di Petovio», *Aug* 18 (1978) 419-434.

DALEY, B.E., *The Hope of the Early Church*, Cambridge 1991.

DANIÉLOU, J., *Gospel Message and Hellenistic Culture*, London 1973.

——, J., *The Origins of Latin Christianity*, London 1977.

DE BOER, M.C., *The Defeat of Death. Apocalyptic Eschatology in 1 Corinthians 15 and Romans 5*, JSNTSS 22, Sheffield 1988.

——, «Paul and Jewish Apocalyptic Eschatology», in *Apocalyptic and the New Testament*, Fs. J.L. Martyn, JSNTSS 24, Sheffield 1989, 169-90.

DELLING, G., «ἀπαρχή», *TDNT*, I, 484-486.

——, «καταργέω», *TDNT*, I, 452-454.

——, «ὑποτάσσω», *TDNT*, VIII, 39-46.

——, «τάγμα», *TDNT*, VIII, 31-32.

DELOBEL, J., «The Fate of the Dead According to 1 Thess 4 and 1 Cor 15», in *The Thessalonian Correspondence*, ed. R.F. Collins, Louven 1990, 340-347.

DU TOIT, A.B., «Primitive Christian Belief in the Resurrection of Jesus in the Light of Pauline Resurrection and Appearance Terminology», *Neot* 23 (1989) 309-330.

DUFFY, N.J., «The Significance of Pauline Apocalyptic for Theological Ethics», in *Apocalyptic and the New Testament*, Fs. J.L. Martyn, JSNTSS 24, Sheffield 1989, 279-296.

DULING, D.C., trans., «Testament of Solomon», in *OTP*, I, 934-987.

DUNN, J.D.G., *Christology in the Making. An Inquiry Into the Origins of the Doctrine of the Incarnation*, London 1989².

——, «The Theology of Galatians», in *Pauline Theology*, ed. J. Bassler, Minneapolis 1991, 125-146.

DYKSTRA, W., «1 Corinthians 15.20-28: An Essential Part of Paul's Argument Against Those Who Deny the Resurrection», *CalTR* 4 (1969) 195-211.

EGAN, R., «Lexical Evidence on Two Pauline Passages», *NT* 19 (1977) 34-62.

FEE, G.D., *The First Epistle to the Corinthians*, Grand Rapids 1987.

FILORAMO, G., *A History of Gnosticism*, London 1990.

————, «Rivelazione ed escatologia nello gnosticismo Cristiano del II secolo», *Aug* 18 (1978) 75-88.

FITZMYER, J.A., *Romans*, AB 33, New York 1992.

FREEBORN, J.C.K., «The Eschatology of 1 Corinthians 15», *StEv* (1964) 557-568.

FRIEDRICH, G., «σάλπιγξ», *TDNT*, VII, 71-88.

FROEHLICH, K., *Biblical Interpretation in the Early Church*, Philadelphia 1984.

GAGER, J.G., «Functional Diversity in Paul's Use of End-Time Language», *JBL* (1985) 325-337.

GARAVELLI, B.M., *Manuale di Retorica*, Milano 1988.

GILLESPIE, T.W., *The First Theologians. A Study in Early Christian Prophecy*, Grand Rapids 1994.

GILLMAN, J., «Signals of Transformation in 1 Thessalonians 4:13-18», *CBQ* 47 (1985) 263-281.

GOULDER, M.D., «ΣΟΦΙΑ in 1 Corinthians», *NTS* 37 (1991) 516-534.

GRANT, R.M., *A Short History of the Interpretation of the Bible*, London 1984[2]

GRILLMEIER, A., *Christ in Christian Tradition. From the Apostolic Age to Chalcedon (AD 451)*, London 1975.

GRUENWALD, I., «Jewish Apocalyptic Literature», in *ANRW*, II, Berlin-New York 1979, 89-118.

GRUNDMANN, W., «δεῖ», *TDNT*, II, 21-25.

HANSON, P.D., *The Dawn of Apocalyptic. The Historical and Sociological Roots of Jewish Apocalyptic Eschatology*, Philadelphia 1983[2].

————, ed., *Visionaries and Their Apocalypses*, Philadelphia 1983.

HARRINGTON, D.J., trans., «Ps-Philo», in *OTP*, I, 297-378.

HARTMAN, L., «Survey of the Problem of Apocalyptic Genre», in *AMWNE*, 329-344.

HAY, D.M., *Glory at the Right Hand. Psalm 110 in Early Christianity*, SBL Monograph Series 18, Nashville 1973.

———, ed. *Pauline Theology. 1 and 2 Corinthians*. Minneapolis 1993.

HELLHOLM, D., ed. *Apocalypticism in the Mediterranean World and the Near East*, Proceedings of the International Colloquium on Apocalypticism, Uppsala, August 12-17 1979, Tübingen 1983.

HENGEL, M., *Judaism and Hellenism*, trans. J.Bowden, Philadelphia 1981[2].

HENNESSEY, L.R., «The Place of Saints and Sinners After Death», in *Origen of Alexandria: His World and His Legacy*, Notre Dame 1988, 295-312.

HÉRING, J., *The First Epistle of Saint Paul to the Corinthians*, trans. A.W. Heathcote – P.J. Allcock, London 1962.

HIERS, R.H., «Day of Christ», in *ABD*, II, 76-79.

HILL, C.E., «Paul's Understanding of Christ's Kingdom in I Corinthians 15:20-28», *NT* 30 (1988) 297-320.

HOOKER, M.D. – WILSON, S.G., ed., *Paul and Paulinism,* Fs. C.K. Barrett, London 1982.

HOOKER, M.D., *From Adam to Christ,* Cambridge 1990.

HORSLEY, R.A., «Consciousness and Freedom Among the Corinthians: 1 Corinthians 8-10», *CBQ* 40 (1978) 574-589.

———, «Gnosis in Corinth. 1 Corinthians 8.1-6», *NTS* 27 (1980) 32-51.

———, «"How Can Some of You Say That There Is No Resurrection of the Dead?" Spiritual Elitism in Corinth», *NT* 20 (1978) 203-231.

———, «Pneumatikos vs. Psychikos: Distinctions of Spiritual Status Among the Corinthians», *HTR* 69 (1976) 269-288.

———, «Wisdom of Words and Words of Wisdom in Corinth», *CBQ* 39 (1977) 224-239.

HURD, J.C., *The Origin of 1 Corinthians*, London 1965.

JANSEN, J., «1 Corinthians 15.24-28 and the Future of Jesus Christ», in *Texts and Testaments*, ed. W.E. March, San Antonio 1980, 173-197.

JENKINS, C., «Origen on 1 Corinthians», *JTS* 10 (1909) 43-48.

JEWETT, R., «A Matrix of Grace», in *Pauline Theology*, ed. J. Bassler, Minneapolis 1991.

JOHNSON, E.E., *The Function of Apocalyptic and Wisdom Traditions in Romans 9-11*, SBL Dissertation Series 109, Atlanta 1989.

JOSSA, G., «Storia della salvezza ed escatologia nell'adversus haereses di Ireneo di Lione», *Aug* 18 (1978) 107-126.

JUEL, D., *Messianic Exegesis. Christological Interpretation of the Old Testament in Early Christianity*, Philadelphia 1988.

KÄSEMANN, E., «Zum Thema der urchristlichen Apokalyptik», *ZThK* 59 (1962) 257-284.

————, «On the Subject of Primitive Christian Apocalyptic», in *New Testament Questions of Today*, Philadelphia 1969, 108-137.

————, «The Beginnings of Christian Theology», in *New Testament Questions of Today*, Philadelphia 1969, 82-107.

KECK, L.E., «Paul and Apocalyptic Theology», *Int* 38 (1984) 229-241.

KENNEDY, G.A., *The Art of Persuasion in Greece*, Princeton 1963.

————, *The Art of Rhetoric in the Roman World*, Princeton 1972.

————, *New Testament Interpretation Through Rhetorical Criticism*, Chapel Hill 1984.

KLIJN, A.F.J., «1 Thessalonians 4.13-18 and its Background in Apocalyptic Literature», *Paul and Paulinism*, Fs. C.K. Barrett, ed. M. Hooker – S.G. Wilson, London 1982, 67-73.

————, trans., «2 Baruch», in *OTP*, I, 615-652.

KLOPPENBORG, J., «An Analysis of the Pre-Pauline Formula 1 Cor 15:3b-5 in Light of Some Recent Literature», *CBQ* 40 (1978) 351-367.

KOCH, K., «What is Apocalyptic? An Attempt at a Preliminary Definition», in *Visionaries and Their Apocalypses*, ed. Paul Hanson, Philadelphia 1983.

KOESTER, H., «From Paul's Eschatology to the Apocalyptic Schemata of 2 Thessalonians», in *Thessalonian Correspondence*, 441-458.

KREITZER, L.J., *Jesus and God in Paul's Eschatology*, JSNTSS 19, Sheffield 1987.

KRENTZ, E., «Through a Lens: Theology and Fidelity in 2 Thessalonians», in *Pauline Theology*, ed. J. Bassler, Minneapolis 1991.

KÜMMEL, W.G., «Futuristic and Realized Eschatology in the Earliest Stages of Christianity», *JR* 43 (1963) 303-314.

LAMBERT, W.G., *The Background of Jewish Apocalyptic*, London 1978.

LAMBRECHT, J., «Paul's Christological Use of Scripture in 1 Cor. 15.20-28», *NTS* 28 (1982) 502-527.

LAMBRECHT, J., «Structure and Line of Thought in 1 Cor. 15:23-28», *NT* 32 (1990) 143-151.

LAMPE, G.W.H., «The Exegesis of Some Biblical Texts by Marcellus of Ancyra and Pseudo-Chrysostom's Homily on Ps. XCVI.1», *JTS* 49 (1948) 169-175.

————, «Some Notes on the Significance of βασιλεία τοῦ θεοῦ, βασιλεία χριστοῦ, in the Greek Fathers», *JTS* 49 (1948) 58-73.

LEBRAM, J.C.H., «The Piety of the Jewish Apocalyptists», in *AMWNE*, 171-210

LEE, J.Y., «Interpreting the Demonic Powers in Pauline Thought», *NT* 12 (1970) 54-69.

LIENHARD, J.T., «The Exegesis of 1 Cor 15, 24-28 from Marcellus of Ancyra to Theodoret of Cyrus», *VChr* 37 (1983) 340-359.

LIETZMANN, H., *An die Korinther I/II*, Tübingen 1949.

LINDEMANN, A., «Parusie Christi und Herrschaft Gottes», *Wort und Dienst* 19 (1987) 87-107.

LITFIN, D., *St. Paul's Theology of Proclamation. 1 Corinthians 1-4 and Greco-Roman Rhetoric*, SNTMS 79, Cambridge 1994.

LONGENECKER, R.N., «The Nature of Paul's Early Eschatology», *NTS* 31 (1985) 77-78.

LÜDEMANN, G., *Opposition to Paul in Jewish Christianity*, Minneapolis 1989.

————, *The Resurrection of Jesus*, London 1994.

McCAUGHEY, J.D., «The Death of Death (ICor 15.26)», in *Reconciliation and Hope. NT Essays on Atonement and Eschatology*, ed. R. Banks, Grand Rapids 1974, 246-261.

MACGREGOR, G.H.C., «Principalities and Powers: The Cosmic Background of Paul's Thought», *NTS* 1 (1954-55) 17-28.

MACK, B.L., *Rhetoric and the New Testament*, Minneapolis 1990.

MACRAE, G., «Apocalyptic Eschatology in Gnosticism», in *AMWNE*, 317-328.

MAIER, F.W., «Ps 110,1 (LXX 109,1) im Zusammenhang von 1 Kor 15,24-26», *BZ* 20 (1932) 139-156.

MARCUS, J. – SOARDS, M., ed., *Apocalyptic and the New Testament*, Fs. J. Louis Martyn, JSNTSS 24, Sheffield 1989.

MARTIN, R., *Reconciliation: A Study of Paul's Theology*, London 1981.

————, *The Spirit and the Congregation. Studies in 1 Corinthians 12-15*, Grand Rapids 1984.

MARTYN, J.L., «Apocalyptic Antinomies in Paul's Letter to the Galatians», *NTS* 31 (1985) 410-424.

MATTILA, S.L., «Two Contrasting Eschatologies at Qumran (4Q246 vs 1QM)», *Bib* 75 (1994) 518-538.

MEEKS, W.A., «Social Functions of Apocalyptic Language in Pauline Christianity», in *AMWNE*, 687-706.

MANKEN, M.J., *2 Thessalonians*, London 1994.

MEYER, B.F., «Did Paul's View of the Resurrection of the Dead Undergo Development?», *TS* 47 (1986) 363-387.

MITCHELL, M.M., *Paul and the Rhetoric of Reconciliation. An Exegetical Investigation of the Language and Composition of 1 Corinthians*, Louisville 1991.

MOLTMANN, J., *The Theology of Hope*, New York 1965.

MONACI, A., «Apocalisse ed escatologia», *Aug* 18 (1978) 139-152.

MOSSAY, J., *La mort et l'au-delà dans Saint Grégoire de Nazianze*, Louvain 1966.

MUNCK, J., *Paul and the Salvation of Mankind*, Richmond 1959.

MURPHY-O'CONNOR, J., «I Cor VIII.6: Cosmology or Soteriology?», *RB* 85 (1978) 253-267;

MUßNER, F., «"Schichten" in der Paulinischen Theologie Dargetan an 1 Kor 15», *BZ* 9 (1965) 59-70.

MÉHAT, A., «Apocatastase: Origène, Clement d'Alexandrie, Act. 3.21», *VChr* 10 (1956) 196-214.

NEUSNER, J., *What is Midrash?*, Philadelphia 1987.

NEYREY, J.H., *Paul, in Other Words. A Cultural Reading of His Letters*, Louisville 1990.

NICKELSBURG, G.W.E., *Resurrection, Immortality and Eternal Life in Intertestamental Judaism*, Cambridge, MA 1972.

⸺, «Social Aspects of Palestinian Jewish Apocalypticism», in *AMWNE*, 641-654.

NORELLI, E., «Il duplice rinnovamento del mondo nell'escatologia di S. Ireneo», *Aug* 18 (1978) 89-106.

OEPKE, A., «παρουσία», *TDNT*, V, 858-871.

O'ROURKE BOYLE, M., «Irenaeus' Millenial Hope. A Polemical Weapon», *RTAM* 36 (1969) 5-16.

PAGELS, E.H., «Exegesis and Exposition of the Genesis Creation Accounts in Selected Texts from Nag Hammadi», in *Nag Hammadi, Gnosticism, and Early Christianity*, ed. C. Hedrick – R. Hodgson, Peabody, MA 1986.

PAGELS, E.H., «"The Mystery of the Resurrection": A Gnostic Reading of 1 Corinthians 15», *JBL* 93 (1974) 276-288.

PATTE, D., *Early Jewish Hermeneutic in Palestine*, SBL Dissertation Series 22, Missoula 1975.

PEARSON, B.A., *The Pneumatikos-Psychikos Terminology in 1 Corinthians*, SBL Dissertation Series 12, Missoula 1973.

PERKINS, P., «Ordering the Cosmos: Irenaeus and the Gnostics», in *Nag Hammadi, Gnosticism, and Early Christianity*, ed. C. Hedrick – R. Hodgson, Peabody, MA 1986.

————, *Resurrection*, London 1984.

PHILONENKO, M., «L'apocalyptique Qoumrânienne», in *AMWNE*, 211-218.

PLEVNIK, J., «The Taking Up of the Faithful and the Resurrection of the Dead in 1 Thessalonians 4:13-18», *CBQ* 46 (1984) 274-283.

PUECH, É., *La croyance des Esséniens en la vie future: immortalité, résurrection, vie éternelle?*, Études bibliques nouvelle série numbers 21 and 22, Paris 1993.

RABINOWITZ, C., «Personal and Cosmic Salvation in Origen», *VChr* 38 (1984) 319-329.

REICKE, B., «πᾶς», *TDNT*, V, 887-896.

RIGGI, C., «Catechesi escatologica dell'Epifanio», *Aug* 18 (1978) 163-172.

RISSI, M., *Time and History. A Study on the Revelation*, Richmond 1966.

ROBERTSON, A. – PLUMMER, A., *A Critical and Exegetical Commentary on the First Epistle of St. Paul to the Corinthians*, ICC, Edinburgh 1914².

ROWLAND, C., *The Open Heaven. A Study of Apocalyptic in Judaism and Early Christianity*, London 1982.

RUSSELL, D.S., *Between the Testaments*, London 1986².

————, *Divine Disclosure. An Introduction to Jewish Apocalyptic*, London 1992.

————, *The Method and Message of Jewish Apocalyptic*, Philadelphia 1964.

————, *The Old Testament Pseudepigrapha*, London 1987.

SACHS, J.R., «Current Eschatology: Universal Salvation and the Problem of Hell», *TS* 52 (1991) 227-254.

SALDARINI, A.J., «Apocalypses and "Apocalyptic" in Rabbinic Literature and Mysticism», *Semeia* 14 (1979) 187-205.

SANDERS, E.P., «The Genre of Palestinian Jewish Apocalypses», in *AMWNE*, 447-460.

———, *Paul and Palestinian Judaism*, London 1977.

SCHENDEL, E., *Herrschaft und Unterwerfung Christi. 1 Korinther 15, 24-28 in Exegese und Theologie der Väter bis zum Ausgang Des 4. Jahrhunderts*, Beiträge zur Geschichte der biblischen Exegese 12, Tübingen 1971.

SCHMITHALS, W., *Gnosticism in Corinth. An Investigation of the Letters to the Corinthians*, Nashville 1971.

SCHWEITZER, A., *The Mysticism of Paul the Apostle*, trans. W. Montgomery, London 1931.

———, *Paul and His Inerpreters: A Critical History*, trans. W. Montgomery, London 1912.

SCHÜRER, E., *The History of the Jewish People in the Age of Jesus Christ*, ed. G. Vermes – F. Millar, I-III, Edinburgh 1979².

SCHÜSSLER-FIORENZA, E., «The Phenomenon of Early Christian Apocalyptic. Some Reflections on Method», in *AMWNE*, 295-316.

———, «Rhetorical Situation and Historical Reconstruction in I Corinthians», *NTS* 33 (1987) 386-403.

SCROGGS, R., «Eschatological Existence in Matthew and Paul: *Coincidentia Oppositorum*», in *Apocalyptic and the New Testament*, Fs. J.L. Martyn. JSNTSS 24, Sheffield 1989, 125-146.

———, *The Last Adam*, Philadelphia 1966.

———, «Paul: ΣΟΦΟΣ and ΠΝΕΥΜΑΤΙΚΟΣ», *NTS* 14 (1967-68) 33-55.

SEGAL, P., *Paul the Convert. The Apostolate and Apostasy of Saul the Pharisee*, New Haven 1990.

SELLIN, G., *Der Streit um die Auferstehung der Toten. Eine Religiongeschichtliche Untersuchung von 1 Korinther 15*, FRLANT 138, Göttingen 1966.

SIDER, R.J., «St. Paul's Understanding of the Nature and Significance of the Resurrection in I Corinthians XV 1-19», *NT* 19 (1977) 124-141.

SIMONETTI, M., «Il millenarismo in Oriente da Origene a Metodio», in *Corona Gratiarum I*, Brugge 1975, 37-58.

SINISCALCO, P., *Richerche sul «de resurrectione» di Tertulliano*, Roma 1966.

SPÖRLEIN, B., *Die Leugnung der Auferstehung. Eine historische-kritische Untersuchung zu I Kor 15*, Regensburg 1971.

STANDAERT, B., «La Rhétorique Ancienne», in *L'Apôtre Paul*, ed. A. Vanhoye, Leuven 1986, 81.

STANLEY, C.D., *Paul and the Language of Scripture. Citation Techniques in the Pauline Epistles and Contemporary Literature,* SNTSMS 74, Cambridge 1992.

STEGEMANN, H., «Die Bedeutung der Qumran Funde für die Erforschung der Apokalyptik», in *AMWNE*, 495-530.

STENGER, W., «Beobachtungen zur Argumentationstruktor von I Kor 15», *Linguistica Biblica* 45 (1979) 71-128.

STONE, M.E., *Fourth Ezra*, Hermeneia, Minneapolis 1990.

STRACK, H.L. – STEMBERGER, G., *Introduction to the Talmud and Midrash*, trans. M. Bockmuehl, Edinburgh 1991.

STURM, R., «Defining the Word "Apocalyptic": A Problem in Biblical Criticism», in *Apocalyptic and the New Testament*, Fs. J.L. Martyn, Sheffield 1989, 17-48.

TEANI, M., *Corporeità e risurrezione. L'interpretazione di 1 Corinti 15,13-49 nel Novecento*, Aloisiana 24, Roma 1994.

THEISSEN, G., *The Social Setting of Pauline Christianity*, ed. and trans. J.H. Schütz, Edinburgh 1990.

THIELMAN, F.S., «Another Look at the Eschatology of Eusebius of Caesarea», *VChr* 41 (1987) 236-237.

THISELTON, A., «Realized Eschatology at Corinth», *NTS* 24 (1977/78) 510-526.

TRAVIS, S.H., «Wrath of God», in *ADD*, VI, 996-998.

TRIGG, J.W., *Origen. The Bible and Philosophy in the Third-Century Church,* London 1983.

————, *Biblical Interpretation*, Wilmington 1988.

VIELHAUER, P., «Apocalyptic in Early Christianity», in *New Testament Apocrypha*, ed. W. Schneemelcher, trans. R. McL. Wilson, Louisville 1992, II, 542-569.

VON RAD, G., *Old Testament Theology*, vol. 2, New York 1965.

————, *Wisdom in Israel*, Nashville 1972.

VORSTER, J.N., «Resurrection Faith in I Corinthians 15», *Neo* 23 (1989) 287-307.

WALLIS, W., «The Problem of an Intermediate Kingdom in 1 Corinthians 15.20-28», *JETS* 18 (1975) 229-242.

WEDDERBURN, A.J.M., «The Problem of the Denial of the Resurrection in I Corinthians XV», *NT* 23 (1981) 229-241.

WEDDERBURN, A.J.M., «Some Observations on Paul's Use of the Phrases "In Christ" and "With Christ"», *JSNT* 25 (1985) 83-97.

WILSON, J.W., «The Corinthians Who Say There Is No Resurrection of the Dead», *ZNW* 59 (1968) 90-107.

WILSON, R.McL., «Gnosis at Corinth», in *Paul and Paulinism*, Fs. C.K. Barrett, London 1982.

WINSTON, D., ed. and trans., *The Wisdom of Solomon*, AB 43, New York 1979.

WINTERMUTE, O.S., trans., «Apocalypse of Elijah», in *OTP*, I, 721-754.

WITHERINGTON, B., *Conflict and Community in Corinth. A Socio-Rhetorical Commentary on 1 and 2 Corinthians*, Grand Rapids 1995.

————, *Jesus, Paul and the End of the World*, Downers Grove 1992.

————, *Jesus the Sage. The Pilgrimage of Wisdom*, Edinburgh 1994.

WRIGHT, N.T., «Adam in Pauline Christology», in *Society of Biblical Literature 1983 Seminar Papers*, ed. D. Lull, Chico 1983, 359-389.

WUELLNER, W., «Where is Rhetorical Criticism Taking Us?», *CBQ* 49 (1987) 448-463.

————, «Paul as Pastor: The Function of Rhetorical Questions in First Corinthians», in *L'Apôtre Paul: Personalitè, Style et Concêption du Ministère*, ed. A. Vanhoye, BETL 73, Leuven 1986.

INDEX OF AUTHORS

TABLE OF CONTENTS

TESI GREGORIANA

Since 1995, the series «Tesi Gregoriana» has made available to the general public some of the best doctoral theses done at the Pontifical Gregorian University. The typesetting is done by the authors themselves following norms established and controlled by the University.

Published Volumes [Series: Theology]

1. NELLO FIGA, Antonio, *Teorema de la opción fundamental. Bases para su adecuada utilización en teología moral*, 1995, pp. 380.

2. BENTOGLIO, Gabriele, *Apertura e disponibilità. L'accoglienza nell'epistolario paolino*, 1995, pp. 376.

3. PISO, Alfeu, *Igreja e sacramentos. Renovação da Teologia Sacramentária na América Latina*, 1995, pp. 260.

4. PALAKEEL, Joseph, *The Use of Analogy in Theological Discourse. An Investigation in Ecumenical Perspective*, 1995, pp. 392.

5. KIZHAKKEPARAMPIL, Isaac, *The Invocation of the Holy Spirit as Constitutive of the Sacraments according to Cardinal Yves Congar*, 1995, pp. 200.

6. MROSO, Agapit J., *The Church in Africa and the New Evangelisation. A Theologico-Pastoral Study of the Orientations of John Paul II*, 1995, pp. 456.

7. NANGELIMALIL, Jacob, *The Relationship between the Eucharistic Liturgy, the Interior Life and the Social Witness of the Church according to Joseph Cardinal Parecattil*, 1996, pp. 224.

8. GIBBS, Philip, *The Word in the Third World. Divine Revelation in the Theology of Jen-Marc Éla, Aloysius Pieris and Gustavo Gutiérrez*, 1996, pp. 448.

9. DELL'ORO, Roberto, *Esperienza morale e persona. Per una reinter-pretazione dell'etica fenomenologica di Dietrich von Hildebrand*, 1996, pp. 240.

10. BELLANDI, Andrea, *Fede cristiana come «stare e comprendere». La giustificazione dei fondamenti della fede in Joseph Ratzinger*, 1996, pp. 416.

11. BEDRIÑAN, Claudio, *La dimensión socio-política del mensaje teológico del Apocalipsis*, 1996, pp. 364.

12. GWYNNE, Paul, *Special Divine Action. Key Issues in the Contemporary Debate (1965-1995)*, 1996, pp. 376.

13. NIÑO, Francisco, *La Iglesia en la ciudad. El fenómeno de las grandes ciudades en América Latina, como problema teológico y como desafío pastoral*, 1996, pp. 492.

14. BRODEUR, Scott, *The Holy Spirit's Agency in the Resurrection of the Dead. An Exegetico-Theological Study of 1 Corinthians 15,44b-49 and Romans 8,9-13*, 1996, pp. 300.

15. ZAMBON, Gaudenzio, *Laicato e tipologie ecclesiali. Ricerca storica sulla «Teologia del laicato» in Italia alla luce del Concilio Vaticano II (1950-1980)*, 1996, pp. 548.

16. ALVES DE MELO, Antonio, *A Evangelização no Brasil. Dimensões teológicas e desafios pastorais. O debate teológico e eclesial (1952-1995)*, 1996, pp. 428.

17. APARICIO VALLS, María del Carmen, *La plenitud del ser humano en Cristo. La Revelación en la «Gaudium et Spes»*, 1997, pp. 308.

18. MARTIN, Seán Charles, *«Pauli Testamentum». 2 Timothy and the Last Words of Moses*, 1997, pp. 312.

19. RUSH, Ormond, *The Reception of Doctrine. An Appropriation of Hans Robert Jauss' Reception Aesthetics and Literary Hermeneutics*, 1997, pp. 424.

20. MIMEAULT, Jules, *La sotériologie de François-Xavier Durrwell. Exposé et réflexions critiques*, 1997, pp. 476.

21. CAPIZZI, Nunzio, *L'uso di Fil 2,6-11 nella cristologia contemporanea (1965-1993)*, 1997, pp. 528.

22. NANDKISORE, Robert, *Hoffnung auf Erlösung. Die Eschatologie im Werk Hans Urs von Balthasars*, 1997, pp. 304.

23. PERKOVIĆ, Marinko, *«Il cammino a Dio» e «La direzione alla vita»: L'ordine morale nelle opere di Jordan Kuničć, O.P. (1908-1974)*, 1997, pp. 336.

24. DOMERGUE, Benoît, *La réincarnation et la divinisation de l'homme dans les religions. Approche phénoménologique et théologique*, 1997, pp. 300.

25. FARKAŠ, Pavol, *La «donna» di Apocalisse 12. Storia, bilancio, nuove prospettive*, 1997, pp. 276.

26. OLIVER, Robert W., *The Vocation of the Laity to Evangelization. An Ecclesiological Inquiry into the Synod on the Laity (1987)*, Christifideles laici *(1989) and Documents of the NCCB (1987-1996)*, 1997, pp. 364.

27. SPATAFORA, Andrea, *From the «Temple of God» to God as the Temple. A Biblical Theological Study of the Temple in the Book of Revelation*, 1997, pp. 340.

28. IACOBONE, Pasquale, *Mysterium Trinitatis. Dogma e Iconografia nell'Italia medievale*, 1997, pp. 512.

29. CASTAÑO FONSECA, Adolfo M., *Δικαιοσύνη en Mateo. Una interpretación teológica a partir de 3,15 y 21,32*, 1997, pp. 344.

30. CABRIA ORTEGA, José Luis, *Relación teología-filosofía en el pensamiento de Xavier Zublrl*, 1997, pp. 580.

31. SCHERRER, Thierry, *La gloire de Dieu dans l'oeuvre de saint Irénée*, 1997, pp. 328.

32. PASCUZZI, Maria, *Ethics, Ecclesiology and Church Discipline. A Rhetorical Analysis of 1Cor 5,1-13*, 1997, pp. 240.

33. LOPES GONÇALVES, Paulo Sérgio, *Liberationis mysterium. O projeto sistemático da teologia da libertação. Um estudo teológico na perspectiva da regula fidei*, 1997, pp. 464.

34. KOLACINSKI, Mariusz, *Dio fonte del diritto naturale*, 1997, pp. 296.

35. LIMA CORRÊA, Maria de Lourdes, *Salvação entre juízo, conversão e graça. A perspectiva escatológica de Os 14,2-9*, 1998, pp. 360.

36. MEIATTINI, Giulio, *Sentire con Cristo. La teologia dell'esperienza cristiana nell'opera di H.U. von Balthasar*, 1998, pp. 432.

37. KESSLER, Thomas W., *Peter as the First Witness of the Risen Lord. An Historical and Theological Investigation*, 1998, pp. 240.

38. BIORD CASTILLO Raúl, *La Resurrección de Cristo como Revelación. Análisis del tema en la teología fundamental a partir de la Dei Verbum*, 1998, pp. 308.

39. LÓPEZ, Javier, *La figura de la bestia entre historia y profecía. Investigación teológico-bíblica de Apocalipsis 13,1-8*, 1998, pp. 308.

40. SCARAFONI, Paolo, *Amore salvifico. Una lettura del mistero della salvezza. Uno studio comparativo di alcune soteriologie cattoliche postconciliari*, 1998, pp. 240.

41. BARRIOS PRIETO, Manuel Enrique, *Antropologia teologica. Temi principali di antropologia teologica usando un metodo di «correlazione» a partire dalle opere di John Macquarrie*, 1998, pp. 416.

42. LEWIS, Scott M., *«So That God May Be All in All». The Apocalyptic Message of 1 Corinthians 15,12-34*, 1998, pp. 252.